CW00750991

Democracy, Conflict and Human Security:

Pursuing Peace in the 21st Century

Democracy, Conflict and Human Security:

Pursuing Peace in the 21st Century

Judith Large and Timothy D. Sisk

This work draws on background studies prepared by a group of contributing authors. The full version of these case studies will be published in a companion volume, entitled *Democracy, Conflict and Human Security, volume II: Further Readings (ISBN 91-85391-75-1)*.

Contributing authors: Reginald Austin, Najib Azca, Feargal Cochrane, Olayinka Creighton-Randall, Andrew Ellis, J. 'Kayode Fayemi, Guido Galli, Yash Ghai, Enrique ter Horst, Aziz Z. Huq, Todd Landman, Gurpreet Mahajan, Khabele Matlosa, George Gray Molina, Arifah Rahmawati, and Paikiasothy Saravanamuttu.

Handbook Series

The International IDEA Handbook Series seeks to present comparative analysis, information and insights on a range of democratic institutions and processes. Handbooks are aimed primarily at policymakers, politicians, civil society actors and practitioners in the field. They are also of interest to academia, the democracy assistance community and other bodies.

International IDEA publications are independent of specific national or political interests. Views expressed in this publication do not necessarily represent the views of International IDEA, its Board or its Council members.

© International Institute for Democracy and Electoral Assistance 2006

Applications for permission to reproduce or translate all or any part of this publication should be made to:
Publications Office
International IDEA
SE -103 34 Stockholm
Sweden

International IDEA encourages dissemination of its work and will promptly respond to requests for permission to reproduce or translate its publications.

Graphic design by: Trydells Forum
Cover photos
Corner photo (right): André Maslennikov © SCANPIX
Photo (upper right): Maria Zarnayova © SCANPIX
Photo on the left: David Isaksson © Global Reporting
Printed by: Trydells Tryckeri AB, Sweden

ISBN: 91-85391-74-3

This publication has been supported by the Human Security Program of the Department of Foreign Affairs and International Trade, Canada

Our main task in today's global community is to accept and live up to the triple challenge of development, security and human rights. These three challenges are together highest on the United Nation agenda. They affect and reinforce each other.

One of the most serious threats to our common security emerges from human desperation in societies which lack in respect for human rights and democracy. Acting for democracy is acting for peace and security. Democracy is also a strong driving force for development. Our efforts to promote respect for human rights and democracy are not only ethically motivated. We can also add the effects on security and development when we promote and defend the fundamental right to vote.

Democratic rights, economic strength – and how it is distributed – social cohesion, environmental balance and well educated people cannot be separated in today's world. We need more than ever to deal with our common future in a holistic way. The only way democracy will prove itself is through a living relationship between peoples and their governments based on trust, accountability and the determination to deliver practical results.

International IDEA has worked for over ten years as an organization dedicated to assistance for democracy based on clear principles which include: local ownership, support for legitimate national processes and multiparty pluralism as well as the belief that democracy is an evolving process.

This publication, *Democracy, Conflict and Human Security: Pursuing Peace in the 21st Century,* gives us a deeper knowledge and understanding on how we can advocate and live up to democratic practice and principles.

It will also challenge us to look at the evolution of democratic systems and democracy assistance, with particular attention to the impact of changes in the world economy and global communications. It argues for the overriding need to address complexity while always returning to basic principles in practice and process.

IDEA reclaims the vision and the viability of democratic approaches. Respecting the voices of the peoples and the values of an open society will be a crucial and fundamental contribution both to global security and development.

Jan Eliasson
President of the 60th General Assembly of the United Nations
Minister of Foreign Affairs, Sweden

i

Preface

International IDEA has entered its second decade of work as an intergovernmental body dedicated to supporting democratization worldwide. The key messages of its founding mandate—the importance of local ownership, dialogue processes and context-appropriate design—are increasingly relevant. For many across the world, democracy is in a crisis of legitimacy and credibility. The idea that people have the right to control their government and that a government is legitimate only if and when it is controlled by the people has won almost global recognition, hardly matched by any other world view in modern history. It transcends cultures, religions and languages; it takes multiple forms and survives in the most inhospitable environments.

However, the way in which the idea of democracy is translated into practice can leave much to be desired. In a world characterized by rising inequality democratic systems will be judged on how they include and deliver to constituent populations.

Democratization processes are in themselves conflictual, involving the reconfiguring of power relations, and competition for resources and representation. Informed analysis and local involvement are key to any positive outcome. In societies emerging from war, they are essential for preventing reversal and securing a just peace. While the promotion of democracy is more central in foreign policy debate and conduct than ever before, it is also true that democracy building is increasingly viewed by many with suspicion. There is polarization of views on both intent and approach, and undemocratic regimes are exploiting the situation.

This book addresses the nexus between democracy, conflict and human security in a way which recognizes that this is highly political, not technical, terrain. It places at centre stage the fundamental need for democratic practice, and reminds us that in every society, North and South, the democratic project is a long-term, ongoing one. This publication is part of IDEA's efforts to contribute to a major ongoing debate and, hopefully, to the strengthening of a democratic practice that responds to the quests for human dignity and development.

International IDEA would like to express particular appreciation to the Human Security Program of the Department of Foreign Affairs and International Trade, Canada, which has supported this project and publication. Additional thanks are due to the Geneva Centre for Security Policy for their cooperation and shared interest in the theme.

A number of individuals have contributed to discussions and input, and you will find quotations from many of them inside this volume, as well as longer papers in Volume II. They include Armineh Arakelian, Reginald Austin, Najib Azca, Ilán Bizberg, James Boyce, Feargal Cochrane, Olayinka Creighton-Randall, Chris Dolan, Kajsa Eriksson,

J. 'Kayode Fayemi, Goran Fejic, Aziz Z. Huq, Khabele Matlosa, Amal al-Sabbagh, Ozias Tungwarara, Arifah Rahmawati, Leena Rikkilä and Paikiasothy Saravanamuttu.

Judith Large, Senior Advisor for Democracy Building and Conflict Management at IDEA, spearheaded the 2004/5 'Confronting 21st Century Challenges' enquiry process and convened our Consultative Advisory Group in April 2005, to whom we also owe our thanks: Abdulkadir Yahya Ali, Ilán Bizberg, Béchir Chourou, Andrew Ellis, Alvaro Garcia, Joao Gomes Porto, Enrique ter Horst, Khabele Matlosa, Arifah Rahmawati, Paikiasothy Saravanamuttu, Massimo Tommasoli, Nkoyo Toyo, and Bernard Wood.

As lead writer, Timothy Sisk provided the initial theoretical framework and manuscript for this meeting, and it was out of robust deliberations engaged with this first draft that the focus on human security emerged for subsequent development. Carlos Jaurez and Monty Marshall have assisted in the finalizing of the work. Our appreciation and thanks go to Tim and Judith for bringing Volume I to completion, for their careful attention to a complex agenda and a multitude of voices, and for offering it as a vehicle for action.

Within IDEA people who have helped directly include Goran Fejic, Sakuntala Kadirgamar-Rajasingham, Andrew Ellis, Abdalla Hamdok and Daniel Zovatto. Several committed staff members have helped us see the process through, including Katarina Jörgensen and Cecilia Bylesjö. Thanks also go to Fran Lesser, Kristen Sample and Ileana Aguilar, to Eve Johansson for her patience and attention to detail, and to IDEA's dedicated publications manager Nadia Handal Zander.

We would also like to thank former IDEA Board member Kuniko Inoguchi, currently Minister of State for Gender Equality and Social Affairs, Japan, for her encouragement at the beginning of this enquiry and for the broader study.

Finally, we express our gratitude to the member states of IDEA, without whose support the work would not have been possible. To them, and to all our readers, we hope that *Democracy, Conflict, and Human Security: Pursuing Peace in the 21st Century* will stand as a useful contribution to the challenges we all face, in varying contexts and circumstances.

Vidar Helgesen
Secretary-General, International IDEA

Contents

Acronyms and Abbreviations

ACE	Administration and Cost of Elections (Project)
ASEAN	Association of Southeast Asian Nations
AU	African Union
CFA	Cease Fire Agreement (Sri Lanka)
DAC	Development Assistance Committee (OECD)
DDR	Disarmament, demobilization and reintegration
DRC	Democratic Republic of the Congo
ECOWAS	Economic Community of West African States
EMB	Electoral management body
EU	European Union
FMLN	Farabundo Marti National Liberation Front (Frente Farabundo Marti de Liberacion Nacional, El Salvador)
FPTP	First Past The Post
HIV/AIDS	Human immunodeficiency syndrome/Acquired immunodeficiency syndrome
IDASA	Institute for Democracy in South Africa
IDEA	International Institute for Democracy and Electoral Assistance
IDP	Internally displaced person
IFES	International Foundation for Election Systems
IFI	International financial institution
IMF	International Monetary Fund
JVP	Janatha Vimukthi Peramuna (Sri Lanka)
LTTE	Liberation Tigers of Tamil Eelam (Sri Lanka)
MDC	Movement for Democratic Change (Zimbabwe)
NGO	Non-governmental organization
OAS	Organization of American States
OECD	Organisation for Economic Co-operation and Development
OSCE	Organization for Security and Co-operation in Europe
POSA	Public Order and Security Act (Zimbabwe)
PR	Proportional representation
PRSP	Poverty reduction strategy paper
RUF	Revolutionary United Front (Sierra Leone)
SADC	Southern African Development Community
SNTV	Single Non-Transferable Vote
SPLA	Sudan People's Liberation Movement
SPLM	Sudan People's Liberation Army
TAC	Treatment Action Campaign (South Africa)
UK	United Kingdom
UN	United Nations
UNDP	United Nations Development Programme
UNIFEM	United Nations Development Fund for Women
USD	US dollar

INTRODUCTION

INTRODUCTION

Introduction: Confronting 21st-century Challenges

The 21st century began with stark challenges worldwide. There is widening inequality between the world's rich and poor. Increased economic ties among states generated by 'globalization' can be exploitative of the global poor, and over a billion people remain below the extreme poverty line of 1 US dollar (USD) a day. New armed conflicts have broken out, as in Côte d'Ivoire, even as protracted violence in nearby Liberia and Sierra Leone is brought to an end through extended peace and recovery processes. For many the policies based on a declared 'war on terrorism' have brought about a changed security environment with severe implications for international norms, human rights and citizenship. Non-state actors wield high leverage through transnational political violence and organized crime; patterns of migration are changing in response to environmental degradation and lack of opportunity; and gender remains one of the strongest benchmarks for disadvantage.

There are also positive developments: accelerations in communications, the growth of worldwide opportunities for networking, visible new social movements, increased regional cooperation, and the election of women to highest office on four continents. Economic growth in some regions (notably East Asia) has lifted many out of the ranks of poverty.

The subject of 'democracy', so celebrated after the fall of the Berlin Wall, now receives a more mixed press. Signs of a loss of confidence in and a decline in the legitimacy of democratic systems, as measured by public opinion surveys, are emerging in many parts of the world. Symptoms include a crisis in representation, poor voter turnout at elections, a loss of trust due to poor performance by political parties, corruption scandals, severe alienation among young people, and the need for innovative responses. In conflict and post-war situations enormous attention is paid and huge resources are poured in to elections as a main showcase of democracy, whereas the affected population may not feel the direct benefits of a representative system in terms of their own personal security. There is an increased de facto equation of democracy with liberalization and the market economy.

Meanwhile, external agendas often drive domestic economic reform with little accountability to the majority of the population. Critics point to the lack of an obvious visible link between democracy and sustainable development, especially given China's tremendous economic gains yet resistance (so far) to full democratization. With previous, structural adjustment policies delivering little on poverty reduction, discourse is now shifting back to the role of the state in infrastructure development, health provision, education and training, and the need for building effective institutions.

At the same time democracy is presented as the solution to multiple national problems and is strongly advocated by the international community and domestic activists across the world. Key factors in this contradiction lie in the nature of the implementation of democratic governance (does it 'deliver' to populations; can it be imposed by external armed intervention?), the design of post-war or post-authoritarian transitions, and liberalization/privatization reforms which may introduce new strains and inequalities unless they are carefully managed. In considering the impact of political restructuring on a population, the 'how' is as important as the 'what'.

This book is based on the premise that, in a world which is increasingly experienced as interdependent, it is essential to understand the linkages between democracy, conflict and human security. Sources of insecurity lie in exclusion and lack of access to power and resources. Human security emphasizes the protection of people from grave threats to their lives, safety from harm and violent conflict, and empowerment against such social threats as disease or crime. Democracy enables protection of peoples through institutional safeguards, equality before the law, and the advancement of human rights, Democratic practice links empowerment of people to critical developmental outcomes such as education, health care, and opportunities for livelihood.

> Paradoxically, at the same time as democracy is presented as the solution to multiple national problems, signs of a loss of confidence in democratic systems are emerging in many parts of the world. In conflict and post-war situations enormous attention is paid to elections as a main showcase of democracy, and huge resources are poured in to them, but the affected population may not feel the direct benefits of a representative system. In many situations there is a danger that dissatisfaction with democracy will lead to its collapse under the strain of social conflicts.

The credibility of democracy as a political system increasingly depends both on *how* it works—practice—and on *what* (whether) it delivers. In other words, it is crucial that democracy be able to move beyond the formal realm of electoral politics to the substantive one of enabling human rights, physical well-being and human development. In this sense, the current emphasis on democratic elections may strengthen certain kinds of political regimes and the competition between political parties, but it does not guarantee state responses to collective needs, the participation of civil society in decision-making processes, or the social and political accountability of the ruling classes in developing and transitional societies.

Democracy has been understood as an instrument for managing conflicting interests in non-violent ways, through electoral systems, checks and balances, power sharing, institutional design, political rights, the rule of law, mechanisms for representation and participation of the citizenry. It is now vital to establish and operationalize the linkages between democracy, conflict and human security. In retrospect, 1990s democratization theory may be seen as in some ways similar to earlier modernization or economic 'take-off' theory—linear in its assumptions and not capable of factoring in shocks, setbacks, or specific defining societal features.

> The credibility of democracy as a political system increasingly depends both on *how* it works—practice—and on whether it can deliver. The current emphasis on democratic elections may strengthen certain kinds of political regimes and the competition between political parties, but it does not guarantee state responses to collective needs, the participation of civil society in decision-making processes, or the social and political accountability of the ruling classes in developing and transitional societies.

1. Democratic Practice: A Linchpin for Realizing Human Security Aims

Democratization may introduce many paradoxes, dilemmas and problematic choices. Often the immediate effect of open competitive politics accentuates social differences. In some instances elections seem to contribute to—or even stimulate—violent conflict, as in the former Yugoslavia in 1989 where it can be argued that an undeveloped democratic political culture resulted in strongly nationalist parties, ensuing division and war. Iraq's January 2005 elections can be seen in this context even though the long-term impact of the US–UK 'guided democratization' there is unknown. At other times, however, it is clear that democracy can contribute to peace and set the stage for socio-economic development to alleviate the root causes of conflict, for example, when parties choose to exchange conflict on the streets for meaningful democratic reform, constitution-making and new elections, as in South Africa's transition from 1990 to 1996. South Korea built institutional strengths which would seem to have cushioned it in part from the Asian financial crisis of 1997/8, if its experience is compared to that of Indonesia. Democratic reform and economic development have in combination contributed to the reduction of levels of violence in Northern Ireland.

Thus, democracy as a system to enable societies to manage conflict through debate, electoral competition, representation and popular participation presents a conundrum. In theory, democracy is the ultimate system of conflict management: disputes are channelled through the political system, competing interests are reconciled through bargaining and problem solving, and the most deprived in society have an opportunity to influence policies that can alleviate the underlying root causes of conflict in poverty, inequality and social exclusion. But, clearly, democracy is not

> Often the immediate effect of open competitive politics accentuates social differences. In some instances elections seem to contribute to or even stimulate violent conflict. At other times, it is clear that democracy can contribute to peace and set the stage for socio-economic development to alleviate the root causes of conflict.

able always and routinely to function as a conflict-management mechanism of final resort. Today, many democratic systems are 'partial', lacking in some fundamental principle or feature of a fully-fledged democratic system (such as the protection of human rights for all), and social dissatisfaction with democracy as a system of governance is borne out in survey results; indeed, in many situations there is a danger that dissatisfaction with democracy will lead to its collapse under the strain of social conflicts.

There is increasing interest in the relationship between policy choices, social–economic development and democratic viability. For example, South Korea and Taiwan pursued their respective national democracy-building projects while holding to protectionist policies which resisted full-scale liberalization and have sustained both growth and development. This is in contrast to Latin America, where market reforms of neo-liberal orthodoxy were embraced fully—the opening of national economies, privatization of public enterprises, unrestricted access for foreign capital, and deregulation. Experience will vary from country to country; Argentina, Uruguay and Venezuela experienced increasing inequality up to 2003, while Brazil (historically the most unequal country in the region) experienced a moderate decline in inequality. The gradual removal of tariff barriers in the East African Community and freedom of movement for citizens in the Economic Community of West African States show a new awareness of the regional dimensions to encouraging trade and jobs.

> In theory, democracy is the ultimate system of conflict management: disputes are channelled through the political system, competing interests are reconciled through bargaining and problem solving, and the most deprived have an opportunity to influence policies that can alleviate the underlying root causes of conflict in poverty, inequality and social exclusion. But, clearly, democracy is not able always and routinely to function as a conflict-management mechanism of final resort.

2. Democracy by Default

Paradoxically, democracy is increasingly a universal value and a 'default' system of governance, with many forms. The *right to* democracy is becoming a universally accepted value, even in societies where underdevelopment or social tensions limit its possibilities. This is also the case during or in the aftermath of war, where 'war-to-democracy' transitions are a reflexive peacemaking strategy by the international community. Its possibilities are also limited during or in the aftermath of war when there are tough policy choices on balancing security and freedoms, and where the socio-economic conditions for the rapid introduction of democracy are not conducive to its quick consolidation.

> Democracy is increasingly a universal value and a 'default' system of governance, with many forms.

Arguing for the universality of democracy in practice in circumstances that are unfavourable to its success is a marked change from arguments that contend that democracy must wait until certain favourable 'preconditions' are achieved. As Amartya Sen suggests: 'Throughout the nineteenth century, theorists of democracy found it quite natural to discuss whether one country or another was "fit for democracy". This thinking changed only in the 20th century, with the recognition that the question itself was wrong: A country does not have to be deemed fit *for* democracy; rather, it has to become fit *through* democracy' (Sen 1999a: 4; see also Sen 1999b).

This distinction applies in highly conflicted societies as well, even in war-torn, weak, less developed or 'failed' states in which state capacities are destroyed, where civil society is weakened, and where political violence and manipulation are the paths of least resistance to securing territory and power. In internationally managed transitions in such war-torn environments (such as those in which the United Nations has exercised trusteeship-type authority), tight control over politics by the UN for a transitional period has been aimed at *building democratic institutions* in order to allow eventually for direct public participation in governance.

> 'A country does not have to be deemed fit *for* democracy; rather, it has to become fit *through* democracy.'

International IDEA, an intergovernmental organization created in 1995, defines democracy not only by institutional forms or processes, but by basic principles or values. The IDEA *Handbook on Democracy Assessment* defines two core principles as essential to democracy: 'popular control over public decision making and decision makers; and equality between citizens in the exercise of that control. In so far as these principles are embodied in governing arrangements we can call them "democratic" . . . Democracy is thus not an all-or-nothing affair, but a matter of degree' (International IDEA 2002: 3–4). It is also a matter of democratic practice (see the following box). Given these core principles, democracy is abetted by core mediating values, among them participation, authorization and choice, representation, accountability, transparency, responsiveness and solidarity (internal tolerance, international support).

> Democracy is not an all-or-nothing affair, but a matter of degree and of democratic practice.

Democratic Practice: A Definition

Democratic practice refers to both formal and informal institutional arrangements for collective decision making and a wide variety of deliberative decision-making processes that incorporate core values of democracy, such as inclusion, consensus building and accountability, in efforts to build and sustain peace.

The concept includes both traditionally conceived *institutional arrangements* of power sharing and *process* options aimed at creating and strengthening democratic values and behaviour and promoting positive outcomes related to human development and human security. In the 21st century, democracy must be able to relate the values of human rights and participation to meeting the challenges of poverty, inequality, and the peaceful management of complex social relations.

This book emphasizes the concept of democratic *practice*. A core principle of democratic practice is the immediate and long-term imperatives of human rights protection—and the more recent concept of a state's responsibility to protect by providing human security. Democracy and conflict management aim for convergent, not divergent, paths to peace.

Democratic practice stresses the traditional focus on democracy as *procedures for collective decision making* based on values of individual equality, participation, and fundamental human rights. In addition, it is concerned with the outcomes, recognizing the stark reality that if democracy fails to deliver just, visible socio-economic and environmental gains, its value as a process is fatally undermined by discontent.

Amartya Sen's admonitions about the imperatives of democracy are buttressed by the fact that, even in the most difficult post-war environments of today, international policy makers agree that a transition to democracy in these deeply divided (and wounded) societies is the ultimate goal of the peace process. This is true of situations in which democracy emerges as a negotiated outcome in a peace process, and in those situations in which outside forces intervene and 'impose' democracy (for an evaluation of the former cases, see Reilly 2003). Democracy's utility in these and other conditions of deep conflict is, as Sen suggests, its *intrinsic value* in promoting political and social participation, its *instrumental value* assuring clean governance through accountability and responsibility, and the *constructive role* of democracy in the formation of collective social values that take into account the relationships between needs, rights and duties for a given society.

There is also an essential link between democratization and development that is often overlooked or underutilized. The (aspired-to) democratic state must be seen not only as a regulatory mechanism for diverse and sometimes conflicting interests but also as an instrument 'for the achievement of socially desired collective goods and the well-being of all of society's members' (Stavenhagen 2003: iv).

Democratic practice, through which individuals and societies address and manage the underlying sources and immediate manifestations of conflict with democratic principles and processes, is the critical intermediary variable between the underlying root causes and the symptomatic expressions of conflict, on the one hand, and more effective realization of human development and human security for the 21st century on the other.

Democratic practice, through which individuals and societies address and manage the underlying sources and immediate manifestations of conflict with democratic principles and processes, is the critical intermediary variable between root causes and the symptomatic expressions of conflict, and more effective realization of human development and human security for the 21st century.

3. Democracy in a Myriad of Settings

Many societies today are in a simultaneous transition from internal war and political crises to recovery, and from authoritarianism or anarchy to a new set of democratically elected—and presumably legitimate—political leaders. Afghanistan, Iraq, Sri Lanka and Liberia capture the headlines. Other societies face the challenges of practising democracy while at the same time waging war against violent rebellions, secessionist struggles, criminal networks and terrorist threats. Sri Lanka is a case in point examined in this volume (see chapter 5). In Indonesia, democratization has run parallel to visible and violent conflicts in varied settings, from Ambon and Kalimantan to Aceh and West Papua. Other countries are required to, or aspire to, hold democratic elections in spite of major unresolved political problems, as in Kosovo and Palestine.

In these settings democracy is challenged and limited by the pursuit of security and protection of the state and society. How can democracy and security imperatives more easily coexist? The same question faces so-called 'mature' democracies of North and South, as demonstrated in the USA, Canada, France, the United Kingdom (UK) and Australia. Democracy is not only a political system but also a social form of processes and interrelationships. It can be fragile or seemingly robust, but will never be static or 'finished', as intense struggles between the executive and legislative and/or judicial branches of government continually show.

> In some settings democracy is challenged and limited by the pursuit of security and protection of the state and society.

For societies which experienced transitions from war to democracy in the 1990s, often with considerable external support, there are continued challenges of sustaining peace and preventing new violence from emerging; South Africa stands as an example of such a successful transition to new-found democracy, yet the country faces deep-rooted social challenges that could jeopardize its democracy and its post-apartheid social contract. Some have argued that in South Africa, or in other settings such as Bosnia, there is a need for 'post-settlement settlements' to reflect the need for a flexible structure of democracy to address the changing challenges of peace building over time. How can the fundamental structures of democratic institutions be revisited in still-conflicted societies when new uncertainties could undermine achievements in resolving old enmities and hatreds?

> Democracy is not only a political system but also a social form of processes and interrelationships. It can be fragile or seemingly robust, but will never be static or 'finished'.

It is also clear that a long period of sustained peace is a prerequisite for socio-economic development, especially in today's world where international capital inflows are critical to participation in a globalized economy; investments by outsiders and domestic investors alike are more likely to occur when there is social peace and some predictability in the political environment. Thus, the democratic management of social relations—especially on ethnic, racial and sectarian lines and across religious boundaries—is essential for achievement of the Millennium Development Goals. As the authors of the 2004 United Nations Development Programme (UNDP) *Human Development Report* argue, 'Cultural liberty is a vital part of human development because being able to choose one's identity—who one is—without losing the respect of others or being excluded from other choices is important to leading a full life' (UNDP 2004: 1).

For long-term social stability, too, democracy cannot be practised in a manner that citizens perceive as a façade masking semi-authoritarian control or 'capture' of the economy by powerful oligarchs. Populations in Bosnia, Georgia, Indonesia, the Philippines and Ukraine have taken to the streets to oppose authoritarian tendencies or perceived economic inequities. 'Democratic reform' is often seen as a disingenuous effort by the powerful to stay in office, or to benefit from privatization of public assets. In parts of Latin America and Africa there is a type of frozen 'presidentialism', effective one-party rule and half-hearted or manipulated reform; surveys of citizens in these regions show a deep concern about democracy that approaches disdain for democratic politics. In parts of the Arab world democracy is viewed as an aspiration by some and as an alien import by others; efforts to create a broader agenda for political reform in the region will face deep challenges and will instigate considerable conflict. Many people see the US and UK-led intervention in Iraq as the imposition of democracy 'at the barrel of a gun'.

> For long-term social stability, democracy cannot be practised in a manner that citizens perceive as a façade masking semi-authoritarian control or 'capture' of the economy by powerful oligarchs. 'Democratic reform' is often seen as a disingenuous effort by the powerful to stay in office or to benefit from privatization of public assets.

Clearly, all these situations have a particular contextual setting and involve deep historical fault-lines that defy broad characterizations. In addressing the interconnectedness between democracy, conflict and human security, this book speaks to a broad range of experience—established democracies, post-authoritarian contexts, transitions from autocracy, transitions from war, 'failed' states, façade democracies, and so on. In evaluating recent experiences of democracy's contribution to conflict management and to the achievement of the broader human security aims, this work seeks to contribute to innovative and effective democratic practices that address the severe social challenges that are surely to be a feature of the 21st-century world.

Two essential arguments underlie the need to articulate more fully the possibilities of democratic practice contributing to peace.

- First, for democracy to flourish over time it should not be introduced or imposed by fundamentally undemocratic means, either by authoritarian governments practising 'façade democracy' or by international actors that lack legal or de facto legitimacy of action in guiding war-shattered countries from violence to democracy. (Both criteria, of legal and de facto legitimacy of action, could in large degree be claimed as a basis for restructuring and assistance to Germany and Japan after World War II.)

• Second, progress towards democracy can be enhanced in myriad ways in divided societies even when national or transitional processes limit the functioning of a fully-fledged, complete system of democracy at all levels of society; in consultative processes, at local levels, in interim measures, or through dialogue processes, practices based on the fundamental values of democracy can lay the foundation for a more extensive and stable system to emerge over time.

4. The Structure and Aims of This Book

Democracy, Conflict and Human Security: Pursuing Peace in the 21st Century is the sequel to an earlier IDEA publication from 1998, *Democracy and Deep-Rooted Conflict: Options for Negotiators* (see Harris and Reilly 1998). As such, it reinforces and updates aspects of the earlier work, such as evaluation of peace processes, power sharing, institutional design, and measures to achieve sustainability of democracy after conflict over time. However, given the human security challenges of the 21st century, there is a need to consider the democracy–conflict nexus through a wider lens. This book outlines the need for democracy to manage conflict through institutional processes, but also to respond effectively in order to achieve tangible outcomes—such as recognition and citizenship, the distribution of public goods and the delivery of services—which contribute to the longer-term amelioration of the deep structures and causes of conflict. Addressing human security needs implies the fostering of 'voice' and participation, which in turn are functions of internal governance practices.

Key Insights from the IDEA Handbook on *Democracy and Deep-Rooted Conflict: Options for Negotiators*

• *The importance of democratic institutions*
Making appropriate choices about democratic institutions—forms of devolution or autonomy, electoral system design, legislative bodies, judicial structures and so on—is crucial in building an enduring and peaceful settlement.
• *Conflict management, not resolution*
There needs to be . . . more pragmatic interest in conflict management: how to deal with it in a constructive way, how to bring opposing sides together in a co-operative process, how to design a practical, achievable, cooperative system for the constructive management of difference.
• *The importance of process*
The process by which parties reach an outcome impacts significantly on the quality of the outcome. Attention must be paid to every aspect of the process of negotiations in order to reach a durable outcome.

Democracy, Conflict and Human Security is designed to clarify core concepts, articulate the meaning of 'democratic practice', highlight key themes of social crises, breakdowns and recoveries, address the peculiar and special challenges of democracy in post-war settings, highlight democracy's relationship to addressing structural causes of conflict, and identify ways to strengthen international democracy building in pursuing human security goals. It is also designed to represent a plurality of 'democracies'—evidence that no 'one size fits all'—and the validity of diverse experience.

The present volume is a distillation of current scholarly research and practitioner experience. Together with its companion volume of selected readings (Volume II) and the additional and online resources that accompany them, it is meant to promote debate and critical thinking so as to inform strategies and policy decisions on several levels. It is intended to reach national actors pursuing political reform agendas or social justice; policy professionals in various local, national, regional and international settings who are negotiating or implementing peace agreements; individuals involved in democratization as a fundamental approach to peace building; and others in international organizations or donor agencies tasked with development assistance. It may be of use to members of the media, who interpret and communicate to the public about these issues, and for educational purposes.

Democracy, Conflict and Human Security seeks to address and be relevant for both North and South, working on the assumption that no democracy is ever perfect or finished, and that populations worldwide face human security needs which differ in degree more than kind. While states calling themselves democracies vary enormously in size and composition, democratic principles may transcend variation, finding different expressions that are appropriate to contexts and local ownership. Volume II, the *Democracy, Conflict and Human Security Source Book*, presents related background papers and case studies—first-hand experience from contexts including Southern Africa and Northern Europe, Sierra Leone and Liberia, Haiti, Bolivia, El Salvador, India, Indonesia and Sri Lanka.

Volume I develops its theme with the following sequence.

Chapter 1, 'Democracy and Human Security', examines in depth the meaning of human security and outlines immediate, intermediate and long-term challenges. It explores the sources of insecurity which lead to deprivation, violence and war, and outlines the meaning of democratic practice.

Chapter 2, 'Democratization after the Cold War: Managing Turbulent Transitions', traces patterns of democratization particularly in the 1990s and 2000s, the role of social mobilization and politics for setting the human security agenda, democratization as conflict-inducing, and 'transition' findings relevant for policy today.

Chapter 3, 'Democratic Practice: Managing Power, Identity and Difference', outlines features of democracy that facilitate conflict management, the critical area of balancing majority prerogatives and minority rights, electoral and institutional design, and consensus building in divided or diverse societies. Measures for social inclusion are a key theme in this chapter.

Chapter 4, 'When Democracy Falters', addresses the crisis in confidence generated by institutional deficits, the failure to deliver, practical inadequacies, crisis or the abuse of power. 'Façade democracy' and 'liberalization without democratization' are examined, as are states of emergency and the importance of international norms.

Chapter 5, 'Democracy in War-Torn Societies', is concerned with human security in the aftermath of war: human rights and local-level participation in peace building, demobilization and security sector reform, power sharing and the question of legitimacy. Election processes in post-war settings and the long-term human security issue of reconciliation are included.

Chapter 6, 'International Democracy Building: Pursuing Peace in the 21st Century', presents a summary of findings, and addresses the question of strengthening democratic practice for promoting peaceful outcomes and social justice. It outlines multi-level options for improved measures, and offers concluding remarks.

The work reflected in these volumes is the result of collective deliberation and engaged, international consultation. One study for Volume II is missing—a paper to have been written for the concluding chapter by Abdulkadir Yahya Ali, co-director of the Center for Research and Dialogue, Mogadishu. Yahya was assassinated in Mogadishu on 11 July 2005. To all those who knew him, he was an inspiration in his work for Somali peace and the beginnings of democratic process as an essential requirement for that peace.

References and Further Reading

Harris, Peter and Reilly, Ben, *Democracy and Deep-Rooted Conflict: Options for Negotiators* (Stockholm: International IDEA, 1998)

International IDEA, *Handbook of Democracy Assessment* (Stockholm: International IDEA, 2002)

Reilly, Ben, 'Democratic Validation', in John Darby and Roger MacGinty (eds), *Contemporary Peacemaking: Conflict, Violence, and Peace Processes* (London: Palgrave Macmillan, 2003), pp. 174–83

Sen, Amartya 'Democracy as a Universal Value', *Journal of Democracy*, 10/3 (1999) (Sen 1999a)

— 'The Importance of Democracy', in Amartya Sen, *Development as Freedom* (New York: Anchor Books, 1999), chapter 6, pp. 149–59 (Sen 1999b)

Stavenhagen, Rodolfo, 'Needs, Rights and Social Development', Overarching Concerns Paper No. 2, United Nations Research Institute for Social Development, July 2003

United Nations, Commission on Human Security, *Human Security Now: Final Report* (New York: United Nations Commission on Human Security, 2003)

United Nations Development Programme (UNDP), *Human Development Report 2004: Cultural Liberty in Today's Diverse World* (New York: United Nations Development Programme, 2004), <http://hdr.undp.org/reports/global/2004/>

CHAPTER 1

CHAPTER 1

1. Democracy and Human Security

In today's world threats to 'security' come as much from factors that occur within states as from the historically significant threat of war between states. Security is being more broadly defined away from the traditional state-centred focus on 'national security' and in terms of the well-being of whole populations, the need for equitable development and sound inter-group relations, and the human needs of both sub-national groups and individuals within a state's borders. The idea of human security shifts the focus away from the state and makes the primary unit of analysis the individual, who is meant to live in *freedom from fear and freedom from want*. The concept has developed in response to the complex emergencies of the 1990s and 2000s.

Most violent conflict—the most immediate and acute threat to human security and to human development—is internal to states. Many analysts see the ultimate 'causes' of conflict in economic deprivation, social exclusion and deep-seated social structures that give rise to group grievances—often exacerbated by cross-border spillover influences. Human security threats emanate from weak state environments. There is therefore an imperative for focusing on improving democracy's capacity to address the underlying sources of human insecurity.

Critical to the mitigation and management of contemporary root causes of conflict is *democracy that strengthens the state* by strengthening social capacities to manage threats to human security. Increasingly democracy is not seen as something that is either–or, but rather as a complicated practice. It finds its meaning in the way in which it is put into operation or application. *Democratic practice* can be applied as a concept to address key governance challenges that relate to conflict mitigation. It strengthens the state and strengthens society by helping to facilitate mutually reinforcing relationships between public authorities and civil society. Precisely because deeply divided societies lack cross-cutting social relationships, democratic practice that focuses on strengthening the state and strengthening society is critically important.

Since the end of the cold war, the international system has experienced dramatic shifts away from the traditional state-centred focus on 'national security'. There has been a marked re-conceptualization of security needs from the point of view of populations themselves. The new awareness is driven by realization that in today's world threats to 'security' come as much from factors that occur within states as from the historically significant threat of war between states, such as the world wars of the 20th century.

The concept of human security represents a significant paradigm shift for scholars and practitioners working in the fields of development, democracy, human rights and humanitarian assistance. Traditional approaches and policies in international relations have placed the state and its interests at the centre of concern, while the interests, grievances and collective experiences of individuals remained subsumed under the larger analytical unit of the state. In such approaches, security is thought of in terms of national security, conceived in such terms as territorial integrity, political viability, power, prestige, sovereignty and economic interests. Threats to national/state security include interstate conflict and warfare; the proliferation of traditional and nuclear weapons; intra-state conflict, rebellion, revolution, and terrorism; trade disputes, retaliation and protectionism; and in some instances environmental degradation.

In contrast, the idea of human security shifts the focus away from the state and makes the individual the primary unit of analysis, who is meant to live under socio-economic and political conditions that seek to guarantee the twin values of *freedom from fear* and *freedom from want*. Here, many of the threats to human security are the same as those that confront states, and the role of the state is by no means diminished. Rather, the state is still seen as the main organ with the capacity to provide the necessary institutions for realizing human security. The key difference is that the idea of human security, like the idea of *human development*, reorients the analytical focus away from state interest to that of human dignity (see the contribution by Todd Landman in Volume II).

> The idea of human security shifts the focus away from the state and makes the individual the primary unit of analysis. The individual is meant to live under socio-economic and political conditions that seek to guarantee the twin values of freedom from fear and freedom from want.

This chapter addresses the essential linkages between the human security concept and democracy, in particular the notion of democratic practice. *Human security* emphasizes the protection of people from grave threats to their lives, their safety from harm and violent *conflict*, and their empowerment against such social threats as disease or crime. *Democracy* enables the protection of peoples through the advancement of human rights. *Democratic practices* provide for the empowerment of people for critical developmental outcomes such as education, health care, and opportunities for livelihood. Democratic practices can also be the ultimate viable mechanism for socio-political conflict management, in which conflicts are managed through non-violent negotiation, dialogue and decision processes. Through the practice of democracy, social tolerance, coexistence and cooperation can be shown as avenues for meeting key development goals—such as measurable improvements in literacy, health, the ability to earn a livelihood, and environmental sustainability.

The need for nation states to counter external threats has not gone away with the end of the cold war. Traditional international conflicts still occur, albeit much less frequently, as in Ethiopia and Eritrea's recurrent war. But the sources of threats to security are seen in a broader context in which serious challenges come not just from other states but from intangible, non-state forces as well. In a globally interdependent world, all states are affected by instability and threats that emanate from external sources—disease and climate change, for example, do not respect national borders. The pursuit of national security requires attention to and the mitigation of threats to the people of states everywhere. Many states are either incapable of providing or unwilling to provide security for all their citizens. It is for this reason that the international community is especially interested in the concept of state building, or creating structures of legitimate authority that can provide a basic political framework and create public goods like health, education, environmental safeguards, a functioning, fair system of law, and sound economic management.

In 2003, the United Nations Commission on Human Security outlined in its final report the interwoven challenges that give rise to the need for new concepts to grasp these realities:

> Human security is concerned with safeguarding and expanding people's vital freedoms. It requires both shielding people from acute threats and empowering people to take charge of their own lives... . The demands of human security involve a broad range of interconnected issues [such as] conflict and poverty, protecting people during violent conflict and in post-conflict situations, defending people who are forced to move, overcoming economic insecurities, guaranteeing the availability and affordability of essential health care, and ensuring the elimination of illiteracy and education deprivation and of schools that promote intolerance (United Nations, Commission on Human Security 2003: iv).

At the 2000 Millennium Summit, the countries of the United Nations committed themselves to the realization of clear and measurable goals for development—the Millennium Development Goals. These goals are more likely to be pursued and reached in countries that are well governed, that feature inclusiveness and participation in decision

> Security is being more broadly defined in terms of the risks and threats to the well-being of whole populations, the need for equitable development and sound inter-group relations, and the human needs of both sub-national groups and individuals within a state's borders.

making, and that allow for the exercise of democratic choice through the ballot box. Realizing them is a matter not just of promoting prosperity and freedom from want, but of achieving national and human security needs worldwide.

1. The 21st Century: Immediate, Intermediate, and Long-Term Human Security Challenges

Security is being more broadly defined in terms of the risks and threats to the well-being of whole populations, the need for equitable development and sound inter-group relations, and the human needs of both sub-national groups and individuals within a state's borders. In sum, the concept of human security refers to the *protection* and safety of society's most vulnerable segments from harm, and the *empowerment* of people in human development terms (enhancing their ability to make choices in pursuing their lives). Without basic security for all citizens, human rights principles and people's practical ability to participate in democracy are rendered meaningless. As the scholar Astri Suhrke writes, 'the concept of human security ... is associated with the pre-eminent progressive values of the 1990s: human rights, international humanitarian law, and socio-economic development based on equity' (Suhrke 1999: 266).

Concerns about human security have their most immediate origins in the complex emergencies of the early 1990s to which the international community seemed especially ill-equipped to respond—war-induced famine in Somalia, ethnic cleansing in Bosnia and Herzegovina, genocide in Rwanda, and complex exits from civil war in places such as Cambodia, Mozambique or El Salvador. 'Hard' security concerns, such as the demobilization of armed forces, came face to face with humanitarian concerns such as mobilizing for the mass distribution of food, health supplies and shelter. As a consequence of the horrors of the 1990s and early 2000s, new norms, such as the protection of civilians in war, and institutions such as the International Criminal Court are designed to enhance international cooperation in protecting whole populations or social groups. In the longer term, the keys to 21st century security lie both in a system of states committed to the resolution of international disputes through universal institutions such as the UN or regional organizations, and in the democratization and development of the political institutions and societies to achieve peace within these states.

Box 1.1: Examples of Human Security Crises: Natural and Human-Induced Catastrophic Events
- The Chernobyl explosion, 1986
- The Horn of Africa crisis, late 1980s
- The global refugee/internally displaced persons (IDP) crisis, early 1990s
- The emergence of HIV/AIDS as a security threat, early 1990s
- 'Non-consensual humanitarian intervention', beginning with the US-led operations in Somalia, 1991–6
- Ethnic cleansing in Bosnia, 1992–5
- The Rwandan genocide, 1994
- Global climate change: expected impact on island states
- The East Asian financial crisis, 1997

- Targeted political violence and transnational bombings
- Severe acute respiratory syndrome (SARS), 2003
- The Darfur atrocities, 2003–2005
- The South-East Asian tsunami, 2004
- The South Asian/Hindu Kush earthquake, 2005

1.1. Defining 'Human Security': Immediate Crises, Structural Injustices

Human security—a concept developed to embrace the new realities—remains an unsettled concept in the international community. There are debates about the boundaries of the term, its utility as a guideline for action, and its relationship to other concepts such as human rights, human development and sovereignty. For example, there is debate over whether human security should refer to narrow definitions of basic human rights, or to broad and all-encompassing goods such as sustainable development (Hampson 2003). Likewise, are natural disasters human security events or does the concept refer primarily to the consequences of violent conflict and/or environmental catastrophes like Chernobyl? When do violations of human security demand immediate international action, for example, through humanitarian intervention, when some problems are urgent and immediate whereas others are long-term?

Despite this debate about the boundaries of the concept, there is at least one element on which broad agreement does exist: attention to human security is necessary to establish the minimal conditions under which formal democracy can be meaningfully practised and domestic and international peace can be secured. Efforts to introduce democratic procedures in conditions of grave insecurity—such as holding an election in the midst of widespread, violent political conflict—will inherently produce limited results.

The term 'human security' originated in the UNDP's 1994 *Human Development Report*, which sought to highlight new concerns about global security and the importance of addressing chronic threats to human life. The report's authors criticized narrow concepts of human security that focus on state security: 'Forgotten were the legitimate concerns of ordinary people who sought security in their daily lives. For many of them, security symbolized protection from the threat of disease, hunger, unemployment, crime, social conflict, political repression, and environmental hazards' (UNDP 1994: 22).

> Attention to human security is necessary to establish the minimal conditions under which formal democracy can be meaningfully practised and domestic and international peace can be secured.

The authors of the 1994 UNDP report cite seven critical areas of concern that continue today to provide a succinct and clear (if expansive) list of the broadest range of possible features of human security to which the international community should aspire for the people in all the world's states. These are:

- freedom from extreme poverty (economic security);

- freedom from hunger, or secure access to food;
- health security: access to prevention and treatment of infectious diseases;
- environmental security, or protection from pollution and the depletion of non-renewable resources;
- freedom from fear for persons, such as protection of one's physical safety;
- freedom from fear for communities, such as protection of traditional cultures and vulnerable groups; and
- 'political security', to include freedom from repression and the ability to enjoy civil and political freedoms and other human rights.

Threats to these elements of human security come from a variety of sources and take many forms; in the UNDP's 1994 analysis, the principal future sources of human security threats will come from deep-seated 'root causes of conflict' such as unchecked population growth, disparities in economic opportunities, excessive international migration, environmental degradation, drug production and trafficking, and international terrorism (UNDP 1994: 22–46). In retrospect, the 1994 definition provided by the UNDP seems a little too broad and unwieldy, and subsequently the definition has been narrowed a little without losing the emphasis on taking a more broadly encompassing view of what constitutes security in today's world. Criticism of the term is valid: the scholar Roland Paris writes 'If human security is all these things, what is it not?' (Paris 2001: 92).

In 2000 the UN Security Council adopted Resolution 1325 on women, peace and security, calling for the involvement of more women in peace-building and conflict-mediation work, and promoting women as advocates for peace. The awareness of gender perspectives on war and peace is growing but progress is mainly visible at policy level. The actual content of Resolution 1325 is to ensure female participation at all levels of peace negotiations. The measure is intended to assist in changing practice after decades of exclusion. A study of women's activism in Timor-Leste (Cristalis and Scott 2006) points out that, even when their physical safety is not in jeopardy, women have been excluded from the negotiation and decision-making processes on the basis that these are solely 'men's business'. These findings are supported by a gender audit of the 1994 post-conflict period and transitional election in Mozambique (Jacobson 1997), which noted that women's organizations had been completely excluded from the peace negotiations, despite the essential role they had played in maintaining the social fabric of the country over decades of war.

With such concerns as gender on the table, it was up to the 2003 United Nations Commission on Human Security (created at the UN Millennium Summit in 2000) to define the concept of human security more carefully and fully, and to underscore its practical application in humanitarian crises, in post-war situations, in achieving gains in education and health, and in preventing violent conflicts. The commission's final report, *Human Security Now*, issued in 2003, carefully lays out two essential components of human security that give meaning to its overall definitional statement, which declares:

Human security: *to protect* the vital core of all human lives in ways that enhance human freedoms and human fulfilment. Human security means protecting fundamental freedoms—freedoms that are the essence of life. It means protecting people from critical (severe) and pervasive (widespread) threats and situations. It means using processes that build on people's strengths and aspirations. It means creating political, social, environmental, economic, military and cultural systems that together *give people the building blocks* of survival, livelihood, and dignity (United Nations, Commission on Human Security 2003: 4, emphasis added).

International IDEA is working on the basis of these two components of human security as:

• *protection*, which seeks to ensure safety from events and forces that are beyond the individual's control, such as a 'financial crisis, a violent conflict, chronic destitution, a terrorist attack, HIV/AIDS, under investment in health care, water shortages, pollution from a distant land' (United Nations, Commission on Human Security 2003); and
• *empowerment*, or the capacity of people to develop and pursue their aspirations as individuals and communities; empowerment equally refers to the strength and ability of people (men and women) to understand and advocate for their rights and interests in democratic processes of elections and in direct participation in decision making (United Nations, Commission on Human Security 2003: 11).

Box 1.2: Analysis: Is Emphasis on Human Security a Response to the Pressures of Globalization?

Globalization has generated its discontents: some see the increased economic ties among states as exploitative of the global poor, as producing new inequities that will generate social conflict, and as weakening local identities and community-level control over people's lives. In an era of globalization, does the world need a new and different vision of what constitutes 'security'? International interdependence and the security threat that emanates from environmental catastrophe were cruelly demonstrated by the Chernobyl disaster in 1986.

Instances such as these and problems of global concern such as climate change have significantly broadened definitions of security and highlighted the weakening relevance of international frontiers. New forms of epidemiological, biological and chemical threats have emerged. Threats have come to be more directly experienced by people than by states as such, and thus the concept of security needs to expand to account for today's 'hard security' (such as international conflict) and 'soft security' (health, environmental effects) threats. At the same time, global governance has improved in the pursuit of international human rights.

For further reading, see Simmons, P. J. and de Jonge Oudraat, Chantal, *Managing Global Issues: Lessons Learned* (Washington, DC: Carnegie Endowment for International Peace, 2001).

The Commission on Human Security organized its findings under topics that evaluate how human security threats appear for people in situations of violent conflict—the special insecurities experienced by migrants (both economic migrants and political refugees and the internally displaced); human security challenges in post-war settings; the relationship between poverty and insecurity; health as an essential element of security; education as the pathway to empowerment; and measures the international community can take to advance human security (see below).

In late 2004, another United Nations panel of eminent persons—the UN High-Level Panel on Threats, Challenges and Change—articulated future security concerns. This group, too, found in its final report, 'A More Secure World: Our Shared Responsibility', that states acting alone are incapable of ensuring security in today's complex world of globalized, interdependent states. The High-Level Panel reinforced the basic logic of the human security concept in arguing that 'Today's threats recognize no national boundaries, are connected, and must be addressed at the global and regional as well as national levels. No State, no matter how powerful, can by its own efforts alone make itself invulnerable to today's threats. And it cannot be assumed that every State will always be able, or willing, to protect its own people and not to harm its neighbours' (United Nations, High-Level Panel on Threats, Challenges and Change 2004: 1).

> 'Today's threats recognize no national boundaries, are connected, and must be addressed at the global and regional as well as national levels. No State, no matter how powerful, can by its own efforts alone make itself invulnerable to today's threats.'

The central message of the High-Level Panel is the need for a new security consensus among states to collectively address the 21st century challenges of both traditional threats, such as the proliferation of chemical or nuclear weapons, border and territorial disputes, and enduring rivalries, and new threats from non-state actors such as transnational terrorism. At the same time, the panel concludes that these 'threats without borders', if not addressed, will create new future human security challenges for weak and strong states alike. The panel's findings highlight poverty and economic stress, the transnational migration of diseases across boundaries, weak states that enable global crime and terrorism, and nuclear, biological and chemical weapons proliferation as the key 21st century security challenges.

Box 1.3: The Concept of Human Security : A Bird's Eye View

Some have likened the human security concept to a diamond, which has a number of facets or vantage points that allow for alternative insights into its multidimensional meanings. This is also true of the human security concept. In sum, three such facets of the concept are succinctly summarized in the categories used by the UN Secretary-General, Kofi Annan, in his March 2005 report 'In Larger Freedom':

Freedom from want. Extreme poverty—more than 1.2 billion people live on less than 1 US dollar per day—together with the associated vulnerability to disease and child mortality, poses immediate, critical threats to the safety of nearly one-sixth of the world's population.

Freedom from fear. Terrorism, nuclear, chemical and biological threats, war and the risk of new wars top the agenda of human security advocates. Terrorism requires a comprehensive strategy that includes the need for a new international convention to coordinate and harmonize international reaction to these threats. Progress towards the elimination of weapons of mass destruction has taken on new urgency with the upsurge in transnational terrorism, with the risk that terrorists would use such weapons against innocent populations. Finally, war-to-democracy transitions are essential because historically, where civil wars have recurred after several years, this has usually been because underlying grievances, including economic relationships, are unresolved.

Freedom to live in dignity. Living in dignity means enjoying fundamental human rights, to include the right to democratic participation, living under the rule of law, and freedom to practise religion, express views, and live in a society that is guided by principles of tolerance. Essential to the pursuit of living in dignity is the state's 'responsibility to protect' groups and individuals in society which are the most vulnerable to violation of their human rights.

See United Nations, 'In Larger Freedom: Towards Development, Security and Human Rights for All: Report of the Secretary-General', UN document A/59/2005, 21 March 2005, <http://www.un.org/largerfreedom/contents.htm>.

Importantly, the panel underscored again the core concerns of the human security approach: it found that there are clear and direct linkages between environmental degradation, disease and violent conflict. 'Poverty, infectious disease, environmental degradation, and war feed one another in a deadly cycle', the panel reported: 'Environmental stress, caused by large populations and shortages of land or other natural resources, can contribute to civil violence' (United Nations, High-Level Panel on Threats, Challenges and Change 2004: 15). The panel takes the term 'human security' to encompass the need to respond to immediate crises—both man-made and natural— that present grave and immediate threats. In man-made crises that are the result of violent conflict and civil war, human security concerns involve principally ending the war as the acute source of insecurity, nudging the protagonists towards peace, and building the peace in the post-war environment; in this context, human security is about achieving a transition away from war towards democracy. Finally, the concept of human security takes the long view according to which the underlying root causes of conflict must be addressed through development if the ambitious aim of providing security for all people is to be realized in the decades ahead.

> The underlying root causes of conflict must be addressed through development if the ambitious aim of providing security for all people is to be realized in the decades ahead.

Box 1.4: Human Security: Immediate, Intermediate and Long-term Dimensions

Immediate-term Human Insecurity

Overview

The early 1990s witnessed the rapid emergence of the concept of 'complex humanitarian emergencies' on the global security agenda. Internal conflicts such as those in Somalia, Rwanda and Bosnia that characterized the early 1990s affected states well beyond their borders through refugee flows and the need to mount a coordinated global response to the humanitarian tragedies they created. These conflicts exposed the lack of capacity of existing relationships and institutions to act quickly or (ultimately) decisively in humanitarian emergencies with international ramifications. Environmental degradation, combined with its effects such as pollution, the rapid spread of infectious diseases, and food insecurity, has also been described as a new human security threat emanating from immediate crises that are spawned by or that accompany such armed conflicts.

Concerns

- providing immediate humanitarian relief for basic human needs—life, food, shelter, health and education;
- enforcing humanitarian law on all parties (state and non-state) to the conflict;
- strategically promoting human rights in the delivery and distribution of aid;
- disarming combatants, eliminating landmines or other indiscriminate threats, and soaking up the private supply of small arms;
- reining in and preventing transnational criminal and terrorist networks that find opportunities in weak-state environments; and
- preventing escalating social violence and inter-group tensions, and managing conflicts over citizenship.

Intermediate-term Responses

Overview

Most wars today end at the negotiating table, not on the battlefield. Consequently, they are usually ended in a political settlement that unfolds over time—a lengthy transition in which war and violence are supposed to be replaced by democracy and the non-violent management of social differences. Such protracted transitions are perilous, and pose human security challenges of their own. After the guns have fallen silent—in countries such as El Salvador, Cambodia, Bosnia or Sudan—the transition itself raises human security challenges of reintegrating the displaced, of pursuing justice when war crimes have been committed, and of undertaking painful and difficult social transformation.

Concerns

- enforcing and gaining commitment to ceasefire agreements;
- managing transitional political violence among the contenders for post-war political power;

- inducing the parties to share power rather than seek a winner-takes-all solution;
- resolving difficult, competing claims for group self-determination;
- creating the parameters of a new democratic political order in which competing social forces can resolve disputes and conflicts and achieve common goals through popular participation and consensus-seeking;
- ensuring accountability for past crimes while pursuing a spirit of reconciliation;
- achieving economic recovery and providing the intermediate-term economic stability necessary to produce a 'peace dividend'; and
- ensuring that short-term political settlements are not reached at the expense of long-term transformational necessities if future violent conflict is to be avoided.

Long-term Challenges
Human insecurity challenges will arise in the future if present-day root causes of conflict go un-addressed. Two-thirds of the world's poorest people—the 1.2 million who live on less than 1 USD a day—live in Africa and Asia. Natural disasters, financial crises that wipe out people's life savings, economic meltdowns that create unemployment, terrorist attacks and conflict all produce conditions of deprivation. The UN's Millennium Development Goals, adopted in September 2000, are designed to put the world on a clear and measurable path to addressing the long-term sources of human insecurity.

Concerns
- promoting economic growth that alleviates the plight of the world's extremely poor;
- addressing the distribution of income and wealth in societies to ensure that the poor benefit through employment opportunities, higher wages, security of assets, and the ability to participate in the economy;
- special attention to the concerns of women, who as a global class are consistently seen in indicators of human development as less well-off in life choices than men;
- reforming global trade to eliminate disparities and distortions—such as unreasonable trade barriers and/or subsidies in rich and poor countries alike—that inhibit the optimal, equitable performance of the international economy;
- developing democratic institutions and processes that empower all segments of society to participate equitably in political, economic and social life and that do not allow for social exclusion, intolerance or bigotry;
- creating conditions for environmental sustainability and the prevention of long-term ecological instabilities that will produce future economic catastrophes;

- preventing to the extent possible future natural disasters or man-made disasters such as famine, and developing adequate and accurate early-warning systems of impending disaster;
- protecting the most vulnerable elements of society, such as those with no livelihood, poor workers, the disabled, the elderly or the diseased; and
- creating opportunity for local action, direct citizen participation, and community-level problem solving.

1.2. Perspectives on Human Security

The human security approach has advanced significantly since its conceptualization in the mid-1990s. In the 1990s, states including Canada, Norway and Japan, together with international non-governmental organizations (NGOs), advanced the concept of human security, which places emphasis on the linkages between political, economic, environmental and health factors as underlying threats to peace. Lloyd Axworthy, former foreign minister of Canada, argued that human security 'means safety for people from both non-violent and violent threats. It is a condition or state of being characterized by freedom from pervasive threats to their rights, safety, or even their lives' ('Chairman's statement', Lysøen Conference on Human Security 1999).

What has been unique about the human security advocates is the alliance of states and NGOs which have worked collaboratively in pursuit of overall and specific policy objectives. Fourteen states are members or observers of the present Human Security Network, including Austria, Canada, Chile, Costa Rica, Greece, Ireland, Jordan, Mali, the Netherlands, Norway, Slovenia, South Africa (observer), Switzerland and Thailand (as of August 2005). The network, which operates virtually at <http://www.humansecuritynetwork.org>, works in close cooperation with dozens of NGOs that conduct advocacy campaigns and provide operational and field support for wide-ranging activities that fall under the human security rubric.

Japan has fostered human security as central to its diplomacy, supporting the establishment of the Commission on Human Security and the Trust Fund for Human Security which implements diverse UN projects (see http://mofa.go.jp/policy/other/bluebook/2004/chapter 3). The European Security Strategy adopted by the European Council in 2003 notes that present and future security challenges cannot be 'tackled by purely military means' (European Union 2003). Human security has emerged in the last decade or so as a leitmotif of a number of elements of the evolving Common Foreign and Security Policy of an enlarged European Union (EU), in part as a response to the recognition that poverty, inequality, crime, corruption, demographic instabilities and environmental degradation generate problems that often spill over national borders. These tangible concerns also relate to the traditional agendas of human rights and democracy promotion, as governance is seen as the linchpin variable between the root causes of insecurity and their positive management.

As the authors of the Barcelona Report of the Study Group on Europe's Security Capabilities argued in September 2004, human security has emerged as a central theme of a common foreign policy for European states because of the moral thrust of its content, countries' legal obligations under international law pertaining to human rights, and 'enlightened self-interest' as the problems of terrorism, organized crime, unchecked migration and 'soft' threats such as environmental degradation pose new types of security threat (Study Group on Europe's Security Capabilities 2004: 9–10).

At the same time, major global powers such as China, the United States and Russia still emphasize national security as the operational principle of their foreign policies, although these states, too, are now fully aware that traditional conceptions of and approaches to security are inadequate, if not altogether obsolete. The United States has not generally—and certainly not officially or overtly—adopted the rhetoric of human security. Indeed, some elites in the US foreign policy establishment have been hostile to the concept since its first introduction in 1994 in UNDP reports and its further articulation by Lloyd Axworthy. US opposition to the 1997 Convention on the Prohibition of the Use, Stockpiling, Production and Transfer of Anti-personnel Mines and on Their Destruction (the Landmines Convention), the unwillingness of the USA to adopt the Convention on the Rights of the Child and the Kyoto Protocol or to ratify the 1998 Organization of Armerican States (OAS) Firearms Convention (the Inter-American Convention Against the Illicit Manufacturing of and Trafficking in Firearms, Ammunition, Explosives, and other Related Materials), and its opposition to the International Criminal Court are examples of the ways in which US policy has clearly and unambiguously diverged from the policies of those states which have more fully embraced the human security approach.

> Human security threats emanate from weak state environments. Governance is seen as the key variable between the root causes of insecurity and their positive management.

Table 1.1: Security—For Whom?

	Traditional	Contemporary
States	Conventional realism (national security)	New security issues (e.g. environmental security)
Society and individuals	Internal conflicts, genocide and forced migration (civilians in war)	Human security (human rights, safety of peoples, sustainable development)

Source: Adapted from Paris, Roland, 'Human Security: Paradigm Shift or Hot Air?', *International Security,* 26/2 (2001), pp.87–102.

2. Sources of Human Insecurity

Violent conflict presents the most immediate and acute threat to human security and to human development. Even without consensus on the definition and utility of human security, there is today a recognized need in virtually all quarters of the international community to clearly articulate those factors that lie at the root of conflict and the dynamics by which such latent causes lead to violence.

2.1. Global Conflict Trends

The trend in global conflict since the end of the cold war at the beginning of the 1990s—that most of the serious violence in the world is seen in settings of social conflict in struggles that are internal to the borders of the states which make up the world system—continues.

> Violent conflict presents the most immediate and acute threat to human security and to human development. Even without consensus on the definition and utility of human security, there is today a recognized need in virtually all quarters of the international community to clearly articulate those factors that lie at the root of conflict and the dynamics by which such latent causes lead to violence.

There is both good news and bad news in an analysis of armed conflict since the end of the cold war. According to a major ongoing tally of armed conflict by researchers at the University of Uppsala's Department of Peace and Conflict Research (most recently extensively updated in 2003), the good news is that the overall number of armed conflicts continues to decline. In 2003, there were 29 active conflicts with battle-related deaths of more that 25 in a year; in 1989, there were 54 such conflicts. Not since 1970 has the incidence of armed conflict been so low—if the measure of conflict is 'battle-related deaths'. The bad news is that between 1989 and 2003 (the last year for which firm data have been reported) there were 116 significant armed conflicts around the globe, of which 92 were essentially internal (Eriksson and Wallensteen 2004).[1]

Although there was a drop in the number of *major* armed conflicts (defined by the Uppsala University researchers as more than 1,000 battlefield deaths in a year) between 1992, when there were the highest number of such wars, and the present, new wars erupted in 2003—notably the Iraq intervention, the fighting in Darfur in Sudan, and the renewal of a violent conflict in Senegal—which temper any nascent enthusiasm that war is becoming obsolete.[2] Widespread continuing violence in relatively newer conflicts such as those in Indonesia (Timor, West Papua, Aceh) or the renewal of conflict in Russia (Chechnya) suggests that conflicts are continuing or emerging as fast as old ones wind down. There were five major wars (more than 1,000 dead per year in battle-related deaths) in 2003—in India

> Most of the serious violence in the world is seen in struggles that are internal to the borders of the states which make up the world system.

(Kashmir), Iraq, Liberia, Nepal and Sudan. These data were reaffirmed by the authors of the 2005 *Human Security Report*, who also found an overall reduction in the incidence of armed conflict while highlighting the new threats that have emerged in recent years and the persistence and even intensification of root causes of conflict (Mack 2005).

Figure 1.1: Global Trends in Armed Conflict, 1946–2005

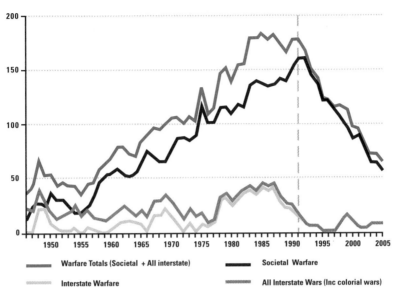

Source: 'Global Trends in Violent Conflict, 1964–2005', in Monty G. Marshall and Ted Robert Gurr (eds), *Peace and Conflict 2005* (College Park, Md.: University of Maryland, Center for International Development and Conflict Management, 2005), p. 14 (figure 3.1), <http://www.cidcm.umd.edu/inscr/PC05print.pdf>, by kind permission.

Explanations for the rise of internal conflicts as the predominant form of war today may be found in analysis that emphasizes the structure of the international system—such as the historical legacy of colonial-era borders that have produced dysfunctional states, or globalization-induced growth of socio-economic inequalities. Some analysts focus on the level of states, suggesting that government policies which promote structured inequality along group lines are a primary cause of violence. Others focus on group and individual-level causes, suggesting that many wars of the last decade or more have been the result of mobilization along divisive ethnic, racial or religious lines amid competition for power. In any event, many of the wars of the last decade or more have been fought with claims of religion, of ethnic identity and security, or over perceived racial differences, and over tough issues such as access to resources, language rights, education, land and territory, and equal status under the law.

2.2. The Root Causes of Contemporary Conflicts
While every conflict will have its specific context and features, there is broad consensus that factors related to grievances over such things as discrimination or inequality are to blame for the rise in contemporary internal conflicts, as well as factors related to opportunistic elite behaviour in pursuit of power. The debate over 'greed and grievance' has been eclipsed by an appreciation that the two approaches are not unrelated. In situations of weak states, unequal distribution of resources, unstable social relations, a history of violence, and the existence of continually excluded subordinate groups, the

emergence of mobilized resistance or 'political entrepreneurs' who organize for violent conflict is more likely to occur. The consequences may be political breakdown, civil war, inter-group riots, acts of violence, mass protests against the state, and in the worst instances crimes against humanity.

The search for 'root' or structural causes of conflict lies in efforts to find the underlying and sometimes elusive source of violence. While ethnic enmity, religious intolerance, or hate speech are often manifestations of conflicts, many analysts see the ultimate 'causes' of conflict in the deep-seated social structures that give rise to group grievances. Issues of natural resource management, especially of high-value commodities such as oil, access to employment, the absence of water and food security, lack of affordable, decent housing, or systematic economic discrimination—all have been seen as strong underlying drivers of conflict that have over time erupted into violent conflict. People are deprived of their basic human needs and will use all means available—including violence—to pursue and fulfil these needs.[3]

> Many analysts see the ultimate 'causes' of conflict in the deep-seated social structures that give rise to group grievances. In situations of weak states, unequal distribution of resources, unstable social relations, a history of violence, and the existence of continually excluded subordinate groups, the emergence of mobilized resistance or 'political entrepreneurs' who organize for violent conflict is more likely to occur.

Factors that reflect human security needs include:

- *Discrimination and 'relative group worth'*. Grievances develop in situations where political and social discrimination produces the systematic exclusion of (usually) minorities from political power. Invidious discrimination and social hierarchies along group lines lead to perceptions of relative group superiority or inferiority. For example, in many Latin American states indigenous groups argue that they are systematically excluded from political power or are not seen as full citizens in their societies. Social psychological approaches that emphasize the group worth idea suggest that many of today's internal conflicts are stimulated by discrimination against groups in terms of political exclusion, denial of language or cultural rights, and lack of opportunities for social advancement through, for example, higher education. Often such exclusion is justified by exclusionary nationalist ideologies that deny the existence or rights of minority groups. These types of 'relative group worth' situations are often described as 'horizontal inequalities'. The war in Sri Lanka, the long history of the 'troubles' in Northern Ireland and the recent 2005 rioting in French urban areas are linked to this dimension of human need and insecurity.
- *Economic dependence on single or especially valuable commodities derived from natural resources*. Such commodities produce significant income streams, usually for the state. Because democracy is weak in many states, lack of accountability allows those with access to natural resources to dominate a power base, with the ability to raise and afford to pay for military power by recruiting, arming and retaining foot soldiers. Examples include Angola during its protracted civil war. State elites

siphoned off wealth from oil revenues and built security forces, and the rebel UNITA faction (União Nacional para a Independência Total de Angola, National Union for the Total Independence of Angola) accessed the diamond wealth in the territory it controlled to maintain a well-equipped army. A more recent example is the close linkage between illegal opium production—emanating from the international demand for heroin—in Afghanistan and the persistence of 'warlord' dominance there. Vulnerabilities are sometimes exacerbated by multinational companies in global markets that unleash local dynamics for conflict in order to extract and retain 'rent' or extraordinary profits.

• *Access to resources or resource revenues.* Internal conflicts, for example in Aceh (Indonesia), Mindanao (the Philippines), Nigeria and Bolivia, may be driven in part by the exclusion of local peoples from access to the extraction of and profit from local natural resources, revenues being controlled by either central government or transnational corporations. Renegotiated revenue sharing is one aspect of successful decentralization or local autonomy. Beyond the issue of returns in revenue there are the implications for capacity and development: are local people also employed and trained to benefit personally and socially? Do revenues work their way into infrastructure improvement, education or health provision?

• *Predatory competition: the political group as organized crime.* In a good number of conflicts in recent years, 'capture of lootable goods'—diamonds and minerals, drugs, timber or oil—is seen as a strong driver of conflict. Research by economists at the World Bank, for example, has found a strong association between the presence of such 'lootable' goods and the onset and persistence of civil wars. The argument of these researchers is that global market conditions in which there is a high demand for such goods, and the opportunity for rent or enormous profit, provide the resource base of money, weapons and paid recruits necessary to wage an effective, long-term struggle against states. The Revolutionary United Front (RUF) in Sierra Leone's tragic war (1991–2000) was partly motivated by capture of the country's rich alluvial diamond beds. There is extensive documentation of similar behaviour in the long-running war in the Democratic Republic of the Congo (DRC) for minerals such as coltan, which is used in the manufacture of cell phones: the DRC has 80 per cent of estimated world reserves.

Box 1.5: Transitions in Doubt: A View on Human Security Concerns in the South Caucasus

In the post-Soviet area, after the collapse of the USSR, within Armenia, Azerbaijan and Georgia, democracy has come to be associated with poverty. The state of democracy is often understood as 'a façade that imitates democracy' and 'a show of elections'. The poverty in the region is different from that in other parts of the world. Rapid and undiscriminating privatization brought about the concentration of financial resources in the hands of a small number of people; only two classes appeared—the rich and the poor—and the gap between them has been growing bigger with every year. The specifics of this region mean that the people in these countries had quite a high level of education. In the Soviet Union, although almost deprived of political and civic rights, people had enjoyed substantial social and cultural rights. The new rules of neo-liberalism and the open, unregulated free-market economy brought quick and unjust social stratification and significant societal polarization, which these states have not been able to overcome during the 14 years of independence.

The majority of the population has no access to power in practice. Everyone has equal social, cultural and economic rights according to the law, but these rights have not traditionally been exercised by the people and the laws have not been enforced effectively and respected in public policies. Lack of knowledge about substantial democracy, lack of civic culture and genuine citizenship, and the low level of social participation in tradition and culture are a hindrance to people's exercising their rights, participating in decision making and fulfilling their duties and responsibilities as fully-fledged citizens of a democracy. The poor (the majority of the society) are not aware of or involved in policy-making processes and not sufficiently empowered or powerful enough to monitor and demand accountability from decision makers. A democratic culture will not appear without a wider, comprehensive knowledge and understanding of the democratic system of governance based on all human rights, social justice and solidarity, and without education for the people on the values and practices of human rights and democracy.

Poverty here is a political and governance issue, rather than a purely economic one.

Armineh Arakelian
International IDEA Resident Representative and Head of Office in Armenia:
a personal view

Understanding economic structures and factors is critical to a full appreciation of the linkages between democracy and human security, for to have any impact on these causes of conflict, action at the national level and—in an era of global economic interdependence—changes in the international economic order are both required. In order to address the economic dimensions of conflict, democracy must be able to generate public goods—things that benefit everyone equally—and to manage the distribution of opportunity and wealth in society equitably. Economic duress is understandably a background 'cause' of conflict, and economic conditions have also prolonged violent confrontation once it has begun. The recent focus on economic conditions reflects the

> Economic duress is understandably a background 'cause' of conflict, and economic conditions have also prolonged violent confrontation once it has begun. Many economists believe that the prevailing opportunity structure affects the ability of a society's political institutions to manage conflict effectively and in such a way that the turn to violence does not happen.

results of research that shows that common ingredients of violent conflict are often found in the economic structures and the factors that underlie social organization and affect political competition.

In sum, many economists believe that the prevailing opportunity structure affects the ability of a society's political institutions to manage conflict effectively and in such a way that the turn to violence does not happen. When governance manages economic benefits efficiently and equitably, conflicts are less likely to occur; when governance distributes economic benefits inequitably, the ingredients for armed conflict—motives and opportunities—are more likely to occur. Weak or less developed states are also less likely to be able to regulate multinational corporations to ensure that their activities provide an overall social benefit to the people in the areas where they operate and to countries as a whole. A case in point is Bolivia (see the contribution by George Gray Molina in Volume II) where popular movements have pressed for a political agenda to redress this imbalance.

The Case of Bolivia

Bolivia is the poorest country in South America and the third-poorest in Latin America, after Haiti and Nicaragua. Average income per head in 2003 was just 900 USD. Since achieving independence from Spain in 1825, the country has had over 190 governments. Although Bolivia had a democratic constitution as early as 1826, periodic breakdown and the return to military rule have frequently derailed democratization in a country of diverse ethnicities and great inequality. Here is a small landlocked country with a population of just under 9 million and the second-largest natural gas reserves in Latin America. The population is one of high diversity: over half are 'indigenous' (Quechua, Aymara, Chiquitano, Guarani and other); and the origins of many indigenous groups go back to the Inca. Spanish is the colonial language, but 70 per cent of Bolivians also speak Aymara, Quechua, and other dialects.

Human security, as evidenced in critical issues of poverty, exclusion, distribution, representation and participation, has proved to be the litmus test for Bolivian democracy. George Gray Molina (who served as coordinator of the UNDP *Human Development Report* in Bolivia) argues that, while social and political conflicts have definitely increased over the years, there was always a sense that underlying, unresolved 'crisis' simmered underneath the political surface. Molina points to how in the 1980s and 1990s most conflicts between state and civil society (or social groups) took the form of 'passive protest' (hunger strikes, rallies, and other forms of peaceful protest). From 2000 conflict escalated to involve active roadblocks, invasions of land, the taking over of public buildings and so on, often pitting civilians against civilians. In 2005, 58 per cent of the population was living below the poverty line, with 24 per cent in extreme poverty. Rural poverty reached 80 per cent, particularly in the indigenous areas of the highlands.

Yet in the 1990s Bolivia was a showcase for the smooth implementation of International Monetary Fund (IMF) reforms, having capitalized (a form of privatization) state industries in oil and gas, telecommunications, electricity, the railways, the airlines and tin between

1995 and 1998. Water privatization in Cochabamba was revoked in 2000 after riots in protest. In the same year, *The Economist* of 24 June 2000 referred to Bolivia as 'a model of democratic stability'. (On the economic and social situation in Bolivia generally, see *Statesman's Yearbook 2006*: 296; see also CAFOD 2005; and, for UN data on the poverty gap in Bolivia, see <http://globalis.gvu.unu.edu>.)

Although there was initially marginal economic growth, this did not translate demonstrably into meaningful development. The failure of economic policies to deliver poverty reduction, and their exacerbation of the profoundly entrenched inequality in the country, led to a backlash and divisions which pushed the country seemingly to the brink of civil war. In October 2003, 67 people were killed by troops under the government of Gonzalo Sánchez de Lozada, in protests calling for the nationalization of Bolivia's hydrocarbons (gas and oil). Sánchez de Lozada was forced to flee. In 2005 residents of El Alto (following the earlier precedent) forced the government to end the contract with the privatized water utility due to rising water prices and its failure to extend the water and sewerage network to many residents. Renewed protests at natural gas nationalization brought the country to a standstill for three weeks, forcing another presidential resignation. General elections in December 2005 brought in a government with populist policies in response to mass discontent and historical inequalities, and seemingly pulled the country back from what many commentators called the brink of civil war. A Constituent Assembly is planned for July 2006 to draft a new constitution, which the recently elected government hopes will assert Bolivia's right to use its natural resources for the benefit of the majority. Severe tests still await Bolivia, not least managing devolution policies amid competing claims for autonomy and more.

The practical linkages between human security needs and democracy in Bolivia are manifold. At its most basic, to be able to vote has long depended on having a recognized identification (ID) card. According to estimates of the UK Department for International Development (DFID), until recently nearly nine in ten people in Bolivia's rural and indigenous communities did not possess ID cards while more than half lacked the birth certificate needed to acquire one. Without a birth certificate, children cannot go to school, which closes off a potential escape route from poverty. 'Without an ID card, people cannot vote, have limited legal rights—which can leave them vulnerable to exploitation by employers or the police—and are effectively excluded from accessing social and health services. These services include Bolivia's national health insurance for mothers and pregnant women, which was introduced to combat the country's high maternal and child mortality rates and yet which is closed to women who cannot produce their ID cards' (see <http://www.dfid.gov.uk/countries/caribbean/bolivia.asp>).

At its most basic, then, *democratic practice* means enabling equality before the law—the right not only to the vote but to the development goals of access to education and health as well. This is alongside the national issues of representation, language rights, economic policy and social justice.

Box 1.6: The Experience of Crisis in Bolivia: Key Points

1. In Bolivia, as in apartheid-era South Africa, in Nepal in the 1990s and before, and in Aceh and West Papua, Israel and Palestine, popular needs for recognition, for rights, for development and for human security have taken on political force when unmet over time. Response to enduring structural inequalities will reflect strongly in the perceived legitimacy of government. Popular movements, as in the case of the indigenous peoples of Latin America, may themselves be forces for democratization.

A first principle of democratic practice is political equality before the law and through recognized rights pertaining to basic education and health. The right to vote should not only be an election practice, but should be a step towards fuller citizenship of the polity as well.

2. There have been over 190 Bolivian governments since 1825 (in spite of the country having had a democratic constitution as early as 1826), and intermittent breakdowns and the return of military rule have frequently derailed democratization. The crisis over foreign direct investment and the terms of trade for Bolivia's hydrocarbons, alongside a worsening in basic conditions (provision for human needs such as water), resulted in major confrontation across historical social divisions and a major political reconfiguration.

To anticipate and manage any divisive mismatch between national politics and international economics, there is a need for trade policies that minimize the adverse effects of trade on poverty and inequality.

3. In one year and five months of President Carlos Mesa's administration (2003–5), the executive power in Bolivia signed 820 accords, pacts and dialogues with non-governmental actors and social groups. A vicious cycle of unfulfilled promises eroded the government's capacity to deliver and, over a prolonged period, negatively influenced the public's perception of democratic governments' ability to deliver public goods, welfare improvements and basic rule of law.

There must be a firm foundation and a viable action plan underlying agreements undertaken between government and social groups or constituencies, lest 'participation' become purely symbolic or rhetorical, thus leading to loss of trust.

4. Political capture by local elites accentuated a patrimonial government style and pushed political reform and disenchantment to the fore in the late 1990s. Today, political parties suffer from the lowest level of public credibility of the past 40 years. (This problem was also faced by Nepal in the lead-up to the king's declaration of a state of emergency. It is not unknown in Northern democracies, where there is disillusionment with parties: in the UK the current government was

elected by one-fifth of the population—25 per cent of registered voters.)

While elitist and populist-dominated political parties represent opposing extremes on the national spectrum, it is their behaviour and responsiveness to the needs of both constituents and the national collective good which will determine their legitimacy, and hence that of the party system.

5. Attempts at political and institutional reform in Bolivia have resulted in a situation that is described alternatively as successfully enabling ethnic politicization and empowerment, or as incomplete in terms of releasing more radical aims of hegemony or self-government: for some the notions of decentralization and autonomy within the state are not enough. (Consider the fragile peace in Aceh, which will depend in large part on winning people over to the viability of autonomy within newly democratic Indonesia. In Canada and in the UK, recent devolution and major political reforms have been essential to meet the needs of Quebec and both Wales and Scotland.)

The social contract and the mutually reinforcing benefits of autonomy or devolution must be visible and sustainable, with built-in mechanisms for both communication and trade-offs between centre and periphery.

In December 2005 after a tumultuous period of social upheaval, peaceful elections in Bolivia brought Evo Morales to the presidency following his campaign on social inclusion, poverty reduction and natural resource management.

The case of Bolivia demonstrates in a practical way the linkages between democracy, conflict and human security. In it we find elements which are clear, strong drivers of social conflict and violence today in many settings. To identify these, researchers have developed comprehensive conflict assessment or analysis models that posit the linkages between the root causes of conflict and the outbreak of violence: the intervening variable is the capacity of governance structures to reconcile competing interests, contain extremism, and allow for peaceful participation in politics.[4] When contributing factors such as inequality, discrimination, extremist ideologies and resource booty are present, societies are especially vulnerable to the rapid emergence of widespread internal conflict. These factors are often exacerbated by cross-border spillover influences such as flows of weapons or refugees, or criminal activity. When these internal and external factors exist, all it often takes is a spark—a riot, a stolen or highly contested election, a politically motivated murder, or an abrupt change of regime—to trigger a rapid escalation of violent conflict.

The focus on the economic causes of human security is reflected in efforts by international financial institutions such as the World Bank to emphasize these conflict drivers in country-level poverty reduction strategies to evaluate macroeconomic, structural and social policies. The bank has conducted comprehensive analyses of poverty reduction in conflict-affected countries such as Bosnia and Herzogovina, Cambodia, Rwanda and Timor-Leste (for its reports on these and other conflict-affected states, see <http://web. worldbank.org/>). Among the findings are that economic policies must be fairer, that subsidies, targets and quotas can help to right economic imbalances, and that equality of outcomes in health, education and income is paramount. One way to achieve such outcomes is participation—in central government processes, in regional and local settings, and by sector (see chapter 6). Countries that have seen success in recent years in addressing such structural drivers of conflict are Macedonia, Northern Ireland (UK) and South Africa. In these situations, fairness emerged as the expected norm in processes that emphasized basic rights and the need to provide essential services and economic opportunities for all.

Box 1.7: Identifying Situations Likely to Lead to Violent Conflict

These factors correlate significantly with violent conflict and may be the most salient indicators of a country or society's vulnerability to the outbreak of violent conflict. Not all are 'causes' of conflict, and indeed some of these indicators (such as high infant mortality rates) may be consequences of conflict.

Legacies—a history of violent conflict in the last ten years, which may recur in an old or new form.

Poverty—countries with low per capita gross national income (GNI) are more prone to experience violent conflict; research has found that increasing rates of infant mortality are indicative of vulnerability to conflict.

Dependence—economies that rely on single or few primary commodity exports (such as minerals) set the stage for competition among different social groups over control of the revenues from such exports.

Political instability, to include both rapid change and/or transformation of existing governance structures or the breakdown of law and order.

Restricted civil liberties and political rights, where constraints on personal freedoms are seen.

Militarization of the state, or situations in which an unusually high percentage of gross national product is spent on defence, security and policing.

Ethnic dominance—situations in which one or more ethnic groups systematically control political and/or economic power.

Active regional conflicts, which harbour the potential for spillovers and contagions.

High youth unemployment, which creates a reservoir of people who can be induced to fight through economic incentives.

Source: Adapted from the World Bank Conflict Analysis Framework, <http://siteresources. worldbank.org/INTCPR/214574-1112883508044/20657757/CAFApril2005.pdf>, by kind permission.

2.3. The Consequences of 21st Century Conflict

Modern internal conflicts are global problems that require a multilateral response (Sisk 2001; and Managing Global Issues web site). Internal conflicts have direct implications for neighbouring states through spillovers, such as refugee flows or the spread of weapons, and indirect implications for the entire international community (such as the violation of international norms on crimes against humanity, or the creation of humanitarian emergencies). Indeed, most conflicts today are regionalized through the involvement of neighbouring states and communities, for example, when there are ethnic groups involved in a struggle that transcends international borders. In the database of Minorities at Risk, 122 of 268 ethnic groups have ethnic kin in neighbouring states (<http://www.cidcm.umd.edu/inscr/mar/>). A principal fear is that restive minorities in one state may provoke grievances in nearby states as well. Such regionalized internal conflicts may be less amenable to peacemaking by the international community because trans-border linkages provide support and encouragement to the combatants.

> Modern internal conflicts are global problems that require a multilateral response. They have direct implications for neighbouring states through spillovers, such as refugee flows or the spread of weapons, and indirect implications for the entire international community.

Increasingly in today's wars, civilians are targeted directly; the historically sharp line between military combatants and civilians has become distinctly blurred. While reliable data on the total number of civilian deaths in today's armed conflicts do not exist, the toll on civilian lives is reflected in the exponential increase in the numbers of refugees today's wars generate. In early 2005, there were an estimated 17 million refugees, internally displaced and stateless persons around the world; the vast number of these refugees and displaced were homeless as a result of armed conflicts.[5] A recent study on the effect of new internal wars on civilians in the 1990s argued that 90 per cent of fatalities in today's conflicts are civilians, as opposed to only 5 per cent in World War I and 50 per cent in World War II (Chesterman 2001). Moreover, international humanitarian law is routinely disregarded in today's conflicts by states and rebel forces alike.

> Increasingly in today's wars, civilians are targeted directly; the historically sharp line between military combatants and civilians has become distinctly blurred. The toll on civilian lives is reflected in the exponential increase in the numbers of refugees today's wars generate.

The costs of humanitarian assistance for emergencies are borne by international donors, and it is no surprise that the interventionist impulses to stem internal conflicts have come from these states. In 2003, for example, total assistance for complex humanitarian emergencies (those generated by wars) and natural disaster aid totalled some 7.8 billion USD (*Global Humanitarian Assistance Update* 2005). As the Carnegie Commission on Preventing Deadly Conflict points out, 'In short, once war has broken out, the costs of violence soar' (Carnegie Commission on Preventing Deadly Conflict 1997: 21). Economists such as Anke Hoeffler and Marta Reynal-Querol have shown that civil wars exact measurable direct and indirect economic costs on societies that last for

Box 1.8: Findings: Democracy and Human Security in Nepal

Extracts from the IDEA Pookara Dialogues Summary, November 2004
(names of speakers withheld)

'We can see in the context of Nepal that the state is trying to invest more in security by equipping the army well without investing on food, education, health and water. We are at a very difficult time in history, but we think towards humanity and human security, qualitative transformation, women participation, Dalit and Janajati's interest, and representation over authority and state resources should be arranged. People should be made strong by providing human security by providing for social, economic and basic needs ... '

'It is said that there is democracy in the country, but only one-third of the people may know its meaning and two-third don't know about it. The word "Loktantra" is better than "Prajatantra". It will take some more time for people in the villages to know about it. People have not been able to understand about democracy because of lack of education and feeling of being neglected. They also don't know anything about the situation of the country. Discussion programmes should be taken to the villages. Village people's economic condition is difficult. Economic resources are centered and there is nothing in the villages. Schools, bridges, roads have been constructed only with people's own efforts. There is no help from higher level. There is no provision of food in homes, which the state and the government must pay attention to.'

'People are more in pain due to the Maoists. They should (under duress) feed them. Otherwise, there is fear of being killed. All the pains and problems are due to power politics. The situation has worsened because the power has always remained confined to the same power holder. For instance, there is no proportional representation in Nepali Congress. Dalits, Janajatis, women are not represented. Maoists have spread because of this. Therefore, if all have proper representation, people may not go to the Maoist party.'

'There is no democracy in the country. Forty two per cent of the people are below poverty line. Democracy and human security: human security should be exercised through democracy. But have we understood where is democracy? It is not that we should go for the same process as in Britain although it is a slow process there. Only democracy makes human security. Democracy cannot work if economic, social structures within it are not strong.'

many years after the violence has stopped, calling civil war 'development in reverse' (Hoeffler and Reynal-Querol 2003). These and other economists suggest that civil war reduced gross national product by an average of 2.2 per cent annually.

Box 1.9: Human Security in West Africa

Researchers investigating the linkages between governance and human security in West Africa have homed in on security sector reform as the most critical and urgent task for promoting human security in the conflict-torn region. They write that security sector reform 'offers linkages and synergies between human security and the more traditional security agendas from the level of regional organizations, through to state institutions and local community. Although the concept of human security is gaining international legitimacy, in practice, countries continue to view security through the prism of the State and rely on military instruments to achieve it... . In the long run, however, it will be critical to develop appropriate strategies and approaches to reconcile human and state security goals and objectives'.

Source: Hussein, Karim, Gnisci, Donata, and Wanjiru, Julia, *Security and Human Security: An Overview of Concepts and Initiatives: What Implications for West Africa?* (Paris: Organisation for Economic Co-operation and Development (OECD) Sahel and West Africa Club, 2004), p. 9, <http://www.oecd.org/dataoecd/60/42/34616876.pdf>.

(For more on security sector reform, see chapter 5; on public participation in police reform, see chapter 6.)

In addition to tangible economic costs, the moral basis of international society is undermined when flagrant violations of international standards on human rights occur. More often than not, the international human rights instruments are violated in civil wars, including in the most egregious situations by the perpetration of crimes against humanity, such as genocide, forced migration or 'ethnic cleansing', and other violations of international covenants (see Schabas 1999). According to international covenants such as the 1948 Convention on the Prevention and Punishment of the Crime of Genocide, states have an obligation to respond to prevent acts of genocide. In some interventions, such as those in Kosovo or Timor-Leste, intervention has been explicitly justified by reference to global norms on the prevention and halting of genocide and crimes against humanity. UN Secretary-General Boutros Boutros-Ghali's efforts to outline an Agenda for Peace in 1992 and the subsequent Supplement in 1995 were efforts to develop 'soft law' on the conditions and types of international intervention that could occur in civil wars.

The global consequences of civil wars are such that no single state acting alone can possibly muster the external legitimacy, resources and staying power to intervene for peace on its own. Even the United States, whose record of unilateral intervention in Central American states is long, was compelled to seek UN Security Council mandates for its multilateral mission to promote peace in Haiti. The greater the spillover effects of wars, the likelier it is that regional and global powers will intervene to end them. Civil wars that affect neighbours and that feature unchecked crimes against humanity require a multilateral response, lest intervention in them become an imbroglio for individual states which often lack sufficient military power to succeed. Multilateral efforts spread the risk of intervention, and UN Security Council mandates, when they are possible, provide the intervention with legal authority and external legitimacy (see chapter 6). What principles should guide international action in promoting human security?

3. Democratic Practice: Enabling Human Security

Today's global challenges require national governments which are responsive to domestic needs, and a network approach—of states, of international organizations, regional and sub-regional organizations, transnational civil society, national, regional and local governments, and local civil society—dedicated to responding to immediate human security crises, facilitating and assisting intermediate transitions from crises such as war to peace, and ameliorating the root causes of conflict through human development. Indeed, the human security concept has seen the rapid development of what is known as a 'global public policy network' to advance the human security agenda (Reineke and Deng 2000, chapter 7). As UN Secretary-General Kofi Annan writes in his 2005 report 'In Larger Freedom',

> Hence, the cause of larger freedom can only be advanced by broad, deep and sustained global cooperation among States. The world needs strong and capable States, effective partnerships with civil society and the private sector, and agile and effective regional and global intergovernmental institutions to mobilize and coordinate collective action. The United Nations must be reshaped in ways not previously imagined, and with a boldness and speed not previously shown (United Nations 2005: 6).

Human security threats emanate from weak state environments, of which the principal feature is often the absence of or inadequacies of democracy. There is therefore an imperative for focusing on improving democracy's capacity to address the underlying sources of human insecurity. Social conflicts occur when governance processes fail to manage conflict adequately through political dialogue, mechanisms for legitimate decision making, and the rule of law. In such situations, societies are left to manage themselves, and, while civil society often steps in to fill the gap—in providing basic social services, for example—ultimately capable, effective states are needed to ensure human security.[6] Thus, critical to the mitigation and management of contemporary root causes of conflict is *democracy that strengthens the state* by strengthening social capacities to manage threats to human security. As the Commission on Human Security concludes in its final report:

> There is an imperative for focusing on improving democracy's capacity to address the underlying sources of human insecurity. Critical to the mitigation and management of contemporary root causes of conflict is democracy that strengthens the state by strengthening social capacities to manage threats to human security.

> A democratic political order, buttressed by physical safety and economic growth, helps to empower people. Respecting democratic principles is a step towards attaining human security and development. It enables people to participate in governance

and make their voices heard. Deepening democratic principles and practices at all levels mitigates the many threats to human security. It requires building strong institutions, establishing the rule of law, and empowering people (United Nations, Commission on Human Security 2003: 133).

3.1. Defining Democratic Practice

To broaden the analysis of the relationship between democracy and the attainment of human security, a further elaboration of the concept of democracy itself can be useful: increasingly democracy is not seen as something that is either-or, but rather a complicated practice. Democracy finds its meaning in the way in which it is put into operation or application. As described in the definition in the introduction, democratic practice involves both formal, institutional (i.e. rule-bound) processes and informal institutions (rules and norms). Democratic practice also addresses events as structured processes (such as major electoral events) and other processes of change, such as the *way in which* rebel forces transform into political parties, or the way a constitution is made. Democratic practice may also be applied as a concept to address key governance challenges that relate to conflict mitigation, such as interim processes for monitoring human rights violations and redressing non-compliance.

The rationale for developing a more sophisticated concept of democracy is twofold.

First, although many of the democratic transitions of the late 1980s and 1990s were the result of closed negotiations among elites (which produced so-called 'democratization pacts'), only those which have managed to broaden support for democracy beyond the elites have successfully sustained democracy while also improving its quality (see chapter 2). It is for this reason that there is much concern about the idea of democratic 'transition' as a temporary condition, or about the inevitability of democratic consolidation after a certain period of time or a fixed number of elections. Partial democracy and dissatisfaction with democracy have much to do with the undemocratic way in which political change has occurred.

> Many of the democratic transitions of the late 1980s and 1990s were the result of closed negotiations among elites. Only those which have managed to broaden support for democracy beyond the elites have successfully sustained democracy while also improving its quality. Partial democracy and dissatisfaction with democracy have much to do with the undemocratic way in which political change has occurred.

Box 1.10: Characteristics of Democratic Practice: Implications for Governance
• *Participation*: all people should have a voice in decision making either through electoral processes, or through civil society and interest group organizations (such as trade unions), and directly through citizen participation and initiatives.
• *Rule of law*: legal frameworks that are fair and impartially enforced are critical to securing human rights.

• *Transparency*: the free flow of information, especially on public needs and services and in decision making, and accountability of those in positions of power (including government and civil society) to the underlying social interests they purport to represent.
• *Responsiveness*: government should be responsive to the concerns of all major stakeholders, striving for consensus whenever possible.
• *Equitability*: all people have the opportunity to improve or maintain their well-being.

For further information see UNDP, 'Governance for Sustainable Development: A UNDP Policy Document', 1997.

Second, recent experience has shown a variety of ways in which democratic practice has occurred in settings where, overall, a country is not a full democracy: democracy can exist at the local level, in dialogue processes, or in 'zones of peace'. Not only is democratic practice desirable in micro-level or issue-specific settings; arguably the gradual and visible introduction of democratic values through such practice is essential to the long-term development of democracy at the national level as well.

Ideally, democratic practices will feature the following elements; this is especially true in societies that face major change processes, in which democratization processes or peace negotiations may last for years before a society finds itself free from devastating social violence.

1. *Deliberative/dialogue processes (ongoing arenas of bargaining and interaction)*. Democratic practice has its roots in a theory of democracy that suggests that the essence of the system is open, free-flowing dialogue that exchanges information and allows all sides to see openly the needs, aspirations, preferences, attitudes and intent of others (Dryzek 2000). From such deliberation—tedious and time-consuming as it may be—problems can be solved and, when possible, consensus solutions can emerge. Moreover, dialogue is a key form of expressing recognition and acceptance.
2. *Contextual appropriateness*. Democratic practice as a concept also rests on the belief that there is no inherent superiority of a single approach or option, and indeed democracy is not a formulaic enterprise that replicates Western ideals or institutions. Arguably, there are democratic practices in a variety of cultural traditions in which the core values of democratic practice are reflected in indigenous institutions. Notwithstanding debates about 'Asian values' or the compatibility or incompatibility of democracy with Islam, cultural characteristics are not an inherently limiting variable in the practice of democracy. 'Local ownership' or relevance in response to local needs is by far the best test for substantive democracy and its practice.
3. *A multifaceted and multi-layered approach*. Democratic practice is similarly based on the notion of a multi-layered approach in which democracy operates at various levels—national, provincial, local, in communities, and in civil society. This multi-

layered approach creates 'complementarity' in which progress towards the realization of democratic values at one level—for example in national contexts—is complementary to the attainment of these values at other levels of society. Similarly, processes that promote democracy may involve formal negotiations with authoritative decision makers and informal—or, to borrow a term from the conflict resolution literature, 'track two'-level—discussions among influential opinion leaders in a society.

4. *Sustainability over time.* Given the concern with partial democracy, or 'one person, one vote, one time', democratic practice must relate to the overall viability of democracy over time. Pacts to end civil wars that lead to democratization, for example, have been criticized for setting the parameters of undemocratic practices over time; for example, while Zimbabwe's initial post-war regime was seen as democratic, the sustainability of its democracy has been questioned anew amid recent concerns about human rights, vote rigging, and authoritarian rule by the government. Likewise, in Bosnia, the 1995 Dayton accord which ended the war has been said to be limiting of democracy in the long run. Sustainability as a concept is preferred to the more static notion of 'consolidation' of democracy, in post-war and in transitional settings alike. Sustainability also suggests flexibility, in that democracy's arrangements need to be able to take into account demographic or other changes; the argument for flexibility is best illustrated in the problems that were seen in Lebanon's national pact, which were due to its rigidity in the allocation of parliamentary seats along confessional lines.

5. *Realism about difficult issues.* At the same time, democratic practice should be realistic about the very tough and sometimes confrontational issues that arise in deeply conflicted societies, especially around questions of representation, inclusion, and the limitations to open deliberation. For example, inclusion is an indisputable principle in democratic practice, but questions arise about the possibility that political forces with anti-democratic tendencies may well be legitimately elected, about whether those with prior records of human rights abuses can participate, about whether exclusive, ethnically narrow parties preaching discrimination should be allowed to campaign for elections, and so on.

6. *Consensus seeking as an optimal decision rule.* This remains the most critical principle of democratic practice in divided societies. The criticisms of majority-rule democracy in deeply divided societies stand the test of time; minimum-winning coalitions (that is, coalitions that are based on the lowest possible number of election winners under a given set of rules), winner-take-all outcomes to electoral contests, and exclusive regimes are tantamount to domination in divided societies which by definition lack a common sense of national unity, a common purpose and a collective destiny. There may be moments when majority-rule procedures contribute to peace—such as the 1998 referendums in Northern Ireland that bolstered the peace process—but these are anomalous situations, not the norm.

7. *Practices that are inclusive of all major elements of a given population.* One of the most enduring findings about democracy's role in managing conflict is that the inclusion of all major social groups is essential. In addition to inclusion, however, participation by minorities or vulnerable groups also implies influence on policy outcomes and not 'token' or powerless representation. Proportionality in representation, in the distribution of resources, and in the allocation of other goods in society is fundamental

to democratic practice. From membership in the armed forces, to the fair distribution of oil revenues, to plum jobs in the civil service, to the appointment of cabinet ministers (and sometimes, as in Bosnia, to the recognition of tangible and intangible values, such as language use), proportionality remains a critical characteristic of democratic practice in divided societies.

In addition to these features, democratic practice must produce essential outcomes if democracy's capacities to enable security are to be realized. These outcomes are the promotion of human rights and the strengthening of state–society relations. The protection of human rights is a, if not the, central element in democratic practice.

In recent years there has been somewhat of a divergence of views between those who have focused on the relative importance in divided societies of human rights as freedom from harm and freedom of action, those who have focused on democracy building in terms of institutional processes and elections, and those who have focused on conflict management and resolution (Baker 1996). In many ways, arguably the differences of emphasis between human rights and democracy building are based on underlying core value differences concerning justice and accountability and conflict management. The divergence is most commonly seen in the principle of inclusion in conflict management processes—the question whether those who have committed acts of violence deserve a place at the democracy and/or peace negotiations table. However, democratic practices for conflict management do not need to trade off democratic accountability for peace, as a number of recent instances of reconciliation processes demonstrate (International IDEA 2003). As the scholar Jack Donnelly has argued, human rights help 'civilize' democracy by giving meaning to the operation of democratic institutions in a way that does not allow for tyranny, be it through broadly-based, majority or minority rule (Donnelly 1998).

Finally, democratic practice strengthens the state and strengthens society by helping to facilitate mutually reinforcing relationships between public authorities and civil society. One of the key arguments against introducing democracy in deeply divided societies is that social conflict weakens the state by reproducing the fragmented nature of society in political institutions. Likewise, democratic practices that empower civil society for advocacy and/or actual service delivery are seen as weakening the state by promoting alternative sources of power that do not allow public authorities to develop capacities for governance. (For a summary of these arguments, and especially on mutually reinforcing state–society relations, see Migdal, Shue and Kholi 1994.) In fact, a key principle of democratic practice is that *the strengthening of state capacities is reliant upon measures to empower civil society and give it capacities for direct participation in governance.* The stronger a society's ability to contribute to governance and the more legitimate the political processes that are inclusive and democratic, the stronger the state will be in implementing its policy goals.

> Democratic practice strengthens the state and strengthens society by helping to facilitate mutually reinforcing relationships between public authorities and civil society.

Democratic practice thus involves the simultaneous focus on the formal processes of democracy that yield capable state institutions, and processes that encourage civil society empowerment through interest-group formation, activism, lobbying and collective action. Precisely because deeply divided societies lack cross-cutting social relationships, and thus the social capital necessary for development success, democratic practice that focuses on strengthening the state and strengthening society is critically important.

Table 1.2: Human Security and Democracy: An Overview

Human Security Dimensions	Conflict Concerns	Democratic Practice
Immediate human security crises	Political processes to achieve the termination of the war through ceasefire Stopping and preventing further war crimes and crimes against humanity Agreements by parties to respect civilian life Provision of immediate humanitarian relief	Emphasis on fundamental human rights Ensuring equitable distribution of humanitarian relief and empowering local actors in its fair distribution to civilians in need Defining a transition to inclusive democracy as a pathway to peace
Intermediate-term transitions from war to peace	Facilitating negotiation processes that allow for settlements that define the transition path and the outcome of the transition Managing political violence and potential spoilers Ensuring the demobilization of factions and community security Providing for immediate benefits of peace, such as economic revival	Designing and implementing a comprehensive plan for supplanting peace process negotiations with institutionalized bargaining structures, such as power-sharing executives, parliaments and local councils Ensuring that the transition is something experienced by people on the ground and not just a process of change negotiated by elites
Long-term human development	Ameliorating the underlying root causes of conflict through an appropriate and sustained programme of socio-economic development Sustainable political institutions that can process social conflict over the long term	Creating conditions—such as literacy and health—through which people are empowered to be able to participate Ensuring through the political process that resources, income and opportunities are fairly shared among all social groups

Notes

1 While these scholars differentiate between civil 'war' and less intensive forms of internal armed conflict, for the purpose of this chapter we will refer freely to all internal armed conflicts as civil wars.

2 The trends also show that earlier hope that 'international wars' (wars between the armies of opposing countries) were on the decline was misplaced. The battles between Pakistan and India high in the Himalayas in the summer of 1999 shattered that myth, as has the eruption of the broadly-based war in the Democratic Republic of the Congo, which has been dubbed Africa's first 'world war'.

3 John Burton observes that human 'needs reflect universal motivations ... From the perspective of conflict studies, the important observation is that these needs will be pursued by all means available' (Burton 1990: p. 36).

4 For such a comprehensive conflict analysis model, see the World Bank's Conflict Analysis Framework, available at <http://lnweb18.worldbank.org/ESSD/sdvext.nsf/67ByDocName/ ConflictAnalysis>.

5 For up-to-date statistics, see the web site of the United Nations High Commissioner for Refugees, <http://www.unhcr.ch>.

6 For further evaluation of 'state building', see the findings of the project at the International Peace Academy (<http://www.ipacademy.org>) which has evaluated, for example, instances of United Nations transitional administrations to build capable states in the wake of violent conflict.

References and Further Reading

Baker, Pauline, 'Conflict Resolution versus Democratic Governance: Divergent Paths to Peace?', in Chester A. Crocker, Fen O. Hampson and Pamela Aall (eds), *Managing Global Chaos: Sources and Responses to International Conflict* (Washington, DC: United States Institute of Peace Press, 1996)

Burton, John W., *Conflict Human Needs Theory* (New York: St Martin's Press, 1990)

CAFOD, 'Why Focus on Bolivia?', 2005, <http://www.cafod.org.uk/news>

Carnegie Commission on Preventing Deadly Conflict, *Final Report* (Washington, DC: Carnegie Commission on Preventing Deadly Conflict, [December 1997])

'Chairman's statement', Lysøen Conference on Human Security, Norway, 20 May 1999

Chesterman, Simon (ed.), *Civilians in War* (Boulder, Colo.: Lynne Rienner, 2001)

Cranna, Michael, *The True Cost of Conflict* (New York: New Press, 1994)

Cristalis, Irena and Scott, Catherine (eds), *Independent Women: The Story of Women's Activism in East Timor* (London: Catholic Institute for International Relations, 2006)

Crocker, Chester A., Hampson, Fen O. and Aall, Pamela (eds), *Managing Global Chaos: Sources and Responses to International Conflict* (Washington, DC: United States Institute of Peace Press, 1996)

Donnelly, Jack, *International Human Rights*, 2nd edn (Boulder, Colo.: Westview Press, 1998)

Dryzek, John, *Deliberative Democracy and Beyond: Liberals, Critics, Contestation* (Oxford: Oxford University Press, 2000)

Eriksson, Mikael and Wallensteen, Peter, 'Armed Conflict 1989–2003', *Journal of Peace Research*, 41/5 (September 2004), pp. 625–36

[European Union], 'A Secure Europe in a Better World: The European Security Strategy', Brussels, 12 December 2003, <http://ue.eu.int/uedocs/cms/Upload/78367.pdf>

Global Humanitarian Assistance Update, 2004–2005, Development Initiatives, 2005, <http://www.globalhumanitarianassistance.org/GHAupdFinal2inccov.pdf>

'Global Trends in Violent Conflict, 1964–2005', in Monty G. Marshall and Ted Robert Gurr (eds), *Peace and Conflict 2005* (College Park, Md.: University of Maryland, Center for International Development and Conflict Management, 2005, <http://www.cidem.umd.edu/inscr/PC05print.pdf>

Hampson, Fen O., *Madness in the Multitude: Human Security and World Disorder* (Oxford: Oxford University Press, 2003)

Hoeffler, Anke and Reynal-Querol, Marta, 'Measuring the Costs of Conflict', Centre for the Study of African Economies, University of Oxford, April 2003

Hussein, Karim, Gnisci, Donata and Wanjiru, Julia, *Security and Human Security: An Overview of Concepts and Initiatives. What Implications for West Africa?* (Paris: OECD Sahel and West Africa Club, 2004), <http://www.oecd.org/dataoecd/60/42/34616876.pdf>

International IDEA, *Reconciliation After Violent Conflict: A Handbook* (Stockholm: International IDEA, 2003)

International Peace Academy, <http://www.ipacademy.org>

Jacobson, Ruth, 'Dancing Towards a Better Future? The 1994 Elections in Mozambique', Centre for Democratisation Studies, University of Leeds, Working Paper, 1997

Mack, Andrew, *The Human Security Report 2005: War and Peace in the 21st Century* (Oxford: Oxford University Press, 2005), also available at <http://www.humansecurityreport.info>

Migdal, Joel, Shue, Vivienne and Kholi, Atul, *State Power and Social Forces: Domination and Transformation in the Third World* (Cambridge: Cambridge University Press, 1994)

Paris, Roland, 'Human Security: Paradigm Shift or Hot Air?', *International Security*, 26/2 (2001), pp. 87–102

Reineke, Wolfgang and Deng, Francis, *Critical Choices: The United Nations, Networks, and the Future of Global Governance* (Ottawa: International Development Research Centre (IDRC), 2000)

Schabas, William, *The Genocide Convention at Fifty*, United States Institute of Peace Special Report (Washington, DC: United States Institute of Peace, 7 January 1999)

Simmons, P. J. and de Jonge Oudraat, Chantal, *Managing Global Issues: Lessons Learned* (Washington, DC: Carnegie Endowment for International Peace, 2001)

Sisk, Timothy, 'Violence: Intrastate Conflict', in P. W. Simmons and Chantal de Jonge Oudraat (eds), *Managing Global Issues: Lessons Learned* (Washington, DC: Carnegie Endowment for International Peace, 2001)

Statesman's Yearbook 2006 (London: Palgrave Macmillan, 2005), p. 296

Stiglitz, Joseph, *Globalization and Its Discontents* (London: Allen Lane, The Penguin Press, 2002)

Study Group on Europe's Security Capabilities, 'A Human Security Doctrine for Europe' (The Barcelona Report of the Study Group on Europe's Security Capabilities), September 2004

Suhrke, Astri, 'Human Security and the Interest of State', *Security Dialogue*, 30/2 (1999), pp. 265–76

United Nations, 'In Larger Freedom: Towards Development, Security and Human Rights for All: Report of the Secretary-General', UN document A/59/2005, 21 March 2005, <http://www.un.org/largerfreedom/contents.htm>

United Nations, Commission on Human Security, *Human Security Now: Final Report* (New York: United Nations Commission on Human Security, 2003)

United Nations, High-Level Panel on Threats, Challenges and Change, 'A More Secure World: Our Shared Responsibility', UN document A/59/565, 2 December 2004, <http://www.un.org/secureworld>

United Nations Development Programme (UNDP), 'Governance for Sustainable Human Development: A UNDP Policy Document', January 1997, <http://magnet.undp.org/policy>

— *Human Development Report 1994: New Dimensions of Human Security* (Oxford: Oxford University Press, 1994)

— *Human Security Report 2005* (New York and Oxford: Oxford University Press, 2005)

World Bank, *World Development Report 2006: Equity and Development,* <http://HYPERLINK "http://www.web.worldbank.org" web.worldbank.org/WBSITE/EXTERNAL/EXTDEC/ EXTRESEARCH/EXTWDRS/EXTWDR2006>

Web Sites

Human Security Network, <http://www.humansecuritynetwork.org>

Managing Global Issues, <http://www.ceip.org/mgi>

Minorities at Risk database at the Centre for International Development at Conflict Management, University of Maryland, <http:// www.cidcm.umd.edu/inscr/mar/>

UK Department for International Development (DFID), <http://www.dfid.gov.uk/countries/caribbean/bolivia.asp>

United Nations High Commissioner for Refugees, <http://www.unhcr.ch>

World Bank, Conflict Analysis Framework, available at <http://siteresources.worldbank.org/ INTCPR/214574-1112883508044/20657757/CAFApril2005.pdf>

CHAPTER 2

CHAPTER 2

2. Democratization after the Cold War: Managing Turbulent Transition

Democratic transitions are problematic. Although democracy is an indispensable goal, the process of introducing democratic practices is inherently troubled. Such processes rearrange political competition, alter structures and power relations, and often exacerbate social problems rather than ameliorating them. The actual process of political reform is destabilizing, and in the short term there may be real and direct threats to peace in democratizing societies as a result of the uncertainty and competition that democracy introduces into unsettled social environments, in particular at times of economic stress. Rapid or ill-considered democratization can also be conflict-inducing.

At what point can a country be considered 'democratic'? There are many qualifiers today that attempt to describe countries at different levels of democratic development—'partial democracy', 'partly free', 'non-competitive democracy', 'transitional democracy' and so on. There is no simple answer to the 'threshold' problem in measuring democratization other than to say that the idea of a perfect 'end-state' of democracy has to be eschewed. More fruitful are the concept of democratic practice, an approach that looks at 'pathways of democratization', and a methodology for the assessment of the state of democracy.

The phenomenon of social movements has been critical in the evolution of democracy, especially in some 'colour' revolutions in recent years, but there is no straightforward equivalence between mass movements and democratic outcomes. Social movements and popular upsurge have been key turning points in the process of ending authoritarian rule, but they are not a basis for sustaining a democracy.

A striking feature of the introduction of democratic reform in both post-war and post-authoritarian settings has been the dominance of economic change with emphasis on a market economy at the same time. Recent liberal democratization agendas see democracy as restricted to the electoral and institutional sphere, not recognizing that political power is also a means to transform unjust socio-economic structures. Too often the social and economic dimension of 'peace building' is ignored.

Democratization has become a goal in multiple transitional settings since the end of the cold war. There are special challenges in understanding the effects of the introduction of democracy (often taken to mean elections) in a variety of social settings, from post-authoritarian to post-war situations, and coupling democratic change with the achievement of developmental and peace-building goals. While democratization should help promote human security, at times the process itself can stimulate conflicts which have the opposite effect. Ideally, democracy is intended to function as the ultimate conflict management system for a society. Practically, however, democratic transitions are problematic. Such transitions rearrange political competition, alter structures and power relations, and often exacerbate social problems rather than ameliorating them.

The interconnections between democracy and conflict at the beginning of the 21st century raise complex questions:

- What factors contribute to social mobilization for democracy by, for example, people seeking justice and human dignity?
- When does democratization work towards peace by helping manage social conflict and facilitating or promoting positive outcomes for development and human security, and when can democratization actually worsen conflict by inflaming social differences and engendering violence?

> Ideally, democracy is the ultimate conflict management system for a society. Practically, however, democratic transitions are problematic. Such transitions rearrange political competition, alter structures and power relations, and often exacerbate social problems rather than ameliorating them.

This chapter puts these questions in context through an evaluation of trends in democratization and peace in recent years. An examination of trends in the 1990s and early 2000s offers insight into the connections between democracy and conflict management and helps to identify when democratization can contribute to furthering human security. More than 70 countries have made dramatic transitions in the last few decades from one-party, dictatorial or authoritarian (e.g. military) rule to democracy. An assessment of the patterns of armed conflict alongside the patterns of war termination suggests that most internal wars today—and intra-state wars are the now predominant type of armed conflict—will end up at the negotiating table where protagonists negotiate the terms of a settlement.

1. Democracy Transitions in the 1990s and 2000s

Since the end of the cold war in 1989, the world has seen an ongoing 'wave' of democratization. Some 100 countries have undergone transitions to democracy since the 1970s, with some 40 countries having done so in the 1990s and early 2000s. In 2005, a wide variety of countries experienced political change seen as having elements of democratization in very varying degrees—Egypt, Hong Kong, Georgia, Liberia, Ukraine, Togo and Lebanon, for example. There is no way of knowing whether such trends will continue, or whether non-democratic countries (such as China at the national level) will find a different pathway to political reform. The democratization trends of the 1990s and early 2000s raise a number of important retrospective questions about the underlying drivers of democratization, the various paths that countries go down on the road to democracy, whether such changes are sustainable over time, and why they are sustainable or not.

Equally important are regional variations, such as those in the experiences of post-Soviet bloc states that are undergoing 'dual transitions' from authoritarianism to democracy and from command to market economies, or in African countries that are emerging from post-colonial one-party rule to multiparty politics. Does the introduction of market liberalization, which often accompanies democratization, heighten

> While democratization may lead to peace over time, the actual process of political reform is destabilizing for societies, and in the short term there may be real and direct threats to peace in democratizing societies as a result of the uncertainty and competition that democracy introduces into unsettled social environments.

(at least in the short term) socio-economic inequality, giving rise to additional tensions? While democratization may lead to peace over time, the actual process of political reform is destabilizing for societies, and in the short term there may be real and direct threats to peace in democratizing societies as a result of the uncertainty and competition that democracy introduces into unsettled social environments.

The very word 'transition' to democracy is rightly questioned: the use of the word here does not imply that there is a point of no return when democracy is 'consolidated' and a country goes from the 'emergent' category to fully formed democracy. Rather, 'transitional' is taken to mean a state of fundamental change

> Does market liberalization, which often accompanies democratization, heighten socio-economic inequality, giving rise to additional tensions, at least in the short term?

from what went before—from protracted war or violent conflict to a new social contract for building the 'peace'; from autocratic centralized government to representative, elected forms; from political subjugation or domination to independence or the redressing of imbalances in power relations. In Volume II Reginald Austin reflects on 40 years of experience, 'intellectual, practical and emotional involvement with both the idea and some of the practice of the international community's efforts to intervene in the affairs of sovereign states in order to bring about a political and governmental transition. These interventions have been combined with "peacekeeping" operations seeking to end violent conflicts associated with one form or another of unrepresentative and/or repressive government, and to bringing about a transition to . . . peaceful means of dealing with conflicting interests'. Also in Volume II, Olayinka Creighton-Randall speaks from immediate experience in the context of Sierra Leone, and Enrique ter Horst addresses specifically the role of the UN in El Salvador and Haiti.

1.1. Trends in Democratization

The present upturn in the number of countries shifting to democratic political systems began in the mid-1970s with Portugal's 'Revolution of the Carnations' in 1974 and in Spain and Greece at around the same time. A wave of societies in Latin America, including Argentina, Brazil, Chile and Peru, moved from authoritarian military rule in the 1980s. These were followed by the dramatic fall of the Berlin Wall in 1989 and the subsequent collapse of the Soviet Union. Many, if not all, of the states of the USSR and Eastern Europe have at least gone through the motions of creating multiparty political systems based on elections and the rule of law; some, such as the Czech Republic, are seen as having succeeded, while others, such as Uzbekistan, are viewed by many as a new form of post-Soviet authoritarianism.

What are the underlying causes of the rapid growth in electoral democracies in recent years? A number of explanations have been offered.

- *Global norms and standards have encouraged open regimes.* Since World War II and the adoption of the Universal Declaration of Human Rights in 1948, there has been a broadening of acceptance of international norms and standards that influence the internal conditions within states. Human rights of freedom of speech, self-determination, and other civil and political liberties can only be accommodated within democratic systems. Incentives such as membership in the European Union may have encouraged countries to take measures in the direction of democracy, as undertaken in some Baltic and Central European states.
- *There has been a diffusion effect.* Some observers suggest that democratization has occurred because people in countries around the world see the growth of personal freedoms in other countries—particularly the right to vote in free, fair, multiparty elections—and demand the same rights for themselves. Some have gone so far as to argue that there is an emerging 'cosmopolitan political culture' worldwide in which the legitimacy of governments can only be justified by reference to popular participation and choice through open, transparent elections.
- *Economic and social development may promote democracy.* However, not all market reform has that effect: indeed, in some cases, such as that of Argentina, market reforms dramatically increased inequalities, undermined the middle class, and unleashed a backlash against neo-liberal economic change. Political liberalization accompanied by the implementation of structural adjustment polices was devastating in many African countries when investment in social services, infrastructure and environmental management was cut heavily. This is echoed in the post-Soviet republics, as in Georgia.
- *Internal economic development may promote democracy if it expands education and access to information and mobility.* There are explanations for the democratization trends that focus on the 'modernization' of economies and on economic development as the impetus for political reform. When economies grow and diversify, and when human development leads to gains in literacy, services and wealth, the result is often an active middle class. This may in turn generate demand for more open and accountable institutions and access to communications and mobility, as well as

contributing to conditions for citizens' associations or locally relevant civil society to develop. Plural (or multiple) interests in a developing economy can be accommodated through democratic openness.

• *The sense of popular grievance makes democracy worth fighting for.* In 2005 leading Nepalese political parties came to agreement on a shared agenda with representatives of the Maoist leadership in the country on principles for restoring multiparty democracy and convening a constituent assembly. The Maoists offered a ceasefire in hopes of a response from the monarchy; by April 2006 popular protest on the streets of Katmandu against the suspension of the democratic process in the country brought about that response. Some had taken up arms, while other Nepalese took to the streets. It was liberation struggles in continental Africa which heralded what Reginald Austin calls the 'first phase' of 20th-century democratization efforts by the broader international community.

The observable trend in democratization around the world raises a critical and, frankly, unresolved question. At what point can a country be considered 'democratic'? This concern revolves around issues of state formation itself, and with it the critical issue of the substance of democracy. Just because a country's ruling government has allowed an election, or liberalized to allow some alternative political parties to form, does not mean that all the criteria for democracy have been met. Similarly it is possible for a 'mature' democratic system to regress or decline.

As a result, there are any number of qualifiers today that attempt to describe countries at various levels of democratic development—'partial democracy', 'partly free', 'non-competitive democracy', 'delegative democracy' or 'transitional democracy'. Add to these qualifiers different forms of democracy that have developed—such as Uganda's state project of a 'no-party' democracy in which opposition parties were not allowed—and the debate intensifies. There is no simple answer to the 'threshold' problem in measuring democratization other than to say that every country or political entity (such as a city) on the globe can be evaluated as to the quality of its democracy through comprehensive assessment practices. To that end, International IDEA has developed a comprehensive assessment guide for both countries and cities available through the State of Democracy project (see chapter 4).

1.2. Pathways of Democratization

While many countries have held initial elections or even had 'alternation' or a change in the ruling political coalition, democracy remains tenuous, human rights are often breached, human security is sometimes threatened, power and resources remain in the hands of the few, and the danger of a return to authoritarianism or civil conflict remains on the horizon. For this reason, critics of the term 'transition' prefer the terminology of 'pathways of democratization'. When does 'democratization' end and a fully established 'consolidated' democracy begin? Because this question is so problematic—it assumes a linear view of history—many analysts have abandoned the idea of a consolidated democracy and instead prefer to evaluate the sustainability of democracy in the light of new, emergent challenges to human rights and participatory politics. The study on

Northern Ireland in Volume II refers to 'stop–go' democracy.

While theories and generalizations about pathways to democracy are elusive, and there is no single or given formula for the introduction of democracy, it is clear that there are some common *types or patterns* of democratic transition. While no country fits any one type exactly, with so many experiences of democratization in the last three decades some patterns are recognizable. The context for analysing these patterns is a general theory of democratization that was articulated in a seminal scholarly article by the late Dankwart Rustow, whose work continues to influence our understanding of the basic elements of democratic transition today (Rustow 1970). His theory contained critical insights that are useful in interpreting democratization experiences. He argued that:

- *Analysis needs to go beyond 'preconditions for democracy'.* The conditions that bring about democratization are not necessarily those that can account for the continued functioning or sustainability of democracy. The historical, social, political and economic elements that pertain at any given point in time are unique to that period; democratization can be stimulated by those conditions but the very same circumstances can doom the success of the enterprise over time. For each situation, it is important to analyse dynamic circumstances. That is, it is not enough to say that there are certain preconditions for democracy—such as a certain level of social cohesion, or a minimum amount of per capita income, or the existence of a middle class—but instead the focus of attention should be on a simple question: 'Under what conditions can a process of democratization emerge from a given set of circumstances in a particular country?'.
- *It's about a process.* The necessary ingredients for a democratization process are a sense of national community or common destiny, a conscious, deliberate and arguably 'rational' adoption of democratic rules, and the interaction of multiple actors in a step-by-step process. Democratization processes thus allow for competition as well as cooperation, for conflict as well as coming together. Much depends on the choices of the protagonists in the process in terms of their own interests and preferences and the type of institutions—or rules—that they choose (in a self-interested way) to govern the new-found democracy.
- *Individuals matter.* In addition to the long-standing focus in the literature on structures of change—such as the role of the military as a social institution, or class relations, or the structures of the state—in democratization processes much depends on the decision making or choices of those involved in the process. In sum, there is a considerable role of human decision making (or 'agency') in the democratization process that is now well accounted for in models of change that focus on structural change or modernization as the precursors of political reform. Social mobilization will be a key element.
- *It is necessary to focus on elite behaviour and negotiations.* While it may be ideal, and indeed romantic, to think of democratization as a process in which there is popular demand for participation, in reality many democratization experiences boil down to

negotiations among powerful elites. Democratization can occur when elites involved in power struggles ultimately decide that democracy—structured, ongoing competition through known rules of the political game—can serve their interests better than the status quo. Rustow called this the 'decision' phase. Over time, however, the ultimate success of democracy depends on whether the process can be expanded to involve society's contending forces in the democratic bargain.

Democratization, then, is both 'contingent' and 'dynamic'. There are arguments for and against the concept of democratic consolidation, in which countries that have experienced a period of political reform are considered to be beyond the point of return to authoritarianism or where the political culture and rules of democracy are so entrenched that other forms of political decision making are simply not conceivable.

Arguments for the consolidation concept include:

• *The 'two elections rule',* ideally with alternation. According to this view, there is evidence that once a country has experienced two democratic elections, and ideally one in which the incumbent regime is voted out and a new government takes power peacefully, the country can be considered to have consolidated democracy. This somewhat minimalist definition suggests that the key to democracy is competition among contending social forces. Two elections signal that such competition exists and is vibrant and healthy, and alternation in governing coalitions signals that peaceful politics and a willing handover of power have replaced power-at-all-costs mindsets of political leaders.
• *The 'only game in town' argument:* when the rules of the democratic game—human rights, tolerance, freedom of association, freedom of speech, elections—become so engrained in a country's political culture that they are the only conceivable rules of politics, democracy can be said to be consolidated. According to this view, when there is a situation in which democratic politics becomes a matter of expectation and habit, consolidation has occurred.

Sceptics disagree. There have been so many cases of failed processes that have not succeeded in yielding functional democracies, or where elections have been violence-ridden or fraudulent, or in which elected elites have behaved undemocratically, that the entire notion of a linear 'transition' is flawed. According to this argument, because some transitions to democracy have been incomplete or unsatisfactory, or have been hijacked and even generated war, the simple concept of a transition that leads to relatively quick consolidation (over a few years) is faulty both in its assumptions and in its application to the real world. In recognizing the fallacy, at least one is being realistic in today's world of dominant-power countries, of predatory (or corrupt) elites, and of weak states with little capacity to fulfil their basic duties of providing for human development and human security.

Box 2.1: Pathways to Democracy: Some Examples

When the incumbent regime collapses—as in East Germany, with the rapid turn away from communism and the fall of the government of Erich Honecker; the former German Democratic Republic (GDR) was simply absorbed into the former Federal Republic of German (West Germany, FRG). Democratization occurred in this instance through the incorporation of a formerly authoritarian state into a pre-existing democracy.

When the incumbent regime is overthrown—as in Serbia and Montenegro, when mass protests led by the Otpor! movement in Belgrade deposed former President Slobodan Milosevic. Democratization in this instance occurred as the result of a popular uprising that threw out the existing government and, through a process of negotiation with the government's security forces and new elections, introduced a new government. (It is a sobering thought that Milosevic had himself been elected in the first multiparty elections in the former Yugoslavia in 1989.)

When the incumbent regime gradually liberalizes but retains control—as in Pakistan, following the military *coup d'état* that brought General (now President) Pervez Musharraf to power in 1999. Following the coup, the military announced a democratization process and a return to civilian rule, but not one in which the incumbent government was willing to risk a loss of power. On the other hand, there are instances of incumbent governments unveiling such processes but being unable to retain control, as the Golkar party in Indonesia attempted to do following the resignation of long-time ruler Suharto in 1998.

When the incumbent regime negotiates with opposition elements—as in South Africa, when in early 1990 the last apartheid government led by then President F. W. de Klerk released opposition figures such as Nelson Mandela and began a six-year process of negotiation that culminated in a new constitution in 1996. These types of transition—also seen when military regimes in Latin America negotiated with opposition political parties—are known as 'pacted' transitions because of the emphasis on bargaining and negotiations.

When democracy emerges from peace negotiations in cases of civil war—as in Bosnia, following the devastating war of 1992–5, which ended in the internationally mediated Dayton agreement. Annex 4 of the peace agreement featured a new constitution for a post-war, power-sharing democracy. From Namibia (1990) to Afghanistan (2004), post-war elections are often seen as the culminating moment in a war-to-peace transition (see chapters 4 and 5).

When the international community introduces democracy through transitional administrations—as in Timor-Leste where, after the bloody referendum on independence in 1999 and military intervention by an Australian-led force, the United Nations was asked to come in and administer the country while it prepared the procedural (e.g. electoral) and institutional or state-capacity requirements for the new country to gain its sovereignty.

2. Democratization as Conflict-generating

In virtually every major region of the world there are examples of ways in which democratic political competition has exacerbated underlying social tensions. Elections have often been the precipitating event for an escalation of violent conflict. Afghanistan, Burundi, Cambodia, Colombia, Iraq, Haiti, Liberia, Nigeria, Sri Lanka and Zimbabwe are just a few 20th and 21st century examples of countries in which electoral processes, or the prospect of elections over the horizon, have sharply heightened social tensions and induced or exacerbated political violence (see Lyons 2002). Violence debilitates support for democracy by polarizing societies and undermining the social cohesion necessary for political compromise, while threatening the very security and human development imperatives that democracy must deliver if it is to remain legitimate (for a poignant example, see Sengupta 2004).

> In virtually every major region of the world there are examples of ways in which democratic political competition has exacerbated underlying social tensions.

In many societies today where ethnic, religious, racial or class divisions run deep, democratic competition does indeed inspire and inflame political violence. Violence is often a tool to wage political struggles—to exert power, rally supporters, destabilize opponents, or derail the prospect of elections altogether in an effort to gain total control of the machinery of government. The misfit between sharp democratic competition and the goals of social peace in deeply divided societies is recognized in modern experiences with democracy in complex societies. In the study on Lesotho in Volume II, Khabele Matlosa describes in detail the role of electoral reform in strategies for reducing violence and overcoming social differences.

Some democratization processes have generated sufficient social tensions to contribute to their own demise. For example, the opening of Algeria to multiparty elections in the early 1990s directly precipitated the armed conflict between the government and Islamist insurgents that followed, with the dissolution of Parliament in January 1992; only in 2002 did Algeria begin to slowly revive its democratization process. While the number of

> In many societies today where ethnic, religious, racial or class divisions run deep, democratic competition inspires and inflames political violence. Violence is often a tool to wage political struggles. Political reform generates new tensions among winners and losers. Elites often attempt to maintain their position by using populist, nationalist themes to mobilize support.

democracies has indeed doubled in the last 30 years, and the number of armed conflicts has declined by 40 per cent at the same time (see chapter 1, figure 1), volatility remains. Political reform generates new tensions among winners and losers. After civil wars, some parties retain the ability to wage violence through their continued organization of militias, for example, and thus may be unwilling to accept loss of power at the ballot box, and retain the military power to challenge the elected regime. Edward Mansfield and Jack Snyder argue that young, immature democracies are more prone to interstate (international) war (see Snyder 2000). They write that 'elites, including some who have parochial interests in empire and war, often attempt to maintain their position by using populist, nationalist themes to mobilize support. When mass nationalism and elite logrolling become pervasive in states characterized by imperfectly developed democratic institutions, the danger of war increases' (Mansfield and Snyder 1996: 197).

Similarly, scholarly research has shown that democratization during times of economic stress is especially challenging and may lead to social conflict. Changes in the governing coalition may fundamentally rearrange economic relationships in society, for example along class lines, and this may unleash social unrest among those whose interests are threatened by such change. Situations of high inequality are not conducive to successful democratization, as the pioneering work of the scholar Adam Przeworski has shown (Przeworksi 1991). Inequality is not a barrier to initial democratization, as situations such as those of India and South Africa show, but the transforming of social relations is exceptionally difficult to achieve over time.

> Democratization during times of economic stress especially may lead to social conflict. It can introduce uncertainty that is intolerable for some protagonists because they fear the consequences of the process. Rapid democratization in particular may be conflict-inducing.

Democratization as a conflict-exacerbating phenomenon is linked to the issues of certainty and uncertainty in the process of political change. Democratization as change can introduce uncertainty that is intolerable for some protagonists because they fear the consequences of the process; violence can occur to stop the process of democratization or to change its direction and outcome. On the other hand, democratization as a process can be too certain; protagonists know they may lose, and lose heavily, in elections or in negotiations and the certainty of such loss prompts violence to influence the process or the outcome.

The debacle of the dissolution of the former Yugoslavia in 1989 underscores the concern with rapid democratization as potentially conflict-inducing. The onset of elections after socialism in a situation where political parties quickly crystallized around ethno-nationalist identities set the stage for the violent break-up of the former state. Democratization introduced divisive tendencies because of the complexity of multilayered identity. There was no experience of plural political party membership or of organizing for advocacy on an issue basis. When competitive electoral politics was introduced (after years of rule by a centralized party) amid financial crisis and uncertainty, the 'fall-back' for mobilization was nationalism (Slovenian, Croatian,

Serbian, Albanian etc.). Electoral competition combined with strong historical identities and sharp economic decline introduced insecurity and fear. The population responded, understandably, by closing ranks in nationalist identity. Electoral competition among political parties quickly became a struggle for group hegemony in the new and untested countries to emerge from the collapsing Yugoslav federation.

Today there is also rightful concern about democratization as conflict-inducing when it is introduced as a control mechanism by authoritarian regimes or by external controlling parties. For example, in South Africa in 1984 the white-minority government liberalized apartheid structures to allow 'Coloured' (a category used by the government of the time) and Asian voters to participate in the system; but the Tricameral Constitution reforms, as they were called, only served to underscore the obvious and unjustifiable exclusion of the country's majority Africans. The ill-considered reforms prompted a regeneration of resistance against apartheid, and conflict between anti-apartheid forces and the white-minority government led to an additional 14,000 deaths in political violence between the onset of the popular uprising in 1984 and the onset of negotiations to democratize fully, which began in earnest in 1990. Still, during the transitional negotiations (1990–4), another 14,000 were to die in political violence before the celebrated elections of 1994 that finally ended legal apartheid.

3. Democratization, Social Movements and Human Security

There is widespread interest in the phenomenon of mass social movements in terms of their potential contribution to democracy, and the role of mass action in national politics. In the last four decades, especially, there has been an upsurge of direct popular activism in Asia, Africa, Latin America, Europe, and more recently in the former Soviet states. Generally, such action is, rightly, seen as a sign of broad popular engagement in democracy. In Serbia and Montenegro, the Otpor! ('resistance') movement grew (with a degree of international assistance) from a student-led anti-government group into a social movement that included local-level authorities, farmers and trade unionists; eventually, by marching on Belgrade, they brought down the government of Slobodan Milosevic, widely seen as shouldering special responsibility for the Balkan wars of the 1990s and some of the crimes against humanity that occurred in them.

Otpor!, like many social movements before it, was celebrated because of its non-violent approach to resistance against the state. The inspiration for such a strategy may be traced to Gandhi's Satyagraha movement which used non-violent resistance to overthrow British colonial domination. From the organization of Solidarity at the Gdansk shipyard in Poland in 1980, to 'People Power' in the Philippines in 1986, social movements demanding democracy have historically been critical to democratization. In what became known as the Philippines' 'Second People Power Revolution', a four-day popular revolt peacefully overthrew President Joseph Estrada in January 2001, bringing the popular then vice-president Gloria Macapagal-Arroyo to power. The Rose Revolution in Georgia in 2003–4 and the Orange Revolution in Ukraine in November 2004 showed anew the role of large-scale demonstrations—an outpouring of public participation—in the process of transition to democracy. Clearly, 'popular upsurge' has been a key turning point in the process of ending authoritarian rule.

Mass protests demanding the ousting of an incumbent, together with new accountability, may be the basis for launching, if not sustaining, a democracy. Historically, even violent uprisings such as the American, French or Mexican revolutions have led to the introduction of democracy. More recently, the fall of Suharto in Indonesia was preceded by mass action in Jakarta and regional centres, as well as sustained long-term work by activists, educators and pro-change, pro-reform networks. In Serbia, Georgia and Ukraine, mass action produced regime change. In other places, such as Venezuela or Hong Kong, this was not the case. In Myanmar/Burma or in Tiananmen Square in China in 1989, pro-democracy gatherings were crushed by the state authorities as threats to national security.

3.1. Social Movements and Democratization
The Rose Revolution in Georgia and the Orange Revolution in Ukraine were seen by some observers as mass public bravery in opposition to post-Soviet leaders in the newly independent states of the former USSR, because they were visible protests against corruption and the usurpation of power, against electoral fraud, and against governments that have created 'new oligarchs' whose rapid accumulation of wealth was unimaginable just a few years ago. Some saw the Orange Revolution as new 'winds of change' blowing across the former Soviet space; the popular revolt is held as indicative both of a new demand for democracy in formerly socialist countries and of a seismic shift of geopolitics away from Russia and towards the West (Karatnycky 2005). Protestors, wearing distinctive orange scarves and waving orange flags, camped for weeks in Kiev's Independence Square demanding the affirmation of now-President Viktor Yushchenko's victory at the ballot box in second-round presidential elections held in late December 2004. Eventually they prevailed. Observers around the world heralded the mass action as a triumph of 21st century democracy. A year later in 2005, however, the victorious Orange coalition fell apart amid factional infighting, allegations of corruption, and personality conflicts.

At the same time, popular movements can be cultivated, supported and assisted by external interests. It is well documented that both US and Russian funds flowed to opposing sides in Ukraine's 2004 election and its aftermath; there was a high degree of vested interest being played out in the name of the masses.

The phenomenon of social movements has been critical in the evolution of democracy. They are significant junctures, sometimes lasting years and at other times fleetingly brief, in which people take to the streets to exercise their democratic right of direct participation. From the Civil Rights struggle in the United States in the mid-1960s (where the issue of voter registration was pivotal), which brought new laws preventing racial discrimination, to the anti-nuclear protests of the 1980s in Europe, to the anti-apartheid mass action that finally brought down apartheid in South Africa in the late 1980s, to the gay and lesbian rights protests of the 1990s and the anti-globalization protests of today, social movements arise to press demands for political change. Clearly, public participation may in some cases be democratic—there are even guides to activism that are described as 'doing democracy' (Moyer et al. 2001).

There is, however, no straightforward equivalence between mass movements and democratic outcomes. Mass mobilization is often mentioned as a key element in democratic development, but in some cases this kind of engagement works in the opposite way, with negative and fatal implications for human security and life itself. Mass mobilization is often characterized by the exclusion (or targeting) of individuals or certain groups on the basis of religion, culture or historical factors, and in such cases it will work against democratic reforms. It is also notable that this is more likely to occur in societies where power has been highly centralized and after the transition a strong hierarchical, authoritarian structure remains, with the ability to control the media, and non-accountability in the use of groups and resources. Examples can be found from history as well as the present time: they include Germany, Rwanda and the former Yugoslavia.

Nazism ostensibly came to power in Germany through democratic means and on the basis of mass mobilization. It is noteworthy that under the Nazi regime in the 1930s, and more recently in Rwanda and in the former Yugoslavia, a strong party message of exclusion was pushed heavily. Propaganda pushed notions of a chosen people's destiny, the inferiority of another people, and justification for violent 'solutions' cloaked in historical language. The evocation of the German master race and the legacy of the 'Volk' were used to demonize the Jews. Tutsis were known in Rwanda as 'Inyenzi', which means cockroaches, and the Biblical myth of Ham was cited by Hutu leaders when they called for the deportation of all Tutsis back to Ethiopia, prior to killing them. The extremist Serbian leadership harked back to 14th-century battles in proclaiming their grudge against Muslim ethnic-Albanian Kosovars.

> Mass mobilization may be the basis for launching a democracy, but not for sustaining it. There is no straightforward equivalence between mass movements and democratic outcomes, and mass mobilization may clearly be used for negative ends.

Mobilization, then, may clearly be used for negative ends. It has been observed that in 1994 Rwanda was regarded by much of the rest of the world as the arch-example of the chaos and anarchy associated with collapsed states. 'In fact, the genocide was the product of order, authoritarianism, decades of modern theorizing and indoctrination, and one of the meticulously administered states in history' (Gourevitch 2000: 95). This is revealing. The state without democratic principles and practice will rest on old forms of coercion, be they benign or lethal. The unleashing of hate propaganda is something many sectors of society and the international community are concerned with and which democratic practice attempts to counteract. Journalists, teachers, writers of stories, songs, plays or films, performers, human rights groups, and media people in television and radio can all take a role in highlighting or counteracting the demonizing of an identity group.

However, in less developed states or in post-war settings, the national democratization project may be curiously divorced from the challenge of state building itself. The international donor community will intervene in fields of 'governance reform', 'development' and 'democracy promotion'. Unintended contradictions in approach can occur if those working in these areas do not talk to each other. Moreover, initiatives spawn cross-cutting governance networks involving state and non-state actors, as civil society or local NGOs have project and reporting lines which go to external governments. These same projects undertake services such as health, housing or education—once seen as 'public goods' and thus the responsibility of the state. Improving the technical capability of the elected to govern in terms of their performance in framing legislation or tabling motions does not necessary link the resulting laws directly to implementation outside the capital. Elections may run smoothly, but underneath the surface, old clientelism and shifting coalitions of bosses and clans are the real power holders.

> The national democratization project may be curiously divorced from the challenge of state building itself. The international donor community will intervene in fields of 'governance reform', 'development' and 'democracy promotion'. Initiatives spawn cross-cutting governance networks involving state and non-state actors. Civil society or local NGOs undertake services such as health, housing, or education that were once seen as 'public goods' and thus the responsibility of the state.

3.1.1. Interim or Transitional Administration

Critics of the international operations in Bosnia and Timor-Leste have pointed to the danger that international involvement not only can fail to build support for political alternatives, but can provide carte blanche for foreign administrators to override democratic processes, on the grounds that local voters are not responsible enough to have the rights granted to citizens in Western states. The implication of this approach is the end of formal democracy, of legitimacy through accountability to the electorate. Democracy as experienced is redefined as its opposite, adherence to outside standards, not autonomy and accountability (Chandler 1999; Chopra 2002).

How can 'democratic government' be developed in a sustainable way appropriate to different settings? This is a daunting challenge, but if it is ignored the ambition to create democracy universally will not only continue—as it has so far—to result in cases of false, unsustainable and discredited 'democracy'; it will also reduce any prospect of real reform.

Box 2.2: Key Points on Phases (and Fashions) in Democratization: What Can We Learn from the Past?

One way to understand the evolution of international approaches to democratization is to distinguish historical phases, and look for clusters in conflict type and democratization approach.

First are the decolonization transitions in Southern Africa (1979–94), each associated with some degree of violent conflict. These were relatively well-defined,

UN-authorized and-monitored transitions from colonization to self-determination and independence. This phase was a good example of the international community carrying out an essentially peaceful, reasonably regulated, cohesive, predictable and clearly articulated international policy.

Second, beginning in the 1990s and still continuing, are the spasmodic and generally UN-authorized ad hoc interventions in 'failed' or conflict-ridden states. These were variously linked to the ending of the cold war and of the totalitarian regimes which had (ironically) survived until then with the encouragement and support of one or other of the major cold war powers. Apart from seeking to end the conflicts, they aimed at a transition which could, with continued support, become a steadily strengthening democracy. They aimed to replace (on an unpredictable basis for selection) some of the repressive, illiberal, unelected (or dubiously elected) regimes, such as that which continued to exist in Cambodia after the overthrow of the Khmer Rouge regime.

Third are the more aggressive/defensive interventions initiated following the attacks by international terrorists based in Afghanistan on the USA in September 2001, and in response to the alleged threat posed by Iraq from what turned out to be Saddam Hussein's non-existent weapons of mass destruction. These interventions involved both deliberate 'regime change' by force of arms and the insertion of democratic institutions, including elections. Such transitions to democracy are claimed to be justified as necessary not only to benefit the targeted society to be 'transformed', but also because they are necessary for the defence of the intervening democracies and democracy everywhere. The distinctive character of this third phase has been the readiness on the part of the international interveners to initiate the regime change and transition by the use of force, with or without UN authority. These initiatives have been undertaken as primarily military-led operations by a newly emerging 'coalition' of like-minded Western democracies determined to inject electoral, representative democracy in place of defeated regimes characterized as 'rogues'.

Some General Problems of Good-Faith Transitions and Governmental Reform

The reform of government systems within the confines of a single state is a difficult and challenging project. Entrenched interests, established institutions, procedures and practices, culture and the fact that one is dealing with unpredictable human beings all make this inevitable.

A common aim of these interventions for systemic and practical reforms can in general terms be described as an intention to introduce a system of representative government similar to that enjoyed in Western-style democracies. With regard to the first phase, such a liberal government system was a part of the liberation rhetoric and was understood by the liberation movements' leaders ... . Thus the context in the first phase generally favoured such a transition. It did not, however, guarantee its success. ... Even less should the apparent ease with which the implantation was accepted in that first context have led to the assumption that it would work elsewhere. However, the concern in general is that the model evolved in that first phase has continued to be applied in the subsequent phases.

Another concern is the degree to which such international activities have become stereotyped and based on the almost automatic application to the 'target' states of concepts and institutions which may be the hallmarks of 'good governance' in the interveners' own polities, with little consideration of the realities and cultures of the targeted societies. On the one hand those intervening in the current era earnestly protest their respect for national values and culture; yet much of the reforms represents a direct challenge to those values. One does not need to share their values to understand how the target society, or significant parts of it, will resist reform to defend them. This can place those implementing the reform and working in that society in a difficult, contradictory position. For example, in Afghanistan the doctrine of political pluralism was enshrined in the 2001 Bonn Agreement, allegedly accepted by the Afghan negotiators. In fact the prospect of active and effective political parties competing for power is anathema to most Afghan leaders for substantial reasons that are connected with their recent brutal history. Similarly, anyone who becomes familiar with that country is conscious that it has a long and deeply ingrained political culture of effective decentralized government. Yet the reformed constitution, shaped significantly by the influential international supporters of democracy, promotes the concept of a powerful centralized government. Again, whatever may be the convictions of the 'internationals' involved in such operations, how as democrats do they deal with such contradictions?

Was the prospect of sustainable democracy in the beneficiary state the real objective or was the motive and reasoning some narrower self-interest of the intervening state?

John Stuart Mill, a classic writer in the Western tradition, had relevant observations. 'Political machinery', he pointed out,

'does not act of itself. As it is first made so it has to be worked, by men and even by ordinary men. It needs not simply their simple acquiescence, but their active participation and must be adjusted to the capacities and qualities of such men as are available. This implies three conditions:

The people for whom the form of government is intended *must be willing to accept it*, or at least not be so unwilling as to pose an insurmountable obstacle to its establishment.

They *must be willing and able to do what is necessary to keep it standing.*

And, *they must be willing and able to do what it requires of them to enable it to fulfil its purposes.*

A failure of any of these conditions renders a form of government... .unsuitable to the particular case' (Mill, J. S., *Considerations of Representative Government* (Amherst, N.Y.: Prometheus Books, 1991), p. 13, fn. 1 (emphasis added).

... .

Is there a need, especially if the democratization project is to be spread with the energy and speed now being suggested, to give more thought to the possibility that 'democratic government' is not simply that form of administration with which Western governments are most familiar? This is a daunting challenge, but one which is important if the objective is a truly universal system which is understood honestly and accepted, 'kept standing' and able to fulfil its purposes. If this challenge is ignored the ambition to create democracy universally will not only continue—as it has so far—to result in cases of false, unsustainable and discredited 'democracy', but also spoil the prospects of various different but reasonable national systems of governance surviving, and reduce any prospect of their real reform.

Source: Extracts from the study by Reginald Austin in Volume II.

An international presence is generally undertaken with the professed intention of helping to improve human security in a given setting; but for the long-term viability of the new state, and for the very purpose of helping it to deliver on poverty reduction and social protection, we must also ask how social movements translate both poverty reduction and social protection needs into political action.

If we understand that, strategically, public goods such as health, education, equal opportunity, poverty reduction and peace require public action, then we must be concerned about whether people are mobilised to participate in political society, or whether their participation weakens or even undermines political society and ultimately the possibilities for a state that is able to achieve poverty reduction and development. When the state is moribund, already in a condition of collapse, or an instrument of extreme predation or extreme repression (for instance, Marcos in the Philippines, Suharto in Indonesia by the 1990's, or Mobutu in Zaire), then the question centres more on support that will strengthen political society towards the transformation of the state. The prescriptions for assistance must be specific in both time and place and can only be found through investigation and *political* analysis (Putzel 2004: 3).

4. After 'After the Cold War': Democratization, 'Good Governance' and Global Neo-liberalism

A striking feature of the introduction of democratic reform in both post-war and post-authoritarian settings has been the strong dominance of economic change with emphasis on a market economy at the same time. After the destruction of war, the need for speedy remedies has been used to justify the use of foreign firms and labour to rebuild infrastructure in settings as varied as Bosnia and Timor-Leste. But local (often skilled) workers are both disempowered and the poorer for this, as evidenced in the well-known phenomenon of well-qualified technicians or engineers (who can speak English) driving taxis in capital cities. The implications of privatization of services go even further. Having gone through years of siege and deprivation, citizens of Sarajevo took to the streets in mass demonstrations in 2000 over changes in labour law which reduced maternity leave and brought in 'reforms' thought to contravene workers' rights under the old communist regime. Work was no longer guaranteed, and those who had work no longer enjoyed the socio-economic rights once associated with it. Following IMF reforms meant to assist the Indonesian economy after the Asian financial crisis in 1998, Jakarta and regional cities alike saw mass protests against the lifting of subsidies on fuel and food.

> A striking feature of the introduction of democratic reform in both post-war and post-authoritarian settings has been the strong dominance of economic change with emphasis on a market economy at the same time.

In 2004 analysts Dani Rodrik and Romain Wacziarg tackled head-on the contention that democratization in developing countries produces political instability, ethnic conflict and poor economic outcomes. They looked at anecdotal evidence of 'democratic reforms that led to economic chaos and eventually a collapse back into autocracy'. Using cross-national regression techniques to look at the relationship between democracy and economic performance in 24 countries coming out of dictatorship or war, their conclusions did not support this contention (Rodrik and Wacziarg 2004). (This approach, however, leaves open the question of social policies on development, distribution, and public goods required for better human security.)

More recently, Astri Suhrke and Julia Buckmaster produced a comparative study on 'Aid, Growth and Peace' (2005). In examining Bosnia, Cambodia, Nicaragua, El Salvador, Guatemala, Mozambique and Rwanda, they looked for the effect of aid on growth and the effect of growth on peace, concluding that there was no obvious relationship between economic growth and peace. But their observations go much further than this:

> Although peace in the sense of no war has been sustained in all seven cases, underlying structures of inequality or political exclusion associated with past violence remain ... In some cases this has produced widespread, low-level forms of violence, as in Guatemala, become transposed into regional conflicts pursued across borders, as seen in Rwanda's role in neighboring DRC, or the political economy of war has left

a legacy of violence associated with the illegal economy whose effects are typically magnified by massive post-war unemployment, as in Bosnia ... If such structural sources of violence remain, what would be the equivalent of structural adjustment for peace? The diagnosis in part gives the answer.... . In all our seven cases, *distributional issues* were central, underlying causes of war, whether relating to class (Central America), regions (Mozambique), ethnic groups (Rwanda) or ethno-political entities (the former Yugoslavia). Distributional issues concerned socio-economic goods as well as access to political power ... the proven violence-generating potential of structures of inequality and exclusion and inequality cannot be ignored.

The consequent policy implications for post-war aid strategies is that structural adjustment for peace should focus on three broad areas:

(i) modify systemic inequalities among groups (horizontal inequalities)

(ii) promote institutional structures for inclusive, political representation

(iii) transform the structures of violence, created by the war itself, whether associated with agents of the state or non-state actors (Suhrke and Buckmaster 2005: 17).

In practice, the limitations of recent dominant democratization agendas are partly reflected in the Bretton Woods institutions and the US approach to democracy. In classic US foreign policy, democracy was restricted to the electoral and institutional sphere, not recognizing that political power was also a means to transform unjust socio-economic structures, nor that social and cultural spheres may also need to be democratized. Democracy has been mainly understood more as polyarchy, or a system in which a small group actually rules, and mass participation in decision making is confined to choosing leaders in elections that are carefully managed by competing elites. Political, human and social rights are hardly valued beyond their instrumental role in economic and socio-economic development, which is expected to be furthered by open markets and a subsidiary state. This approach fits well into the dominant trend of emphasis on 'good governance', with its view on governing a (developing or industrializing) country as a technocratic, non-political function. Moreover, this approach to democracy holds that democratic politics needs a thriving free market economy and vice versa.

It is noteworthy that Thailand also saw mass protests in 2005 against plans of the Thaksin administration to privatize the Electricity Generating Authority of Thailand (EGAT). On 3 March 2005 some 50,000 state enterprise workers from all 41 state enterprises were joined by private-sector workers, students and activists in front of EGAT's headquarters in the biggest demonstration to date against the Thaksin government. It was the largest protest in Thailand since the 1992 democracy uprising, and the largest union-led protest in Thai history. At the same time lively debate forums were scrutinizing Thai democracy, raising questions of accountability and policy.

International programmes and conditions for developing and post-communist countries were extended from the economic to the political terrain, and to governance issues. The recent dominant democratization agendas see democracy as restricted to the electoral and institutional sphere, not recognizing that political power is also a means to transform unjust socio-economic structures, or that the social and cultural spheres may also need to be democratized. Too often the social and economic dimension of 'peace building' is ignored.

One year later popular momentum had grown on multiple issues to the point that the prime minister had to step down from office.

Arguments and positions on democracy and the free market will be questions of degree and kind. While a new constitution may be formally or apparently 'inclusive', the market may have the effect of exclusion, depending on purchasing power and the positioning of groups and needs. (Ironically, one of the most 'privatized societies' today may be Somalia, where the state cannot provide but education, telecommunications and medicine are very much for sale.) The key point here is that by privatizing or settling for market forces to meet social needs, donors and governments risk weakening, even de-legitimizing, the state. Too often the social–economic dimension of 'peace building' is ignored, with little investment in jobs and training. In Timor-Leste, in Bosnia, Sierra Leone, Sudan and Afganistan, local people want work in order to both earn and share in their own reconstruction. Rural women in Kosovo after 1999 complained that they were offered trauma counselling and human rights education but could not access small loans to restart businesses or family farming.

> By privatizing or settling for market forces to meet social needs, donors and governments risk weakening, even de-legitimizing, the state.

Suffice it to say that popular protest is severely challenging the 'Washington Consensus', as seen in Sarajevo (above), in Bolivia, in Venezuela, and recently in Mongolia. Critics in developing countries have a point when they label the pro-democracy development agenda as 'market fundamentalism' and a projection of the Western model of development. The often-imposed blueprint of economic and political reform reflects the post-cold war thesis that neo-liberal policies will be successful and legitimate in the context of democratic regimes. Due to this consensus, the international programmes and conditions for developing and post-communist countries were extended from the economic to the political terrain, and to governance issues. The political outcome of the international democracy agenda is thus very problematic. For people living in countries that were previously ruled by an authoritarian regime, democratization is a major step forward, although for those striving for more equal social and economic relations the new democracies can still be restrictive. In settings with an international presence or strong donor influence, the roles of political representation, political struggle and true consensus building are diminished. Dominant realms of decision making are far from democratic if power is centred within the international community through the ability to control standards and money.

5. Managing Democratization: Some Lessons Learned

Experiences of democratization since the mid-1970s yield a number of useful findings about managing the uncertainty that such political reform processes generate. The lessons that follow may be useful when thinking through strategies by which local actors and the international community may better facilitate the process of political change.

1. *Democratization processes are conflict-inducing; societies with a proliferation of conflict prevention and conflict management mechanisms are better able to weather the turbulent moments of change.* Conflict itself is not necessarily problematic, as it can be a constructive means of social change in situations where the status quo is unfair or illegitimate. What is problematic, however, is when democratization unleashes social or widespread political violence—either by incumbent governments seeking to retain power through force, or among clashing social forces vying for influence or control—which creates acute human security challenges. Transitions may be anticipated as turbulent processes; international and local actors alike should be encouraged to foster resilience through communications and access to information, crisis prevention measures and conflict management mechanisms which can facilitate intervention, bargaining and negotiation, at different levels. Civil control of the military and the professionalization of policing (including community approaches and public order policing) are important.

2. *Early warning mechanisms for crises are critical in democratization situations.* This applies also to electoral processes. From the review or preparation of the electoral law through to the election events and the formation of a government after the election, there are any number of critical turning points that pivot a society towards, or away from, democratization and peace. Identifying potential crisis points early on and developing appropriate responses—such as monitoring missions, independent electoral commissions, political party pacts on non-violence, human rights reporting, engaging civil society, civic and press education, or working with governments and opposition in dialogue processes—are critical in managing the crises that democratization processes can present.

3. *Local-level processes should be promoted.* The need for multiple methods of engagement to manage crises highlights the relevance of local-level processes for conflict mitigation. A multi-tiered approach is called for in which top-level bargaining bolsters the work of community-level mediators, and local-level confidence reinforces the transitional processes at the top. This also raises the notion of complementarity in processes of change, in which efforts at different levels of society reinforce each other (Bloomfield 1997). In Volume II, Arifah Rahmawati and Najib Azca illustrate the value of 'bottom–up' security sector reform in Indonesia through work with the police in different conflict settings within Indonesia.

4. *Inclusion must be fostered.* The most consistent finding of the comparative analysis of democratization is that processes and institutions must be broadly inclusive of major social groups and/or factions. In some instances there will be 'spoilers' whose positions are extreme and who refuse to participate in peace and democratization talks, and every effort must be made to ensure that the general peace and democratization talks are as inclusive as possible while recognizing that there are limits to inclusion from both domestic and international perspectives (e.g. those who have committed serious human rights abuses or, in transitions following war, are under indictment by international criminal courts). Although there are no

universally applicable lessons learned with regard to inclusion and exclusion, it is clear that the 'stakeholder' approach is vital; room must be made for women's and minority interest representation.

5. *International norms in keeping with local needs should be emphasized.* Finally, and fortunately, international norms on the promotion of human rights and democracy evolved rapidly in the 1990s and early 2000s, and their further development is critical to building and maintaining peace. In 1992, the United Nations General Assembly adopted a resolution on the fair treatment of minorities and indigenous groups. The Organization for Security and Co-operation in Europe (OSCE) established a High Commissioner for National Minorities, who seeks to prevent the eruption of ethnic violence in Europe through quiet diplomacy, particularly in the newly democratic states of the former Eastern bloc. Electoral assistance is now readily available from the United Nations, the Commonwealth, regional organizations, and a plethora of non-governmental groups. It is increasingly recognized that where there is a local basis for consensus building and participation, this should be built upon when possible for new national strutures to ensure viability and legitimacy.

6. *It is essential to take a long view of democratic development, to include not just the transitional process itself but also changes in underlying social conditions needed for democracy to be sustained.* Finally, there is a need for better understanding of both the historical roots of patterns of inequality and how to gauge the political implications of development in order to transform these patterns. For example, recent studies undertaken by the World Bank echo the work of earlier 'structuralist' or '*dependencia*' schools of thought. The bank's 2003 study *Inequality in Latin America and the Caribbean: Breaking with History?* confirms that the unequal distribution of resources that characterizes the region today follows a pattern set with specific traits of European colonization in the region, when elite populations shaped institutions and policies to serve their own interests first. Political choice has determined that low levels of support for basic education contrasted with generous financing for universities, where the children of the elite are trained. Political institutions in the region, typically, have been weak. Political choice and social policy development must be further extended; hence recommendations to:

i) Build more open political and social institutions, that allow the poor and historically subordinate groups, such as Afro-descendants and indigenous people, to gain a greater share of agency, voice and power in society;
ii) Ensure that economic institutions and policies seek greater equity and allow for saving in good times to enhance access by the poor to social safety nets in bad times;
iii) Increase access by the poor to high-quality public services, especially education, health, water and electricity, as well as access to farmland and the rural services the poor need to make it productive. Protect and enforce the property rights of the urban poor (World Bank 2004).

Some degree of turbulence, then, in the form of advocacy, awareness raising and mobilization for action, such as meetings, voting, protesting, asking for accountability or inclusion, challenging a status quo which does not deliver, or fighting for justice and change, may thus be seen as a necessary, possibly ongoing and dynamic feature of democratization.

6. Looking Forward: Current Trends and Beyond

Both internal and external factors contribute to popular demand for democratic change. Conditions in Bolivia, however divided and stratified the society, were sufficiently 'open' and historically influenced by the idea of democracy for mobilization to lead from popular protests to a referendum, the revision of the rules for standing for office, elections, and eventually a Constituent Assembly. Regional and international actors joined a process to prevent violence and enable dramatic but nevertheless peaceful changes through the ballot box. There is now a wave of change in Latin America driven by majority demands for accountability, inclusion and attention to socio-economic grievance.

In Burma (Myanmar), by contrast, sufficient openings for public voice and domestic mobilization do not exist. A centralized military power base resorts to the use of armed violence or negotiated accommodation with localized and/or ethnic leaderships and groups. Even in Burma, however, there are consistent pressures for further reform. In these and more open societies, it is likely that there will continue to be the open social protests that have characterized internal pressures for democratization in the past. Such protests are often staged at moments when demands for reform are at a peak, as in situations of strained or collapsing economic conditions or when the government steps up repression in its efforts to retain power. Such demands are threatening for governments in power, as well. They face choices of whether to attempt liberalization as a type of safety valve while maintaining ultimate control. From the former Soviet Union to South Africa to Egypt, liberalization without full democratization can generate new challenges to governments that are increasingly hard to control.

When is full democratization—beyond liberalization—likely to be initiated? Classically, democratic transitions are believed to be more likely if two types of conditions apply:

(a) when there are clear splits among existing autocratic leaders, in which some urge reform in order to accommodate popular demands for change, while others in the ruling group seek to preserve the current order at all costs. Such splits, often involving the top military officers as well, can under certain circumstances lead to a new, 'democratizing' coalition of opposition leaders and reform-minded insiders (Stepan 1986). This was the case in many of the transitions to democracy in Latin America during the 1980s and the pattern can be also seen in some of the so-called 'Colour' revolutions of the early 2000s—notably that of Ukraine, where top military officers sided with the Orange revolutionaries in November 2004. It may yet apply to Nepal, where the monarch has increasingly isolated himself against the people and the political parties and in the face of armed opposition which holds territorial control of most rural areas; and

(b) when power has been strongly centralized in the person of a charismatic leader who has ruled for many years, sometimes for decades. When such leaders centralize power in their own person, usually with a cadre of loyalists around them, the end of a leader's tenure—often from natural causes—can induce a political vacuum in which there is rapid political change. This is especially true when such leaders have come to power through revolution or liberation politics, where 'neo-patrimonial' (father-figure) rule has occurred. Today, there is considerable speculation in countries where there is a long lineage of personalized or highly charismatic rule as to what will happen when the incumbent leader inevitably passes from the scene: Cuba under President Fidel Castro, Egypt under President Hosni Mubarak or Zimbabwe under President Robert Mugabe are all seen in this light. In such situations, political crises may be quickly precipitated even though change has been anticipated for years.

One significant consideration about the future of democratization is the question of political reform in the world's most populous state, China. China's phenomenal economic growth in recent years, its increasing openness to the world through trade and investment, and galloping advances in international communication technologies have raised anew the question of democratization in China. In many ways, the politically charged question of democratization in China has evolved dramatically since the government suppressed popular protests in Tiananmen Square in the spring of 1989 following the declaration of martial law in response to what the government of China refers to as a 'political storm'. In 1989, a group of students, disgruntled labourers and intellectuals had coalesced to demand democracy, the combating of corruption, and job security; in Tiananmen Square some students erected a statue of the 'Goddess of Democracy' to press their claims.

In examining the prospects for democratization in China, the country's dramatic economic growth and demographic change must be borne in mind. With mass migration from rural to urban areas, and subsequent moves by the Chinese Communist Party government to undertake political reform, there is a long-term imperative to deal with deeper social trends. Dealing with national poverty and inequality is high on the agenda. The advent of village-level elections in the 1980s and the practice of local elections are sometimes seen as the beginning of bottom–up democratization that will eventually reach higher levels of political authority (Pei 1995). Today elections at the local level are beginning to occur in urban areas as well, with initial elections in cities having occurred in some areas of Shanghai in 2003, lending support to the 'creeping democratization' thesis.

Likewise, some interpret the 'consultative' rule-of-law regime as an intermediate step on the path to full democracy, in which there is widespread consultation of citizens in public policy decision making together with improvements in the judicial processes and the rule of law; others, however, see this as a desirable end state that does not imply China's full embrace of democracy per se (Zhao 2006). Critics of democratization in China point to the likelihood of widespread social disruption and the collapse of order—

creating a crisis of human security—and to the purported incompatibility of democracy (especially Western conceptions of democracy) with mainland Chinese cultural values. There is also the possibility that democratization in China could accentuate demands for autonomy in outlying provinces such as Xinjiang or Tibet, where there are separatist claims. At the same time, democratization and decentralization could be seen as a way or ameliorating the tensions created by diversity (such as those described in chapter 3) in these regions.

Another perspective for China involves a longer-term analysis that would suggest that democratization there, if not 'inevitable', is very likely in the future. As the Chinese economy grows, so too does its middle class. In the context of 21st century globalization, and especially the diffusion of international telecommunications (which transmits ideas as well as entertainment), the Chinese people and especially the new middle class may increasingly demand accountability, a voice in public affairs, and the ability to oust those political leaders who do not perform well or who behave badly. Urbanization, along with the growth of the middle class, has historically also led to demands for democracy and thus pressures for democratization are likely to be especially strong in urban areas. Thus, some see China's democratization not as a matter of 'if' but of 'when' and 'how' (Diamond 2006). Given the popular protests for broader participation and more accountable democracy in Hong Kong and the practice of multiparty democracy in Taiwan (a province of China that may one day be reunited with the mainland), clearly the issue of democratization in the world's most populous and increasingly prosperous state is one of the great questions of the 21st century.

This brief evaluation of democratization's future suggests that there are many ways in which the international community can 'think ahead' about ways to build democracy and to facilitate the realization of human security. If past experience is any guide, future transitions will be fraught with their own uncertainty and turbulence, such that in some situations there may well emerge threats to security during the period of rapid political change. The recommendations in section 5 of this chapter offer some lessons from prior experience in approaching future crises. In this context, anticipating transitions and acting proactively to help manage the turbulence of transitions may well be one of the most important aspects of the international community's early warning and preventive action in the years to come.

References and Further Reading

Bloomfield, David, *Peacemaking Strategies in Northern Ireland: Building Complementarity in Conflict Management Theory* (New York: St Martin's Press, 1997)

Chandler, David, 'The Limits of Peacebuilding: International Regulation and Civil Society Development in Bosnia', *International Peacekeeping*, 6/1 (1999)

Chopra, Jarat, 'Building State Failure in East Timor', from *Development and Change*, 2002, Blackwell-synergy.com

Comparative Politics, 'Transitions to Democracy: A Special Issue in Memory of Dankwart A. Rustow', special edn edited by Lisa Anderson, April 1997

Diamond, Larry, 'The Rule of Law as Transition to Democracy in China', in Suisheng Zhao (ed.), *Debating Political Reform in China: Rule of Law vs Democratization* (Armonk, N.Y.: M. E. Sharpe, forthcoming 2006)

Gourevitch, Philip, *We Wish to Inform You That Tomorrow We Will Be Killed With Our Families: Stories from Rwanda* (London: Picador, 2000; originally published in New York: Farrar, Straus & Giroux, 1998)

Karatnycky, Adrian, 'Urkaine's Orange Revolution', *Foreign Affairs*, March/April 2005

Lyons, Terrence, 'Post Conflict Elections, War Termination, Democratization, and Demilitarizing Politics', George Mason University Institute for Conflict Analysis and Resolution Working Paper 2, February 2002, <http://www.gmu.edu/depts/icar/Work_Paper20.pdf>

Mansfield, Edward D. and Snyder, Jack, 'Democratization and the Danger of War' (Correspondence), *International Security*, 20/4 (1996)

Moyer, Bill, McCallister, JoAnn, Finlay, Mary Lou and Soifer, Steve, *Doing Democracy: The MAP Model for Organizing Social Movements* (Gabriola Island, BC, Canada: New Society Publishers, 2001)

Pei, Minxin, 'Creeping Democratization in China', *Journal of Democracy*, 6/4 (1995), pp. 65–79

Przeworksi, Adam, *Democracy and the Market: Political and Economic Reform in Eastern Europe and Latin America* (New York: Cambridge University Press, 1991)

Putzel, James, 'The Politics of Participation: Civil Society, the State and Development Assistance', London School of Economics, Crisis States Discussion Paper no. 1, London, January 2004

Rodrik, Dani and Wacziarg, Romain, 'Do Democratic Transitions Produce Bad Economic Outcomes?', December 2004, <http://www.aeaweb.org/annual_mtg_papers/2005/0108_1015_0403.pdf>

Rustow, Dankwart A., 'Transitions to Democracy: Toward a Dynamic Model', *Comparative Politics*, 2/3 (1970), pp. 337–63

Sengupta, Somini, 'Violence Jolts the Still Fragile Democracy in Nigeria', *New York Times*, 24 May 2004

Snyder, Jack, *From Voting to Violence: Democratization and Nationalist Conflict* (New York: W. W. Norton, 2000)

Stepan, Alfred, 'Paths Toward Redemocratization: Theoretical and Comparative Considerations', in Guillermo O'Donnell, Philippe C. Schmitter and Laurence Whitehead (eds), *Transitions from Authoritarian Rule: Comparative Perspectives* (Baltimore, Md.: Johns Hopkins University Press, 1986), pp. 64–84

Suhrke, Astri and Buckmaster, Julia, 'Aid, Growth and Peace: a Comparative Analysis', Bergen, Chr. Michelsen Institute, 2005

World Bank, *Inequality in Latin America and the Caribbean: Breaking with History?* (Washington, DC: World Bank, February 2004) (see also <http://lnweb18.worldbank.org/LAC/LAC.nsf/ECADocByUnid/4112F1114F594B4B85256DB3005DB262?Opendocument>)

Zhao, Suisheng (ed.), *Debating Political Reform in China: Rule of Law vs Democratization* (Armonk, N.Y.: M. E. Sharpe, forthcoming 2006)

CHAPTER 3

CHAPTER 3

3. Democratic Practice: Managing Power, Identity and Difference

Consensus seeking is an overriding principle of the search for democracy in divided societies, even if complete consensus by all parties in society is an elusive ideal. Consensus-based democracy has emerged as a distinct alternative to traditionally conceived competitive democracy; but there are both intrinsic and empirical problems with the consensus principle.

Majority rule and elections themselves can be conflict-inducing: many conflicts have been generated by fears and uncertainties surrounding elections. The electoral system chosen in a particular context is crucial, affecting several major aspects of the development of a conflicted country's politics, in particular the way in which a majority is constituted, the types of political parties that develop, and thus their ability to cut across lines of conflict, and the chances of elections generating stable and inclusive governing coalitions.

It is important to consider the invisible social and cultural barriers, as well as legal ones, that may hinder inclusion along group identity or gender lines, so that access to agenda setting and decision making may be furthered. Historical and cultural factors will influence effective democratic institutional design, but the principles of power sharing, political equality, representation and participation are key to democratic practice.

Historically, peoples have struggled for democracy in order to reconfigure power relations while expressing identity and difference within a shared polity. Such aims require long-term measures that are suitable to particular contexts and needs. The formal instruments of democracy may be used and abused, as when elections are marred by political violence, campaigns stoke and give voice to long-held grievances, and extremist appeals gain favour in ways which threaten others. It may seem a paradox that Nepalese demonstrators took to the streets in 2005 to protest against elections called by the king, but in fact this an example of a formal instrument's legitimacy being challenged: there was a strong public perception that an election was being used in a non-democratic way.

Democracy is defined by the fundamental principle that its political institutions treat all citizens equally. In practice the force of law is only as strong as the underlying moral consensus. It is also subject to structural constraints. That is, the right to vote may be clear, but people living in outlying areas far from the polling station have no access or means of travel; or good legislation is passed but illiteracy and lack of information mean that individuals are not aware of and do not benefit from it. Institutions that are considered as characteristic of modern democracy—free elections, political and civil rights protected under the rule of law, and checks and balances through a division of powers between, for example, the executive, the legislative and the judiciary—are not the same thing as politics. The introduction to this book has referred to the duality of formal and substantive democracy, with formal democracy being selected and established arrangements for organizing political competition, provisions for legitimacy and accountability, and channels of representation, while substantive democracy refers to social relations themselves and the wider distribution of power and access. Ultimately, both spheres are essential for protection against the abuse of power and the exploitation of identity and difference, and for the furthering of human security.

This chapter offers approaches to institutional democratic design, with an emphasis on mechanisms for consensus building. Western liberal democracy assumes certain 'building blocks' for democracy based on centuries of historical development, and these must match prevailing political conditions or adapt, as with recent devolution in the United Kingdom to allow for a Welsh National Assembly and Scottish Parliament. The search for democratic systems that are more appropriate to complex societies has developed principally since the rapid expansion of new states that followed post-World War II decolonization. The design of the constitution of India following independence in 1947 is a particularly striking example of adapting formal democracy to a population of great size, diversity and complexity, as highlighted by Gurpreet Mahajan in the Volume II study.

Subsequently the rise of highly diverse post-colonial states in the 1960s has prompted the need to cultivate forms of democracy that are better suited to differing contexts and conditions. Democratic 'design' may be challenged by deep social divisions, problems of unconsolidated borders and national identities, as well as acute underdevelopment. (For an overview of the literature on approaches to consensus-oriented democracy, see Sisk 1996. For a recent treatment of the role and importance of democratic governance for human development, see United Nations Development Programme (UNDP) 2002.)

While there are debates over how cooperation can best be fostered (described below), consensus-based democracy has emerged as a distinct alternative to traditionally conceived competitive democracy. Consensus-oriented democracy is also closely linked to the concept of democratic deliberation, or democracy as a conversation. These views place a greater premium on democracy's ability to foster discourse that can eventually produce policy solutions that are conflict-resolving through a decision-making process that is based on more than a simple majority, even if complete consensus by all parties in society remains an elusive ideal. Consensus must also be based on interests. To date, much of the work on consensus-oriented democracy has been focused on evaluating institutional options for linking democracy more closely with the hard realities of conflict in societies deeply divided by class, ethnic, racial or religious differences.

> Consensus-based democracy has emerged as a distinct alternative to traditionally conceived competitive democracy.

A central principle for democratic practice should be representation for all, and consensus as a basis for decision making. In institutional terms, whether broadly-based coalitions are formed following electoral processes (as in consociationalism) or prior to elections (as in integrative approaches), the overriding principle of consensus seeking remains a core feature. The search for consensus, however, is difficult in the light of conflicts over power, identity and difference—especially in societies that are going through transitions. For example, in societies that are going through transitions or emerging from violent conflict full consensus is simply not possible. Stakes will be high. Some voices may feel or be marginalized. There may well be spoilers who either cannot or should not be part of the new process. The question who is a spoiler capable of inclusion in a consensus decision, and who should be excluded from the broad majority, is a difficult one that is common both to democratization processes (e.g. should former dictators' or security forces' views be accommodated?) and to peace processes (e.g. should perpetrators of mass violence have a place at the negotiating table?). It is answerable only in application to specific situations. (For an evaluation of these difficult choices in peace processes, see Stedman 1997.)

> In many societies fraught with conflicts over power, identity and difference—especially those that are in transition, for example, emerging from violent conflict—full consensus of all elements in society is simply not possible.

1. Balancing Majority Prerogatives and Minority Rights

Competition and conflict are intrinsic to definitions of democracy. They are evident in the participation of citizens at the ballot box and in civic life, and the competition between candidates in elections for votes, those elected serving as representatives of the people in decision-making institutions. Democracy defined as *competition to secure majority rule* is an enduring concept in contemporary theory and practice, for good reason. This is true even though most systems with strong majoritarian features also feature institutions and practices that encourage compromise and consensus building. There are very few pure majoritarian systems in the world. (Andrew Reynolds, for example, distinguishes between majoritarian systems and 'qualified majoritarian' systems. See Reynolds 1999.)

1.1. Majority Rule: Merits and Demerits
Does democracy-as-majority-rule in plural societies make conflicts worse? This burning question resonates in many societies around the world that have intense

identity conflicts, in countries rich and poor. The rationale for a majority-rule form of decision making remains compelling. Indeed, the argument that the determination of collective decisions in society is most fair and just under conditions of simple majority rule is a strong one. In the view of eminent social contract theorists, majority-rule decision making is arguably the fairest way to make collective decisions, for a very good reason. In *A Theory of Justice*, for example, John Rawls argues that under the 'veil of ignorance'—the original condition in which a group of people come together to make collective decisions without knowledge of the preferences of all the others—ultimately majority rule will emerge as the democratic principle on which every rational person will eventually agree (see Rawls 1972). Liberal democracy, conceived of in this way, is the outcome of simple reasoning. That is because for each individual majority rule is the decision-making system that will maximize their opportunities to be in a winning coalition and minimize the likelihood that they will be among the losers on any given policy decision.

> Democracy is essentially a majority-rule form of decision making. Majority rule treats all individuals as equals. Each voter's preference has an equal chance of influencing the outcome.

As long as democratic decisions benefit even the least well-off in society (an important assumption, especially in complex multi-ethnic societies), majority rule is an idealized way to determine basic issues of fairness and justice in a society. Under majority rule, all voters' preferences are weighted equally, that is, each voter has an equal chance of influencing the outcome. The *Encyclopedia of Democracy* succinctly captures the clear allure of majority rule as a 'default' decision rule in democratic systems:

> Majority rule treats all individuals as equals. The decision of a numerical majority thus carries the most weight; in contrast, accepting the decision of the minority would mean a relative devaluation of the vote of each member of the majority. Because majority rule respects the individual choices made by the majority of the citizenry, it implies a utilitarian theory of justice. If people vote according to their own perceived best interest, majority rule will result in policies that are perceived to benefit most people.
> Majority rule presumes that all individuals are capable of understanding their own interests and that no single group has the monopoly on truth or political wisdom. Majority rule is therefore not compatible with claims to possess and enforce the singular truth about human nature, the good life, or the just society (Grossman and Levin 1995: 788).

While there are those who suggest that, in high-conflict societies, majority-rule decision making is invariably conflict-inducing, critics also point out the efficiency and coalition-building gains that majority-rule democracy offers. Policy makers as well still cling to the view that there are instances in which majority-rule procedures are just and fair. The principle of majority rule as the defining approach to democratic decision making is alive and well, even in its application to the most contentious issues in today's complex societies.

For example, the use of referendums today to address even the most difficult decision for a society—whether to stay together or to separate through secession—is commonplace. In contested territory such as Serbia (Kosovo), Sudan (Southern Sudan), Morocco (Western Sahara) and Papua New Guinea (Bougainville), there is a reflex reaction by policy makers to determine the will of the people in disputed territories by simple majority decision. In all these societies, referendums are seen as the legitimate way to determine the will of the people on the most essential element of the social contract—sovereignty. That is, in these and other similar situations there is apparently broad acceptance that simple majority rule is a legitimate way to determine the question: Who constitutes the 'people'? These concerns suggest a strong need to put into place appropriate safeguards of human rights for those who lose out in majority-rule electoral processes. The same need can apply in other settings (consider Timor-Leste) to those who win.

> Does majority rule in conflicted societies make conflict worse? As long as democratic decisions benefit even the least well-off in society (an important assumption, especially in complex multi-ethnic societies), majority rule is an idealized way to determine basic issues of fairness and justice in a society.

Box 3.1: Considering Referendums: Promises or Perils?

Promises

Referendums offer certain promises, among which are:
• a definitive resolution of a public dispute;
• a clear and easily understandable mechanism for citizen participation and direct decision making;
• the opportunity for citizen initiatives to put the question on the ballot paper;
• clear and unambiguous determination of the popular will and the precise level of support or opposition among voters; and
• opportunities for public education on important issues.

Perils

• Referendums often lend themselves to decisions taken by bare majority rule. On contentious issues, this can lead to 'winner-take-all' politics, which can induce community conflict rather than resolve it.
• Questions can be written in such a way as to mislead or obfuscate the issues, rather than clarifying them.
• Sometimes the referendum can become a vote on the legitimacy of the incumbent government instead of the merits of the particular issue at hand.
• Some issues require deliberation and compromise rather than clear Yes or No answers.
• Some issues require specialized knowledge and information that the public may not be able to easily digest and decide upon, particularly if the issue is highly technical or emotionally charged.

> • Sometimes what may be in the individual interests of a bare majority of voters is not really in the broader interest of the community as a whole, such as tax cuts that then undermine funding for education and schools.
> • The issue can effectively become closed or frozen out of future public debate.

Thus there are—even in societies with strong identity differences—arguably conditions under which majority-rule systems may be appropriate for the definitive resolution of social disputes. This conclusion will be further investigated in the course of this chapter, but at present the following hypothesis is offered: majority-rule approaches to democratic practice, while generally a source of concern in societies splintered by conflicts over identity, cannot be excluded from consideration as a means for contributing to the peaceful management of conflict. The core features of majoritarianism—accountability (responsibility for the success or failure of governance), alternation (the ability to replace governments with oppositions), clarity of decision-making outcomes, and efficiency in determining the will of the people—are all maximized under majority-rule decision making.

The question remains, however: How should a 'majority' be constituted?

1.2. Human Rights, Minority Rights

In societies that are prone to internal conflicts the human rights agenda becomes more complicated because of the very fight over the boundaries of the political community. In secessionist struggles such as those in Chechnya or Aceh, some members want to leave the political community and the country's very identity is under threat. When the very existence of the country is at stake, some leaders decide that the survival of the country justifies limiting (disregarding) human rights in pursuit of secessionists—particularly if the secessionists are using armed struggle in their fight for liberation. In these and many other situations the protection of human rights is 'trumped' by concerns for national security—although historically there are have been other behaviours as well, as with the 'velvet divorce' undertaken in the former Czechoslovakia, the 2006 referendum in Montenegro, or the peaceful split of Norway from Sweden in 1905.

Even where the state's very existence is not directly at stake, for example, when minority group claims are made for autonomy or a share of power, as in Sudan or Burundi, the balance between individual freedoms, security for the state and society, and autonomy and self-determination for minorities is fraught with complexities. In integrative plural societies such as India or South Africa, questions of defining and promoting human rights are constantly re-evaluated in terms of changing conditions. In India and South Africa the rights of traditional leaders to wield traditional powers (e.g. in land allocation or in family law) is an issue. The legal scholar Kristin Henrard, who carried out a comparative evaluation of minority rights provisions in countries and in international law, observes that: 'A full-blown system of minority protection is a conglomerate of rules and mechanisms that enables an effective integration of relevant population groups while allowing them to retain separate characteristics. The two pillars on which such a system rests are: the prohibition against discrimination on the one hand, and measures designed to protect and promote separate identity of the minority groups on the other' (Henrard 2004: 40).

There are no easy or universally applicable rules on the balance between majority rights and minority prerogatives, although there is broad and increasing consensus in favour of cultural autonomy and in some instances territorial autonomy for minority groups. Historically and in recent years the international community has sought to help define more clearly the rights of minorities through global norms in various human rights treaties, conventions and guidelines (see box 3.2).

> There are no easy or universally applicable rules on the balance between majority rights and minority prerogatives, although there is broad and increasing consensus in favour of cultural autonomy and in some instances territorial autonomy for minority groups.

Box 3.2: Some Global Norms Defining Minority Rights

Article 27 of the 1966 International Covenant on Civil and Political Rights provides a right to identity and by inference t o minority protection. The article states that in those states in which ethnic, religious or linguistic minorities exist, persons belonging to such minorities shall not be denied the right, in community with other members of their group, to 'enjoy their own culture, to profess and practice their own religion, or to use their own language'.

Article 3 of the 1992 United Nations Declaration on the Rights of Persons Belonging to National or Ethnic, Religious Minorities provides a right to participate in politics.

Article 1 of the 1978 UNESCO Declaration on Race and Racial Prejudice describes and prevents discrimination on the basis of race or other identity.

The 1991 Copenhagen Agreement of the Conference on Security and Co-operation in Europe (CSCE, later to become the Organization for Security and Co-operation in Europe, OSCE), together with the 1999 Guidelines for Effective Participation of National Minorities in Public Life, drafted for the OSCE by the High Commissioner for National Minorities (known as the Lund Guidelines). The latter provide a well-considered overview of specific public policy recommendations for reconciling democracy and diversity.

The Inter-American Commission on Human Rights reports regularly on the conditions of indigenous peoples in the Americas and has prepared a draft American Declaration on the Rights of Indigenous Peoples, which remains under consideration by the Organization of American States (OAS) for formal adoption. (For updates and rapporteur reports on the work of the Commission as it pertains to indigenous peoples, see <http://www.cidh.org>.)

Box 3.3: 'Self-Determination' at the UN: A Global Norm for Minority Rights Democracy

Self-determination, articulated in article 1.2 of the United Nations Charter, can be interpreted as a broad right to democracy within multi-ethnic societies.

• Civil wars that pit claims of self-determination by aggrieved minority groups against claims of state sovereignty and territorial integrity are among the most deadly and intractable conflicts on the peace and security agenda of the UN. Where minorities seek secession, the resulting conflicts pose almost uniquely difficult challenges for conflict resolution.
• There is a general consensus that secession should not be encouraged. However, there is no consensus on three important issues.

1. Should a right to secession be conceded where all other means of protecting minority rights have been exhausted?
2. Should there be international action when a self-determination struggle leads to gross violations of human rights?
3. Should secessionist claims be recognized when denial of minority claims to cultural or local autonomy augurs violent conflict?

• The *minority rights interpretation* implies that self-determination means that minority peoples have the right to cultural and political autonomy within existing multinational states. In this view, the principle is articulated both in emerging norms of minority rights formulated in the covenants of regional and international organizations and in the human right to participate in governance. It also applies to freedom from religious discrimination.
• The *democratic governance interpretation* means that people have the right to determine their own destiny within existing states through democratic practices, such as free and fair elections, and freedom of speech, thought and association.
• The *international community's capacity* for monitoring of and fact-finding about minority rights has begun to develop in recent years, but is in need of further improvement. Some advocates have argued for the creation of an international ombudsperson for minority rights, with a mandate, profile and mission similar to those of the OSCE's High Commissioner for National Minorities. Another option proposed is to create an International Conciliation Commission to mediate ethnic disputes.

See Chesterman, Simon, Farer, Tom and Sisk, Timothy, 'Competing Claims: Self-Determination and Security at the United Nations', International Peace Academy Report, 2001.

2. Electoral Processes and Conflict Management

From Afghanistan to Burundi to Liberia to Palestine, today's headlines are full of situations in which electoral processes go forward in the face of tremendous challenges for conflict management. The reason is clear: in today's world, no government can claim to rule legitimately without some degree of deference to the will of the people; and this will is usually (although not always, as in the case of China's village-only polls) determined by national elections in which candidates affiliated with political parties compete for votes at different levels of governance, in presidential, parliamentary, and regional and local elections.

What lessons have been learned? This section explores the complex relationships between electoral processes and conflict management. It begins with an overview of one of the most critical choices made for any political community—the rule by which votes are translated into seats in the legislature, or the *electoral system*. Because the electoral system has such strong influences on the political party system, the implications of these relationships are drawn out here. With these structural determinants in place, the focus turns to the election process: from issues of timing, sequencing, campaigning and mobilizing, to voting, tabulation, the determination of the result and electoral process dispute resolution. The section concludes with recommendations for addressing the paradox of using elections for conflict management.

One of the most critical decisions a country faces in determining the relationship between elections and conflict management is the choice made—either historically or in a more recent decision—for its electoral system. Electoral systems have, rightly, been described as the 'most manipulable' element of politics, but they are critically important to the ways in which votes cast are translated into seats won—or, more coldly, raw political power. In many cases it turns out that electoral system choice is in some way or other a matter of historical accident. At some time, for some reason, in the past decisions were made at pivotal moments in a country's history to choose a particular electoral system.

Often choices were made by constitutional lawyers involved in drafting a country's constitution, and these crafters of a country's system have long since passed away—as have the conditions under which that choice was made. For example, research has shown that in the wave of independence that swept Africa from 1960 to 1975, many countries simply adopted the electoral system of the former colonial power without reflecting sufficiently on the appropriateness of these choices to their own social conditions. Former British colonies often adopted a First Past The Post (plurality) system, which tends to produce victory for parties (or coalitions) whose share of the total vote is relatively small—even less than 50 per cent. This can exclude minorities from power, and may not have been such a problem historically in Britain's (formerly) rather homogeneous society.

> The electoral system of a country determines how votes won are translated into seats in the legislature—or raw political power. One of the most critical decisions a country faces in evaluating the relationship between elections and conflict management is the choice of electoral system.

When it has been transferred to Africa, where local ethnic, tribal or religious identities straddle electoral district boundaries, the result has generally been disastrous. For this reason, many African states today have shifted or are considering a shift to proportional representation (PR) for their very diverse societies.

> Many countries simply adopted the electoral system of the former colonial power. Former British colonies often adopted a First Past The Post (plurality) system, which tends to produce victory for parties (or coalitions) whose share of the total vote is relatively small. In Africa, where local ethnic, tribal or religious identities straddle electoral district boundaries, the result has generally been disastrous. For this reason, many African states today have shifted or are considering a shift to proportional representation.

Beyond rectifying certain historical accidents, those concerned with electoral system design today come to the subject from a very specific understanding of the sources of conflicts and the various transitions that have unfolded. The lesson learned is that many conflicts have been generated by fears and insecurities around elections, and in particular by the nefarious role of political elites who mobilize on ethnic, exclusive nationalist or religious themes. Slobodan Milosevic's disastrous rise to power in the former Yugoslavia is often cited as a case in point. Can the electoral system be designed to prevent, or at least make more difficult, the rise of extremist leaders through the ballot box?

> Electoral system design gives the opportunity to purposefully engineer the electoral system to achieve certain effects. At least one of these effects may be an electoral system that contributes to, rather than detracts from, the goal of managing conflict in a society.

2.1. Electoral 'Design' for Conflict Management

Today, many countries are reviewing their basic constitutional arrangements to include a re-evaluation of the suitability of their electoral system to present circumstances. Often these reviews and renegotiation of the basic rules of politics are precipitated by a crisis. This may be either a political crisis, such as a disputed or high-conflict election, or an even more disastrous event in the life of a country, such as a civil war. The implication for elections and conflict management is stark. There are important, even pivotal, moments in the evolution of a country in which an electoral system is determined to be ill-suited and another system is chosen. In these crucial decisions there is the opportunity to

> Many conflicts have been generated by fears and insecurities around elections, and in particular by the role of political elites who mobilize on ethnic, exclusive nationalist or religious themes.

purposefully select the electoral system in order to achieve certain effects. It is possible to have an electoral system that contributes to, rather than detracts from, the goal of managing conflict in a society.

The idea of design, or 'engineering', is partly about thinking through the incentives that electoral systems create for political behaviour. Studies show that people who seek political power by running for office are highly capable in exercising 'analytical imagination'. That is, they understand how the electoral system establishes the rules of the game, and they know what they might reasonably do to 'win' in the election— either for an individual simply gaining a seat in parliament, or for a political party or coalition winning a majority to be able to form a government.

When electoral systems change, those doing the 'choosing' are really negotiators for political parties, legislators and legal specialists, international specialists, and, in some cases, international mediators. Increasingly, the trend is for constitutional specialists to be tasked with reviewing and recommending options (as in Fiji in 1995 or Zambia in 2005) through expert-led constitutional review processes.

To summarize, there has been increasing awareness in recent years that choices made in democratization or peace-through-democracy negotiations are critical to the way electoral contests are to unfold. These decisions can influence the *process* of elections, for example, how candidates campaign, and the *outcome* of elections, for example, producing winners for decision making in a post-election government. They must be made with due regard to the politics of identity and leadership in given settings, and are highly political as well as technical exercises. This is further elaborated by Andrew Ellis in Volume II.

> Can the electoral system be designed to prevent, or at least make more difficult, the rise of extremist leaders through the ballot box?

2.2. Electoral System Choices: Bewildering Options, Real Opportunities
The main electoral systems are the following.

Plurality/Majority Systems
Under plurality/majority systems, when the votes have been cast and totalled, those candidates or parties with the most votes are declared the winners, sometimes subject to additional conditions.

> *First Past The Post* (FPTP). This is the simplest system. In single-member districts, the candidates (not parties) which receive more votes than any other candidate win the seat; this does not necessarily mean that the candidate received an absolute majority of votes, simply a plurality.
>
> *The Two-Round System* (TRS). Most commonly this is a candidate-centred system used in single-member districts in which, if no candidate receives a set level of support (usually an absolute majority of the votes) in the first round, a run-off is held between the top two (or, sometimes, more) vote-winners. Whoever receives the highest number of votes in the second round is declared elected, sometimes regardless of whether they have achieved the support of an absolute majority of the voters or not.
>
> *The Block Vote* (BV). Used in multi-member districts, the Block Vote allows voters as many votes as there are candidates to be elected (e.g. if there are three seats, each voter has three votes). Voting is candidate-centred and counting is identical to that

for FPTP, with the candidates with the highest vote totals winning the seats.

The Party Block Vote (PBV). This is a party-centred electoral system used in multi-member districts. Voters vote for party lists, and the party with more votes than any other party wins all the seats in the district.

Alternative Vote (AV). This is a candidate-centred system in which voters specify their first and alternative (second, third etc.) preferences on the ballot paper; it is most often used in single-member districts. A candidate who receives over 50 per cent of first preferences is declared elected. If no candidate receives an absolute majority of first preferences, votes are reallocated from the candidates with the lowest level of support according to second and lower preferences until one candidate has an absolute majority of votes cast.

Mixed Systems

A portion of the seats are filled using a proportional system while others are filled using a plurality/majority system, and the same voters contribute to the election of both kinds of seats.

The Parallel System. Proportional representation is used in conjunction with a plurality/majority system but the two systems run in parallel, and the PR seats do not compensate for any disproportionality (i.e. between the proportion of votes and the number of seats won) arising from the election of candidates in the plurality/majority districts.

Mixed Member Proportional (MMP). A portion of the seats is selected by plurality/majority methods, and another by List PR. The PR seats are used to compensate for any disproportionality that may occur in the non-PR seats so that the overall calculation leads to proportional outcomes in the assembly as a whole.

Proportional Representation

These are systems in which the vote-to-seat allocation is roughly proportionate.

List Proportional Representation systems (List PR). List PR systems enable each party to present a list of candidates to voters who choose among parties. Parties receive seats in proportion to their overall share of the vote. Winning candidates are drawn from the party lists. List systems can be closed (the order of the candidates on the lists cannot be influenced by the voters) or open (voters can indicate their preferences among candidates on the list). In some instances, parties can link their lists together through a mechanism known as *apparentement*.

The Single Transferable Vote (STV). A proportional candidate-centred preferential system used in multi-member districts. To gain election candidates must exceed a specified quota of first-preference votes. Those who do are immediately elected. In successive counts, votes are then redistributed from least successful candidates, who are eliminated, and votes surplus to the quota are redistributed from successful candidates, until sufficient candidates are declared elected.

Other Systems

Some systems do not fit into the above categories because of their specific characteristics. Historically these systems have been rare, and to this day they are only found in a small number of countries.

The Single Non-Transferable Vote (SNTV). In this system, FPTP methods of vote counting are combined with multi-member districts, with voters having only one vote. Thus, the highest one, two, three, etc., vote-getters are declared elected.

The Limited Vote (LV). As with SNTV, FPTP methods of vote counting are combined with multi-member districts. Under LV, voters have more than one vote but not as many votes as there are seats to be filled. Those candidates with the highest level of support are declared elected.

The Borda Count (BC). This is a candidate-centred preferential system used in either single- or multi-member districts in which voters use numbers to mark their preferences on the ballot paper and each preference marked is then assigned a value using equal steps. These are summed and the candidate(s) with the highest total(s) is/are declared elected.

(See also Reynolds, Reilly and Ellis (eds) 2005.)

In electoral system choice, the devil is in the details. Electoral design can potentially affect the following outcomes.

• *The structure of the party system,* for example, how many parties form, whether and when they may form coalitions, their prospects for gaining power, and potentially their very make-up in terms of their transcending (or reproducing) the various social divisions that might exist within any given political community (e.g. municipality, region or country).

• *The ways in which candidates craft their appeals.* In some situations it may be possible to induce candidates for office to adopt certain types of appeal (see section 2.4 below). A common example is requirements for presidential elections for the winner to carry a certain minimum percentage of the votes in a very large and often dispersed set of regions. With this rule, in order to win it is almost essential for a candidate to appeal to at least some voters in every part of the country. The intention is that presidential candidates will be unifiers, not dividers, of society as a result.

• *The overall character of the contest* in terms of what the competition is for. The electoral system, which in more technical terms translates votes into seats in the legislature or positions in office, is about determining how ruling coalitions are put together. Winner-take-all systems, including plurality/majority systems, give the winners of a certain threshold of votes—say, 50 per cent in strict majority-rule systems—all the power to make decisions for the entire community. Other systems, too, such as the Alternative Vote or Two-Round systems, can have similar winner-take-all effects. Proportional systems give different political parties an equal share in political power for an equal share of overall votes cast. In winner-take-all systems, candidates and parties are competing for unbridled rule, trying to form coalitions of people and groups to cross the magical threshold within a given system that produces a majority. How many votes are needed, minimally, to 'win'?

In proportional systems, candidates and parties are competing for a proportional share of power, trying to maximize their share or slice of the seats in the overall pie. The greater their share of the pie, the more power they have in bargaining with other parties to form the government. They ask, How can we gain the greatest possible share of the electorate? If they are particularly successful, they may be able to form the government without entering into coalitions, but they may need the support of the opposition to pass critical legislation, such as constitutional changes, which gives the opposition some degree of power.

> The choice of electoral system can affect the structure of the party system, whether the make-up of the political parties transcends or reproduces the social divisions that might exist within a given political community, and whether the political parties craft their appeals and programmes in such a way as to cut across dividing lines in society.

In winner-take-all systems, in general we can say that winning coalitions in plurality/majority elections are often formed prior to the election in 'big tent' (or, usually, nationalist) political parties, whereas in proportional systems the coalitions are formed after the election in coalition-cobbling negotiations (except where there is a clearly dominant party, as in South Africa or Namibia). The question is, can either approach be said to be better for conflict management in today's diverse and complex societies?

Some of the principal considerations in electoral system choice are the following.

- *The electoral formula*—how voters' votes are added up, or aggregated, to determine the winners of seats or places in a legislature or a city council, or the winner of an office such as that of president. Elements of the electoral formula are critical for assessing how electoral systems may or may not contribute to conflict management.
- *The district magnitude*, or how many seats are allocated in a particular district; a key distinction is that between single-member districts (which return one winner to office) and multi-member districts. At the end of the scale is the entire country as a single district, using PR, as was done in the 1994 elections in South Africa and the 2005 parliamentary elections in Iraq. District magnitude is critical because of its effects on the inclusion and exclusion of significant social forces through proportionality of representation: the greater the district magnitude (the more seats allocated to any given district), the greater the proportionality of the results. With greater district magnitude, as in multi-member district systems, it has been shown that the outcome is more inclusive, for example, of women, or better representation of ethnic diversity.
- *The vote-to-seat ratio.* One critical issue for conflict management is considering the vote-to-seat ratio—the minimum number of votes for a party or candidate it takes to win a seat, for example in parliamentary elections. The ratio is important because it affects core concerns for conflict management: which parties or candidates are included in parliament, for example, and who may be excluded from representation because their share of the vote was insufficient. The vote-to-seat ratio varies by electoral system, and generally majority-rule systems require a larger share of votes (in a district, for example) to win representation than do PR systems. The precise number of votes

needed to win representation is a function both of the number of votes cast and of the number of seats to be filled.

The other mechanism for determining the ratio is certain rules, usually found in electoral laws or in provisions in a country's constitution, that require a minimum share of the vote in order to win representation. These provisions are often designed in PR systems to ensure that the party system does not become too fractured and, by implication, to exclude small extremist parties with a narrow base (although not all small parties are necessarily extremist). For example, after the devastating experiences of the Weimar period, when the party system fractured extensively, allowing the Nazi government to form in 1933, post-World War II Germany adopted a representation threshold of 5 per cent, meaning that parties with less than that proportion of votes would not win seats in the Bundestag. The German 5 per cent threshold has generally been seen as successful in helping to promote more stable governing coalitions and, given the rise of far-right parties in the years since reunification, preventing parties which some allege are neo-fascist from gaining parliamentary representation.

On the other hand, a too-high threshold could exclude from representation some key parties which should be included. In sum, there is no general rule or best practice on electoral thresholds. The principal issue to consider for conflict managers is that it is important to be aware of the vote-to-seat ratio in any given setting in terms of the effects it may have in determining inclusion and exclusion in the outcomes of electoral contests.

• *Boundary delimitation.* One of the most contentious issues in electoral system design, which also affects the overall electoral formula, is the delimitation of electoral district boundaries. How many districts will there be, and how do the districts relate to the spatial distribution of voters (for example, along ethnic, racial or religious lines)? Should electoral districts in multi-ethnic societies coincide with living patterns along ethnic lines (when they are present), or should they explicitly cross-cut such lines? Answering these questions in any given situation is critical because boundary delimitation can affect the voters' ability to choose among different candidates with different identity or party political profiles.

Box 3.4: Electoral Processes… for What? Routine and Special Uses of Varieties of Voting

Routine	*Examples*
Presidential positions	Indonesia 2004, Chile 2005
Parliaments: Unicameral, bicameral	India Lok Sahba elections, 2004
Votes within political parties	Internal leadership decisions
Primaries	US presidential and congressional
Provincial elections	Sri Lanka provincial elections, July 2004
Local councils	Sierra Leone local elections, 2004
By-elections	Australia, Werriwa, New South Wales, March 2005

Issues referendums	Swiss stem cell referendum, 2004
Transnational elections	European Parliament elections, May 2004
Recall votes	Venezuela, some US states (e.g. California)

Special	*Examples*
National referendums on constitutions	Burundi, March 2005
Elections to constitution-making bodies	South Africa, April 1994, Bolivia 2005
Votes within political parties	Likud Party on Gaza withdrawal, May 2004
Post-war elections	Afghanistan presidential election, October 2004
Externally administered elections	Kosovo Assembly elections, November 2004

2.3. Is There a 'Best' Electoral System for Diverse or Ethnically Divided Societies?

It is a common prescription for countries with significant social divisions, especially along ethnic, religious or other identity lines, to move from a winner-take-all system to one that arguably more consistently mirrors the diversity of society in the halls of the legislature—PR. From the experiences of recent years, there is good reason to consider this advice. PR elections in countries such as South Africa or Northern Ireland have been seen as an excellent, almost necessary, choice for peace: they give a premium to inclusion over exclusion and ideally to broad as opposed to narrow representation.

Electoral systems matter—a great deal. Because electoral systems establish the rules of the electoral game, the system chosen helps to determine how that game is played. But there is no consensus on whether any single electoral system is always 'best'. While many specialists looking at plural societies argue for avoiding majority-rule elections, and favour PR instead, there are some specialists who, with good reason, see strong benefits to majority-rule systems in certain circumstances.

> It is a common prescription for countries with significant social divisions, especially along ethnic, religious or other identity lines, to move from a winner-take-all system to one that arguably more consistently mirrors the diversity of society in the halls of the legislature—PR. From the experiences of recent years, there is good reason to consider this advice. However, some specialists see strong benefits to majority-rule systems in certain circumstances.

Those involved in electoral system choice thus have tough choices to make about precisely how an electoral system will operate in a particular society. For example, it was long believed that presidential elections were clearly a bad idea in exceptionally diverse societies because presidential candidates are rarely able to truly represent the entire diversity of a country: some voters will always identify them primarily on an ethnic, racial or religious basis, for example. Better, it was argued, to have legislative elections so that all segments of society can have a chance at winning seats. Recent presidential elections in Afghanistan and Nigeria, however, have shown that under certain conditions direct presidential elections for a single office can contribute to nation building if the candidate elected is committed to that goal.

In presidential elections, electoral system choices are crucial in influencing the extent to which an elected president can be a unifying force in the country, especially in large, diverse societies, or whether a candidate can win the presidency on the basis of a narrow, communal appeal. Countries as varied as Indonesia and Nigeria have opted for distributional requirements (to win, a candidate must win a minimum number of votes in a wide distribution of electoral districts) that ensure that the winner should have support from a wide spectrum of society. This is in contrast to some presidential election systems where less than 50 per cent of the vote can potentially win a candidate the presidency, as in Costa Rica, Argentina and the United States.

Even other majority-rule electoral processes (such as referendums), which are usually not advisable for conflicted societies, can reinforce efforts for peace building (e.g. the Northern Ireland referendum of May 1998—a 71.2 per cent 'Yes' to the Good Friday Agreement; and Macedonia's 11 November 2004 referendum on the Ohrid Accord) as well as precipitate the slide into civil war (e.g. Bosnia in March 1992).

Exclusion in terms of electoral outcomes—where the 'losers' are excluded—is a strong predictor of violence. When a highly insecure party or faction expects to be systematically excluded from political power, it may well turn to violence either to prevent being excluded or to prevent the election succeeding. Angola is the outstanding example of this. Conflict-exacerbating election outcomes can be mitigated by pre-election agreements which anticipate scenarios before the ballots are cast; the negotiation of pre-election pacts is strongly encouraged when there are significant spoiler challenges to elections or when an especially powerful party or faction seeks to boycott an election.

> Exclusion in terms of electoral outcomes—where the 'losers' are excluded—is a strong predictor of violence. When a highly insecure party or faction expects to be systematically excluded from political power, it may well turn to violence either to prevent being excluded or to prevent the election succeeding.

What are the criteria for evaluating an electoral system's contribution to conflict management? Part of the picture is clearly the intended or expected consequences of electoral system choice in a general sense, and the other is the unintended or unexpected consequences of the system in a given society. Key issues are questions about voting behaviour. How does the electoral system affect how people consider and cast their votes? How should they vote to advance their preferences and views most effectively?

The effects of an electoral system are seen in the factors identified above, such as proportionality, voting behaviour and consensus building, within given structures and contexts. At the same time, perhaps the strongest effects of electoral system choice are the effects on two major considerations in conflict management: the development of the political party system and—critically—the chances for generating a stable, majority-plus coalition that is broadly inclusive and governs moderately. Because of the strong effects of electoral system choice on the party system, and the effects of the party system on the formation and stability of governing coalitions, the implications of these relationships for conflict management should always be considered.

2.4. How Electoral Systems Affect Party Systems

The relationship between electoral systems and party systems can be easily summarized: the ways in which votes are translated into seats affect the incentive of candidates or representatives to coalesce into larger units such as parties. Here are the key findings.

- Plurality/majority rule systems tend to lead to a stable two-or-three party system. This principle, known as Duverger's Law, is one of the most stable and consistent findings in scholarly research.
- PR allows for the emergence of new parties more regularly because they can have a meaningful opportunity to try to win a seat on their own more often than they might under a single-member district system.
- PR can tend to lead to a proliferation of political parties, meaning the fracturing of the party system as existing parties split and new parties emerge. This can be limited through the use of thresholds.

The structure of the party system—the number and size of the political parties and the range of their policies—is important for its effects on conflict management. That is because fewer parties mean a greater likelihood of the survivability of the governing coalition. Party wrangling in broad coalitions can mean very ineffective government because of a lack of continuity in policies and programmes, and governments may collapse. Some scholars assert, for example, that stable governing coalitions are better able to generate sustainable economic growth than coalitions that frequently collapse and require new elections or negotiations to bring in new coalition partners. 'Polarized pluralism' or the existence of too many parties can lead to 'cycling' or recurring collapses of governing coalitions, as has happened in post-war Italy with its 50 governments since 1945. In 1993 Italy enacted electoral system reform in an effort to redress the 'polarized pluralism' problem.

Electoral system choice also affects the ways in which political parties seek to represent different elements or segments of society. When regionally strong parties are able to win in wider majoritarian elections, they may become sole representatives of their areas. This can institutionalize regional competition into the political debate, with the consequences of intensifying differences, increasing enmity and deepening divisions along identity lines. In other situations, it is argued that single-member district or majority-rule systems lead to the creation of broad umbrella parties because of the need to maximize vote share across the entire country in a effort to form a stable governing coalition. One of the most dramatic effects of these relationships is seen in the United States, where the electoral college system essentially requires political parties to win a majority of votes in a wide distribution of states. The Republican and Democratic parties have shown the ability to win under such a system, but upstart third parties do not really have much of a chance to win. The result is that both major parties aim for the broadest possible appeal in order to maximize their share of the vote.

The key to the success of formal institutional design will be the degree to which it offers meaningful engagement for group interests and needs. A decline in public interest in political party activity (as opposed to civic or single-issue concerns) is of concern in settings such as United Kingdom, where it has been observed that:

> The response of the political system to post-industrialism and to political disengagement has been either technocratic or self-interested in the sense that the [political] parties have adapted their policies and campaigning simply to win elections. The political strategy of 'triangulation' for example, is democracy by numbers. It is a mathematical equation that secures power but in the end drives down people's desire to be politically engaged. It hollows out democracy because it inevitably means by-passing party members who want debate and neglects the democratic channels of engagement which might get in the way of strategy (Power Inquiry 2006: 19).

The implication of 'democracy by numbers' is that political parties craft strategies to win on the basis of calculation and the advice of consultants who concentrate on statistics, rather than thinking through policy positions based on values and interpretation of the common good. Elections under such conditions are an instrumental route to power for party elites rather than mechanisms for providing voters with choices among competing programmes based on well-considered values the policy positions reflect.

> The key to the success of formal institutional design will be the degree to which it offers meaningful engagement for group interests and needs.

2.5. The Ethnic Party Debate

At different points in time, in different societies, ethnically-based political parties have emerged as the fundamental building blocks of the party system, with few political parties that transcend particular identities. In post-war Bosnia and Herzegovina, for example, ethnic parties dominate the political landscape. In other situations, however, ethnic parties have been banned in law to prevent their development precisely because it was believed that this could generate violent conflict. As the Nigerian military designed a return to civilian rule in 1999, ethnic parties were effectively banned; parties had to reflect the 'federal' character of the state, which meant that they must seek to bridge the country's religious and ethnic divisions. Indeed, the military government of General Ibrahim Babangida tried to decree that there would be only two political parties, one slightly to the left, one slightly to the right. Likewise, for many years Uganda opted for a 'no-party' system in which candidates for office stood only as individuals; this system was also seen as a way to avoid ethnicity-oriented political parties.

Box 3.5: Concerns about the 'Ethnification' of Electoral Politics

Some countries decide that the way to manage the tendency of party politics to contribute to ethnic enmity is to ban political parties that purport to represent an ethnic, tribal or racial identity. If politics is perceived as a 'zero-sum' game between differing identity groups or regions—particularly in situations of structural strain, competition for resources and a history of severe conflicts—then both divisions and relations can worsen. A deciding factor, however, is the 'mindset' of the parties, including those which are in the dominant majority position. If there is agreement that the nation is inclusive of other groups and that multiple interests can be accommodated, the likelihood of violence is diminished.

It is also important to consider how political parties that define themselves as broadly 'nationalist'—or standing for everyone in a united country—define the political community. The concern with identity-based parties is that, in the cacophonous environment of newly-formed or transitional democracies, political parties with very narrow mandates can seize power on divisive ethnic, racial or religious themes and end democracy, ironically, through the ballot box.

The examples below raise some important considerations.

• Uganda and President Yoweri Museveni's 'no-party' political system. In Uganda, did the 'no-party' system of elections (each seat is contested by individual independent candidates) limit the salience of ethnic politics? Or does it deny/exclude full regional representation, as the Acholi in the north of the country may feel?
• In Burundi, ethnic parties and power-sharing arithmetic. Should ethnic parties be allocated seats in Parliament roughly equivalent to their proportion of the population, even if this would lead to majority domination of a small and vulnerable minority?
• The 1989 elections in the former Yugoslavia. When do parties based on an ideology (such as socialism) find it in their electoral interests to switch identities and become narrow nationalists? In this case the ideological grounds were shifted amid economic crisis and uncertainty. There was a lot to lose and uncertainty as to how to organize.
• South Africa's African National Congress (ANC)—nationalist, Africanist . . . and inclusive? What conditions lead to the electoral success of 'broad tent' political parties that are generally inclusive of elements from a very diverse population?
• New Zealand and indigenous representation. Should long-standing vulnerable minorities such as indigenous groups be guaranteed a minimum number of seats in parliament through quotas, like the Maori in New Zealand? The same question may be asked regarding women in many societies, and quotas for women may be utilized to reduce barriers which limit women's participation.
• The choice of electoral system will also have an impact on the nature of the political parties and the way in which they frame their programmes.

2.6. The Paradox of Elections for Conflict Management

Elections, for better or for worse, are an essential step in the process of reconstituting political order after civil war, despite the clear and evident risks they involve that violent conflict will be reignited in the heat and passion of the contest for power.

The litmus test for the credibility of post-war regimes is the credible election of new representatives and electoral mandates for ruling elites in processes that are widely perceived as being free and fair. From the setting up of the electoral management body, to the evaluation of statutes on political party registration, to voter registration, candidate nomination, laws on press freedoms, to the design and distribution of ballot papers, to the management of security, to election day itself and the certification of the results, the entire process must be considered for elections to be legitimate and fair. The declaration of the relative freeness or fairness of an election is closely linked with its observation, both by domestic observers (such as official monitors, civil society or the press) and increasingly by international observers. While 'free and fair elections' are not in themselves sufficient for conflict management, they are necessary as a critical contribution of democracy to resolving social differences by democratic means.

> While 'free and fair elections' are not in themselves sufficient for conflict management, they are necessary as a critical contribution of democracy to resolving social differences by democratic means.

It is important to reiterate the basic functions of electoral processes and their intrinsic role in democracy, for it is often easy to focus on the faults of the processes rather than the clear public benefit they serve. Among the key functions of elections in helping manage social conflict are the following.

- *Generating legitimacy.* The key feature of a legitimate electoral process is that it is free and fair in both political and administrative terms. That is, it is inclusive of all elements of society through a well-considered law of citizenship and of voter registration, and it offers meaningful choices to the population. Without vigorous opposition and debate, and without an accountable electoral administration, it is impossible to have a free and fair election that is ultimately perceived as a legitimate way to choose who will wield state power to govern society. Legitimate governments are more likely to manage conflict positively than illegitimate ones.

- *Choosing representatives.* Good electoral processes must be appropriate for the needs of a given society. Electoral system design is critically important in that electoral processes are about not just choosing representatives but also what is meant by 'representation'. That is, a good electoral process will allow society on its own to determine how its diverse interests will be reflected in representation. In some situations it is true that ethnicity or religion may be a salient basis of representation, whereas in other situations issues such as the alleviation of poverty, gender equality, geographic representation or economic interests may be more important. 'Representation' is generated in the election campaign. Candidates put forward their views of who in the electorate they represent and why, and voters are able to choose among them. Quality representation is key to constructive bargaining among a society's diverse interests and communities.

• *Agenda-setting.* Electoral processes help to establish what issues are laid before the community. By articulating different plans, policies and programmes, electoral processes help to define which issues the community must decide collectively, the challenges it faces, and the alternative options to respond to those challenges. Campaigns set agendas when candidates articulate what is important. They choose their 'message' among all possible issues that could be stressed because they think that emphasizing these issues and placing them on the public agenda will generate the maximum number of votes for their cause. Clearly articulating the issues before the community allows the most urgent social problems to be tackled first.

• *Voice and awareness-raising.* Ideally, electoral processes give voice to the citizens in that they provide an opportunity for each individual in the political community to (on polling day) 'speak' as political equals as they cast their vote. It is intended that each vote, and each person's voice or view, is heard equally on that day. At the same time, it is the candidates who present the policy issues.

> A good electoral process will allow society on its own to determine how its diverse interests are reflected in political representation. Quality representation is key to constructive bargaining among a society's diverse interests and communities.

Box 3.6: Some Summary Findings on Electoral Processes and Conflict Management

• Electoral systems matter, but there is no consensus on whether any single electoral system is always 'best'. Those involved in electoral system choice thus have tough judgements to make about precisely how a particular electoral system will operate in a particular society.

• Electoral processes in conditions of violent conflict require a prior degree of progress on the security front: basic safety and security for electoral administration personnel, and the elimination of 'no-go' zones for campaigning by all parties.

• In electoral processes there are key, pivotal decision-making moments in which the process can be tipped in the direction of conflict management on especially divisive issues.

• Exclusion in terms of electoral outcomes—if the losers are excluded—is a strong predictor of violence. When a highly insecure party or faction expects to be systematically excluded from political power, it may well turn to violence either to prevent its own exclusion or to prevent the election from succeeding.

• Conflict-exacerbating election outcomes can be mitigated by pre-election agreements covering scenarios for after the ballots are cast; the negotiation of pre-election pacts is strongly encouraged when there are significant spoiler challenges to elections or when an especially powerful party or faction seeks to boycott an election.

• Perceptions of fraudulent or stolen elections are a strong predictor of violence. When they happen, elections can precipitate armed conflict and even civil war. At the same time, vehement minorities who have lost out in election contests may also turn out in the streets to protest against the outcome. Governments may repress protests when they have conducted a fraudulent poll. Mass protests cannot be a substitute for professional election monitoring.

• Paradoxically, election-related violence is found both in situations when the outcome of the election is wholly uncertain—when power is up for grabs—and when there is a high degree of certainty about the outcome, when a particular party or faction is clearly expected to win. Much depends on the motivation of prospective losers to do everything they can, including waging a violent struggle, to avoid losing political power through an electoral process.

2.7. Electoral Administration

Last but not least, a final set of concerns are the fundamental considerations of electoral administration (for comprehensive information on electoral administration, see the web site of the ACE Electoral Knowledge Network at <http://www.aceproject.org>). Research has shown that the structure, balance, composition and professionalism of the electoral management body (e.g. an electoral commission) is a key component in successful electoral processes that generate legitimate, accepted outcomes. Some questions that routinely arise and that must be satisfactorily answered in order to ensure the fairness necessary if electoral processes are to be conflict-mitigating are the following.

> Elections themselves can be conflict-inducing. Many conflicts have been generated by fears and uncertainties surrounding elections. Perceptions of fraudulent or stolen elections are a strong predictor of violence.

• Is the electoral management body (EMB) balanced along a wide range of social variables, such as political party affiliation (in situations where the EMB is not made up solely of experts), gender, ethnicity, race, religion and the regions of a country? Is the body free from political control or undue interference?

• Are citizenship laws fair and fairly applied? Are some important social segments, such as internally displaced persons (IDPs) or those outside the country, denied representation because they are not legally defined as citizens or because they cannot physically access the opportunity to vote? How can such problems be addressed?

• Is the process of voter registration carried out comprehensively, efficiently and without bias?

• Are the political party registration criteria reasonable and transparent? Is political party funding a level playing field? Are political parties able to canvass all possible voters, or are there 'no-go' zones?

• Is media access guaranteed to all parties, and are the media independent and free from pressure or intimidation? Do journalists abide by the highest professional standards and ethics?

• How appropriate is the design of the ballot paper for the society, and does the design contribute to ease of voting and limit misunderstandings and 'wasted votes'?

• Is balloting carried out in secrecy, where voters are free from influence, intimidation or repercussions for their choices?

• Is the counting process professionally handled and transparent such that the process is verifiable throughout, down to the last ballot cast?

• Are electoral disputes handled in a professional and legal manner? Are those elected installed in office?

(See also the forthcoming IDEA *Handbook on Electoral Management Design* (International IDEA 2006).)

3. Towards Consensus-seeking Democracy in Today's Complex Societies

Both in theory and in recent practice there are concerns about consensus-based approaches to democracy in historically conflicted societies. For example, concerns focus on possible perverse effects of consensus seeking as a decision rule, and on some of the specific features of the two major consensus-based approaches—consociationalism and the integrative approach. (Further detail may be found in the annex to chapter 5.)

The consociational approach emphasizes unity governments formed among various political parties representing social interests, often ethnicity or religion (as in the Ulster Unionist Party in Northern Ireland), whereas the integrative approach emphasizes the need for political parties that themselves cut across society's divides and offer broader platforms that transcend any particular (ethnic or religious) identity, as the Congress Party in India does.

Practical concerns for consensus democracy have risen to new heights in recent years, driven by frustration with systems based on nationalist parties in countries such as Bosnia and Herzegovina, and by doubts about the application of principles of inclusion in countries such as Afghanistan which arguably lead to concerns about the development of 'warlord democracies' (Wantchekon 2004).

3.1. Criticisms of Rigid Power Sharing

From the theory side, a key feature of consociational power sharing—the mutual veto, whereby decisions are only taken with the widest possible consent and only with a near-consensus—often leads to the use of 'political blackmail'. In Cyprus, for example, power sharing failed in the period 1960–3 because of the workings of the mutual veto. (On consociationalism as blackmail in Cyprus, see Jarstad 2001.) Without consensus among contending social forces, governance stagnates, policy making drifts and tensions mount. When power-sharing agreements lead to such political inertia (the inability to make or implement policy due to protracted disagreement), frustrations emerge and one or more parties defect from the accord. Violence frequently ensues.

Consociational democracy suffers from a second problem, too. These institutions are based on elite consensus, and they do not seek to build bridges across the segments of society that are in conflict. While pacts between the leaders of ethnic groups halt ethnic strife temporarily, in the long run a durable and peaceful solution to ethnic conflict depends on citizens' tolerance and their willingness to cooperate across conflict lines. Power sharing may be desirable, and necessary, as an immediate exit from deadly strife such as civil wars. Parties at the negotiating table may demand the fixed representation, the mutual veto, and the hard and fast guarantees that formal power sharing offers. Arend Lijphart insightfully argues that, despite the concerns expressed about consociational democracy, 'Long before scholars began analyzing the phenomenon of power-sharing democracy in the 1960s, politicians and constitution writers had designed power-sharing solutions for the problems of their divided societies . . . Political scientists merely discovered what political practitioners had repeatedly— and independently of both academic experts and one another—invented years earlier' (Lijphart 2004: 97).

However, such institutions are not a viable long-term solution to promoting democracy in societies with sharply polarized differences—particularly in those that have experienced deep enmity and protracted violence (as opposed to other multi-ethnic societies that do not have a history of violence, such as Belgium or Switzerland, where consociationalism seems to work well). Thus, for plural societies emerging from violent conflict, a critical question emerges: What are the ways in which formal power sharing can evolve into more flexible institutions that can foster cross-cutting political allegiances and a cosmopolitan national identity? Specific dilemmas encountered along the way are illustrated in Feargal Cochrane's case study in Volume II (see also box 3.7).

Box 3.7: Managing Power, Identity and Difference: Northern Ireland

The Northern Ireland Civil Rights Association, formed in 1967, was a response to historical discrimination and the subordination of the Catholic community. The movement had specific demands: one person, one vote in council elections; the ending of gerrymandering of electoral district boundaries; provisions for preventing discrimination by public authorities and to deal with complaints; fair allocation of public housing; and the repeal of the Special Powers Act and the disbanding of the 'B Specials', a predominantly Protestant auxiliary police force. The civil rights campaign mobilized Catholics politically for the first time since the formation of Northern Ireland (within the United Kingdom) in 1921. A major complaint was the manipulation of electoral district boundaries in Londonderry to safeguard power for unionists.

What started as a civil rights protest by the Catholic community against the Protestant/unionist government evolved into a war of liberation waged by the Irish Republican Army (IRA) against the British Government and Army and against the local police. There followed decades of bitter polarization, the extension of violence to mainland Britain, and intervals of attempted negotiation and political settlement.

The Belfast Agreement, or Good Friday Agreement, of 10 April 1998 provided Northern Ireland's divided society with a political framework to resolve its differences. *A model of governance based on 'parity of esteem' replaced the old, divisive system of majority rule.* The two political traditions of unionism and nationalism agreed to proportional inclusion of each group in government.

A power-sharing devolved government would be formed with ministerial posts distributed according to party strength. The involvement of parties representing paramilitaries (primarily the Ulster Democratic Party, the Progressive Unionist Party and Sinn Fein) depended on the maintenance of ceasefires and 'decommissioning' of paramilitary weapons.

A copy of the agreement was delivered to every household in Northern Ireland, and in May 1998 the accord was approved by referendum in both Northern Ireland and the Republic of Ireland; by a narrow margin, even unionist voters gave their approval. The inclusive nature of the negotiations was a vital element in terms of building a constituency of support for the agreement eventually reached.

The plan for the Assembly was based on a form of *consociational democracy,* predicated on the need for *cross-community power sharing between nationalist and unionist parties to lock both main ethno-national blocs into a positive-sum relationship of interdependence.*

1. The Good Friday Agreement was based on the consociational logic that institutions should be built which primarily contain and manage societal divisions and that regulate existing sectarian tensions, rather than attempting (at the outset) to transcend or overcome them. This system of governance was based on the *prioritization of group rights and identities over individual ones,* the premise being that *checks and balances* in the distribution and exercise of power had to be *woven into the fabric of the institutions,* to reflect and obviate the central political cleavage between Ulster unionism and Irish nationalism.

2. This produced a form of sectarian mathematics within the new political system where, to ensure cross-community support, all members of the Legislative Assembly were required to designate themselves as unionist, nationalist or 'other'.

3. Critical voices suggest that the institutions which evolved out of the Good Friday Agreement contained the seeds of their own destruction, by institutionalizing sectarian divisions within the fabric of the Assembly, rather than transcending or overcoming them. *A fundamental problem with consociationalism is that it may formalize precisely the division it is supposed to solve.* It assumes that identities are fixed and difference entrenched: good fences, in other words, make good neighbours.

4. Others argue that the Good Friday Agreement did not go far enough; key elements such as demobilization processes had not been decided on, leading to difficulties in achieving full implementation. *This view holds that consociationalism in itself does not lock people or parties into behaviours or attitudes, or should not over time.*

The Northern Ireland example illustrates that *negotiating a political settlement is often more straightforward than implementing it* within deeply divided communities that have experienced violent conflict. When revisiting the Good Friday Agreement it is essential to understand both the dynamics of the negotiations leading to it and the specific terms of the agreement itself.

While it is often seen as a negotiated settlement, *the agreement can more accurately be viewed as being a framework for a settlement*, setting out a number of institutions and relationships that could, over time, develop into an agreed settlement capable of transcending political and cultural differences within Northern Ireland's deeply divided society. By viewing it as a *framework* for, rather than the *achievement* of a settlement, it is easier to understand why it has been beset by so many implementation problems.

Source: Based on the study by Feargal Cochrane in Volume II.

3.2. Broadening and Deepening Participation

A broader and deeper foundation of moderation, rooted in informal political institutions and social organizations, is essential for sustainable peace and durable democracy. A dense network of informal institutions connecting different conflicting groups strengthens moderation in four ways.

First, if citizens identify themselves not only as Irish Catholics or Protestants (as in the case of Northern Ireland), or as Pashtun, Kurds, Abkhaz or Hutus, but also as union workers, parents and members of certain neighbourhoods, interests and grievances are not exclusively identified with and expressed through one's ethnic community. An 'intense struggle over economic resources' might then be not for one's ethnic group but for all union members irrespective of their ethnic affiliation. In short, by cross-cutting various interests, institutionalized cooperation between communal groups mitigates mobilization along ethnic lines.

Second, cross-cutting organizations in the short term monitor and oversee those members who violate social/organizational rules and norms through discrimination or prejudiced behaviour, and in the longer term they cultivate new tolerance across lines of conflict. Ashutosh Varshney, for instance, cites examples where Indian neighbourhood peace committees, consisting of Hindus and Muslims, have played an important role in preventing tension from turning into violence. These committees 'policed neighborhoods, killed rumors, provided information to the local administration, and facilitated communication between communities in times of tension' (Varshney 2001: 375). In the 1990s women in Wajir, Kenya, organized similarly to transform local clan relations and work together for the reduction of tension, from making sure that no one was abused or excluded in market settings to negotiating with elders (this eventually resulting in the appointment of a woman elder as well). The Centre for Peace and Justice in Osijek in Croatia and linked organizations in Vukovar worked on human rights and improved relations in the aftermath of severe killings and forced removals based on 'ethnicity', or rather on the nationalist identities of Croat and Serb. Activists in Osijek protected vulnerable groups during the war as well.

Third, civic groups are important agents of socialization. If organized across conflict lines, they promote norms and values of ethnic tolerance and cooperation. And a tolerant culture is arguably the best guarantor for a durable peace among ethnic groups. In contrast, in societies that are deeply fractured along ethnic or sectarian lines, social organizations that reflect those ethnic or sectarian divisions are unlikely to be sponsors of ethnic peace. If groups in conflict (such as sectarian communities in Northern Ireland or in the Israeli–Palestinian context) are organized 'from womb to tomb' exclusively according to identity or religious affiliation (kindergartens, schools, labour unions and retirement communities), ethnic polarization and isolation are clearly not ameliorated but further increased. In addition, without communication between members of different communities there are few if any opportunities to overcome the insecurities and prejudices that divide them.

A fourth aspect of expanding and deepening consensus-based democracy is the cultivation of cooperative links with representatives of organizations across conflict lines. John Paul Lederach speaks in this regard about an 'organic approach' to peace building. Lederach has argued convincingly that three levels need to be involved to achieve ethnic reconciliation (Lederach 1997). At the top level, political and military leaders are involved in high-level negotiations to achieve settlements between contending groups. At the middle level, economic, religious and humanitarian leaders organize problem-solving workshops and peace committees, and provide training for conflict resolution. At the grass-roots level, local leaders and officials organize neighbourhood committees and workshops for prejudice reduction.

> A broader and deeper foundation of moderation, rooted in informal political institutions and social organizations, is essential for sustainable peace and durable democracy. Institutionalized cooperation between communal groups mitigates ethnic conflict. Without cooperation at the middle and grass-roots levels it will be difficult to speak of democratically-based consensus.

Top-level negotiators have the greatest capacity to influence the peace-building process, yet they are often unaware of specific problems that exist in certain local areas. Without cooperation at the middle and grass-roots levels it will be difficult to speak of democratically-based consensus, as leaders at community levels are able to upset carefully crafted elite settlements. Lederach observes that it is illusory to expect that the accomplishments at elite levels will automatically translate to, and move down through, the rest of the population.

3.3. Gender Difference and Participation

Finally, and intersecting (rather than additional to) all of the above, there is the issue of gender as a determinant of roles and participation. Societies can be deeply divided along gender lines, often with elaborate justification through historical narrative, culture and practice. For women this can be a cross-cutting identity issue for mobilization, as it has been with the Northern Ireland Women's Coalition, a cross-community political party working for inclusion, human rights and equality. Members are both women and men, young and older people, and from nationalist, unionist and other backgrounds. The courageous campaigns led by mothers and widows against war or state repression in Argentina, Russia, Sri Lanka, Uganda, Croatia and Serbia, Israel and Palestine are examples of the unifying force of female identity, as are women's groups globally, from Latin America to the United Kingdom to Indonesia, campaigning against sexual violence.

Box 3.8: Reflections on Gender and Democracy in El Salvador, Nicaragua and Guatemala

When we focus on formal gender equality, it becomes evident that women have increased their participation in the new parties that grew out of the Central American guerrilla movements. The evidence . . . strongly supports the thesis that measures of positive discrimination are indispensable tools in the fight to strengthen female participation in political party structures and increase the number of women holding public office. The Salvadoran experience, in particular, demonstrated that quotas and gender-based candidate lists can be effective mechanisms to open previously closed doors for women. Yet such measures are by no means sufficient to guarantee greater access for women to positions of authority and power. Measures of positive discrimination are ultimately mere tactical tools to be used by committed women and men in the fight for gender equality.

The most effective tools are of no value if the environment for their successful application does not exist. In the final analysis, it is the level of organisation and coordination that women achieve that determines whether these measures can be used effectively. In particular, coalition-building with open-minded men who can be enlisted in the struggle is essential. In the case of Guatemala, the tools for increasing the percentage of women in the party's decision-making structures were put in place, but a male-dominated leadership lacked the political will to apply them. In Nicaragua, male FSLN [Frente Sandinista de Liberacion National, Sandinista National Liberation Front] militants who opposed any effort to increase female representation successfully managed to subvert women's efforts to guarantee the effective implementation of measures of positive discrimination at the local and regional level.

Source: Luciak, Ilja A., *After the Revolution: Gender and Democracy in El Salvador, Nicaragua, and Guatemala* (Baltimore, Md. and London: Johns Hopkins University Press, 2001), p. 228.

A number of factors hinder women's access to decision-making bodies, including socio-cultural barriers, lack of access to information, education or entry points, the type of electoral system, the system of candidate funding, the domestic responsibilities of aspiring candidates, the cultural and political environment, and access to decision making. Political parties are the key to candidacy for elective office and present significant barriers to the election of women. Political parties have largely been reluctant to accept responsibility to act, demonstrating their lack of commitment to making progress on achieving the universally proclaimed goals of greater gender equality. In many cases, significant increases in women's participation have been achieved through the use of quotas—a form of affirmative action in favour of women. Over 40 of the world's more than 190 countries apply some form of official quotas for women in politics (Dahlerup 2006). Elections held in 23 countries in Sub-Saharan Africa between 2000 and 2002 saw increases in the number of women parliamentarians in 14 of them.

South African women played a key role in the national liberation struggle and today benefit from a quota system adopted by the ruling African National Congress (ANC). In a striking example of how crisis also creates openings for change, Rwanda, which reserves 30 per cent of seats in each of the two houses of Parliament for women, is now known for having the highest proportion of women in parliament worldwide, at 49 per cent overtaking Sweden's 45 per cent. The challenges in sustaining this post-genocide development and rebuilding the social fabric are enormous. Women's representation in national parliaments across Sub-Saharan Africa stands at the world average of about 15 per cent. Despite its being one of the poorest regions in the world, the level of women's representation in parliaments in sub-Saharan Africa is higher than that in many wealthier countries (United Nations Development Fund for Women (UNIFEM) 2003).

In contrast, in the USA, France and Japan women hold slightly more than 10 per cent of parliamentary seats. Quota systems may be provided for constitutionally, through election law (provisions are written into national legislation), or by quota systems in the political parties whereby parties themselves adopt internal rules to include a certain percentage of women as candidates for office. Political parties in over 50 countries have introduced voluntary quotas (Dahlerup 2006). To be effective quotas must be understood as a valid opportunity to redress historical imbalances. There is no given guarantee that women will effectively represent social concerns which include the specific interests of women, but such instruments as a women's caucus can be helpful for collective deliberation and strategy. Carefully designed training will assist this entry point into the formal sphere of representative politics. Women's representation can further aid inclusion and participation across group dividing lines and can in some cases add policy dimensions in keeping with human security needs.

Besides quotas, the design of the electoral system itself can advance women's representation and participation (see e.g. Reynolds, Reilly and Ellis 2005: 37, 121). However, Luciak's observation that 'The most effective tools are of no value if the environment for their successful application does not exist' (see box 3.8) is a reminder of the need for multiple entry points into social change and politics in order to encourage gender equality and broaden and deepen participation. Below, Amal al-Sabbagh makes a comparable observation from another region.

Box 3.9: Human Security and Political Participation: Perspectives from the Arab World

UNIFEM's publication *Progress of Arab Women 2004* stresses in the chapter on political participation that 'women are not active in politics because politics is not a safe and secure space'. While this is a legitimate observation in the Arab region, as in several other countries of the world, I believe that for Arab women in particular, lack of human security in its comprehensive sense is also a major contributing factor to women's low political participation.

Women's exclusion in so many aspects of life—the sometimes de jure and often de facto treatment of women as 'dependents' on male relatives' good offices—is totally incompatible with the modernization trend. It does not tackle the core issues of traditionalism, nor does it approach participation in political life as based on each and every citizen's ability to do so. All this in the end leads to women, in general, not enjoying the freedom from fear and want that is basic to human security, hence their low political participation, especially if such participation is viewed in its broader sense rather than restricting it to voting or running for parliamentary elections.

Unfortunately, political participation is often restricted in our minds to voting or running for parliamentary elections, since this is probably the most available indicator. Often in the Arab world, other aspects of political participation are not looked at as seriously simply because of lack of available data.

Interview with Amal al-Sabbagh, scholar, practioner and activist on Middle East gender issues, previously Director of the Jordanian National Commission for Women

3.4. Processes for Inclusion

Beyond institutional reforms to improve participation, there is also increasing concern about the processes by which democracy is introduced and sustained. For example, with constitutional review processes under way in so many states, there has been a concerted effort to revisit the ways in which basic laws can be drafted in a more open, accessible way that involves the public in their creation. Constitution-making or review processes in Afghanistan, Fiji, Rwanda and South Africa that have featured public consultation are contrasted with those in Bosnia, Nigeria or Iraq which have been generally insulated from public debate (arguably to ill effect). As Yash Ghai and Guido Galli argue in Volume II, consitution-building processes themselves can be inclusive consultation opportunities for dialogue and visibility, for raising awareness, and for helping to shape, learn about and build consensus for the national social contract.

Voter education is itself a means of outreach and inclusion, as is the resolution of problems of access and mobility on election day. Do gender roles limit the ability to vote, and if so what practical measures could remove such barriers and enhance participation? How does the education system inculcate the mechanisms and channels which a democratic system can offer in such a way as to strengthen the political culture? Public policy considerations can factor in minority and gender implications, using tools such as gender audits, social mapping or expert advice. Public hearings on proposed legislation offer an avenue for exchange. Ombudspersons or monitoring to oversee and respond in cases of exclusion or discrimination can form a mediating link between the powerful and the less powerful.

By definition, as societies, every democracy will have deficits and space for democratic politics, in the formal realm of constitutional and institutional arrangements, and in the way in which power relations are played out in group relations. Democratizing political institutions and parties themselves will be integral to setting agendas and action relevant to differing group needs for human security. Table 3.1 summarizes some entry points and linkages for managing power, identity and difference.

Table 3.1: Democracy Deficits and Democratic Politics

	Democracy Deficits		Spaces for Democratic Politics
	In formal constitutional and political arrangements	**In substance or practice of power**	
Citizenship	– Socially or ethnically exclusive definitions of citizenship – Poorly protected civil and political rights – Legal/political barriers to freedom of expression and organization – Non-recognition of social and economic entitlements – Access to legal and administrative systems skewed against minorities, the unorganized, the poor	– Major social inequities (class, gender, regional, religious, ethnic, etc.) – Exclusion from public sphere of women, minorities etc. – De facto disenfranchisement of the poor due to lack of resources and organization – Uncivil society: cultures of intolerance, lack of respect for difference – Violence, intimidation, especially against marginalized groups	– Grassroots organizations (in villages, slums, of women etc.) – Both class-based (e.g. trade unions, peasants) and new (gender, environment etc.) social movements – Non-exclusive identity politics (minority rights or ethnic associations etc.) – Participatory development initiatives – 'Islands of civility' in conflict zones

	Democracy Deficits		Spaces for Democratic Politics
	In formal constitutional and political arrangements	**In substance or practice of power**	
Vertical accountability of rulers to citizens	– Elections not free and fair – Electoral systems distort outcomes or disenfranchise minorities – Weak or absent formal accountability procedures – Over-centralization of constitution and structures of governance – Few contact points between civil society groups and political/administrative structures	– Electorates have little effective choice between alternative political programs – Few autonomous, effective, broadly based civil society groups – Weak interest aggregation by political parties, especially of interests of the poor and marginalized – Civil and political society reproduce hierarchies of class, gender, race etc. – Political processes weakened and social capital destroyed by violent conflict	– Consensus on rules of political game – Issue-based, non-zero sum politics, not based on gender, racial or ethnic hierarchies – Synergies between strong civil society groups and political parties – Effective, internally democratic parties – Inclusive forms of corporatism, responsive to pressure from below – Robust regional/local/municipal democracy
Horizontal accountability	– Majoritarianism: politics as a zero sum game – Non-recognition by constitution of regional and social diversities – Weak constitutional checks and balances – Rule of law absent or weak – Executive not sufficiently accountable to legislature – Governmental secrecy, lack of transparency – Weak democratic control of military, police and intelligence bodies	– A narrowed public domain: diminished scope for collective political action – Patrimonial politics: government manipulation via patronage, ethnicity etc. – Endemic corruption – Political processes suborned by elite economic and social interests – Judiciary weak or co-opted – Weak opposition parties – Media lacking in independence – Legacies of military/authoritarian governance	– Societal consensus supporting supremacy of constitution, rule of law – Robust parliamentary processes – Plural sources of wealth, status and power – Strong traditions of regionalism – Civil society groups able to articulate democratic values (rights groups, anti-corruption campaigns etc.) – Independent, broadly based media
International accountability	– Key decisions made by largely unaccountable international bodies (International Monetary Fund, World Bank, UN Security Council, major corporations etc.) – Democracy deficits within these international bodies – Constraints on national sovereignty built into non-renegotiable international agreements (e.g. World Trade Organisation)	– Vulnerability in international markets – Hegemony of international firms – Exposure to capital flight – Donor pressure via conditionality etc. – Difficulties of aggregating democratic politics across national boundaries	– Donor support for political reform (despite its contradictions) – International human rights law and practice – Embryonic global civil society (e.g. human rights, development of environment NGOs) – South–South and South–East political alliances

Source: Bastian, Sunil and Luckham, Robin (eds), *Can Democracy Be Designed? The Politics of Institutional Choice in Conflict-torn Societies* (London: Zed Books, 2003), pp. 26–27, by kind permission.

References and Further Reading

Bastian, Sunil and Luckham, Robin (eds), *Can Democracy Be Designed? The Politics of Institutional Choice in Conflict-torn Societies* (London: Zed Books, 2003)

Chesterman, Simon, Farer, Tom and Sisk, Timothy, 'Competing Claims: Self-Determination and Security at the United Nations', International Peace Academy Report, 2001

Dahlerup, Drude, 'Increasing Women's Political Representation: New Trends in Gender Quotas', in International IDEA, *Women in Parliament: Beyond Numbers*, rev. edn (Stockholm: International IDEA, 2005)

Grossman, Joel B. and Levin, Daniel M., 'Majority Rule, Minority Rights', in Seymour Martin Lipset (ed.), *The Encyclopedia of Democracy 3* (Washington, DC: Congressional Quarterly, 1995)

Henrard, Kristin, 'Relating Human Rights, Minority Rights and Self-Determination to Minority Protection', in Ulrich Schneckener and Stefan Wolff (eds), *Managing and Settling Ethnic Conflicts* (London: Hurst & Co., 2004)

International Crisis Group (IGC), 'Bosnia's Nationalist Governments: Paddy Ashdown and the Paradoxes of State Building', Balkans Report no. 146, Brussels, 22 July 2003

International IDEA, *Handbook on Electoral Management Design* (Stockholm: International IDEA, forthcoming 2006)

International IDEA, *Women in Parliament: Beyond Numbers*, rev. edn (Stockholm: International IDEA 2005)

Jarstad, Anna, 'Changing the Game: Consociational Theory and Ethnic Quotas in Cyprus and New Zealand', Doctoral dissertation, Department of Peace and Conflict Research, Uppsala University, 2001

Lederach, John Paul, *Building Peace: Sustainable Reconciliation in Divided Societies* (Washington, DC: United States Institute of Peace Press, 1997)

Lijphart, Arend, 'Constitutional Design for Divided Societies', *Journal of Democracy*, 15/2 (2004)

Luciak, Ilja A., *After the Revolution: Gender and Democracy in El Salvador, Nicaragua, and Guatemala* (Baltimore, Md. and London: Johns Hopkins University Press, 2001)

Power Inquiry, 'Power to the People: The Report of Power, an Independent Inquiry into Britain's Democracy', 2006, <http://www.powerinquiry.org>

Rawls, John, *A Theory of Justice* (London, Oxford and New York: Oxford University Press: 1972)

Reynolds, Andrew, *Electoral Systems and Democratization in Southern Africa* (Oxford: Oxford University Press, 1999)

—, Reilly, Ben and Ellis, Andrew (eds), *Electoral System Design: The New International IDEA Handbook* (Stockholm: International IDEA, 2005)

Sisk, Timothy, *Power Sharing and International Mediation in Ethnic Conflicts* (Washington, DC: United States Institute of Peace Press, 1996)

Stedman, Stephen, 'Spoiler Problems in Peace Processes', *International Security*, 22/2 (1997), pp. 5–53

United Nations Development Fund for Women (UNIFEM), *Progress of the World's Women, 2002* (New York: UNIFEM, 2003)

United Nations Development Programme (UNDP), *Human Development Report 2002: Deepening Democracy in a Fragmented World* (New York: UNDP, 2002)

Varshney, Ashutosh, 'Ethnic Conflict and Civil Society', *World Politics*, 53 (April 2001)

Wantchekon, Leonard, 'The Paradox of "Warlord" Democracy: A Theoretical Investigation', *American Political Science Review*, 98/1 (February 2004), pp. 17–33

Web Sites

For comprehensive information on electoral administration, see 'ACE: The Electoral Knowledge Network' at <http://www.aceproject.org>

CHAPTER 4

CHAPTER 4

4. When Democracy Falters

The results of the introduction of democracy have at times been disappointing. Democracy has been partial; it has failed to deliver hoped-for economic advances and greater social justice; elected governments have lost legitimacy; there has been 'liberalization' without democratization; crisis has constrained democracy. The HIV/AIDS pandemic in particular is leading to crisis in large parts of the world.

Moreover, democracy is not only about elections. It is also about distributive and social justice. If democracy fails to provide for justly distributed socio-economic development, human security is likely to be threatened. The nature of the special powers currently being used in the name of counter-terrorism is a further, recent concern. Checks and balances on the use of power and for the protection of rights are essential for a healthy democratic system.

The quality of democratic process, including transparent and accountable government and equality before the law, is critical. There is a need for systematic tools of evaluation in specific contexts. The annex to this chapter introduces the IDEA democracy assessment approach and methods, highlighting that systematic analysis across the broad range of democratic practice can help yield insights for its improvement and reform.

No democracy will ever be perfect or 'finished'. By definition, democracy is complex and dynamic, ever changing and altering according to national events and processes. Low voter turnout, poor accountability levels or failures in visibility of representation, concerns over the validity of elections or questionable voter registration practices can all affect the quality of democratic processes. Human security needs, as evident in situations of social conflict, severe inequality, health crises, or responses to threats of political violence and/or terrorist incidents, pose challenges for and place additional strains on the maintenance of democratic systems.

In Latin America and in post-Soviet contexts such as the Caucasus, recent surveys reveal dissatisfaction with democracy following once heralded 'transitions'. There is frustration that the 'turn to democracy' does not adequately address human security needs and has failed to significantly reduce poverty or to create the kind of development expected in the wake of authoritarianism's demise.

For the United States, Canada, Western Europe and Australia, the nature of the special powers being used in the name of counter-terrorism is currently being debated lest such measures severely compromise democracy itself. There is no doubt that both the international and the domestic arenas have been seriously affected by developments related to the US response to the attacks on New York and Washington in September 2001. It is a challenge for governments and peoples to manage incidents, response, risk and prevention in a manner which upholds democratic principles of accountability, rights, checks and balances, and the rule of law.

> There is frustration that the 'turn to democracy' does not adequately address human security needs and has failed to significantly reduce poverty or to create the kind of development expected after the demise of authoritarianism.

This chapter considers democracy as 'faltering', (a) when it loses credibility in the eyes of a given population and is not seen to perform institutionally and in terms of service delivery or economic benefits nationally, (b) when it is unable to deliver human security in the face of social crisis, (c) when powerful ruling elites use democratic practices to control political outcomes, fix elections, or disregard popular public attitudes or evade open accountability, and (d) when governments take special powers in response to an external threat and thus erode the checks and balances that are intended to guard rights and liberties. In the latter case, the very protection of human security may be invoked to justify non-democratic means. 'Faltering' may apply in both senses in a single country, as seen in the recent severe deterioration of democratic practice in countries as different as Russia, Zimbabwe and Nepal. The faltering of democracy is of concern not only in developing or transition countries, but also in the global North.

These contemporary concerns underscore the fact that, as a system of exercising and contending for power, democracy is vulnerable to abuse and characterized by a wide variety of restrictions. Whether restricted by incumbent executive abuse of political power, constrained by social tensions within, or limited in the face of internal or external terrorism, or where the population is fed up with the government when it fails to delivers basic human needs—shelter, food, livelihood, education and health—democracy in today's world is prone to falter. Indeed, democratic practice in its most extensive sense, with its emphasis on broad and deep participation, is fragile in many settings. When democracy is limited, overcome by social conflict,

> When democracy is limited, overcome by social conflict, manipulated by the powers that be, or confronted with collective fear of new terrorist threats, popular frustration can build up not only against the government in power, but also against the concept of democracy itself. In the longer term, social discontent may lead to political frustration and the growth of movements that question the fundamental principles of democracy.

manipulated by the powers that be, or confronted with collective fear of new terrorist threats, popular frustration can build up not only against the government in power, but also against the concept of democracy itself.

> **Box 4.1: Democratic Practice: Recapping**
> Democratic practice refers to both formal and informal institutional arrangements for collective decision making and a wide variety of deliberative decision-making processes that incorporate core values of democracy in efforts to build and sustain peace:
>
> - institutional arrangements of power sharing;
> - checks and balances for the responsible and accountable use of power;
> - 'process options' for public policy which meets local needs for development and human security; and
> - equality in human rights and political participation.

In many countries today, populations are deeply frustrated that democracy is faltering, and support for democracy has declined. If a less-than-democratic system can deliver basic human security needs, then should non-democracy be preferred? There are a variety of concerns about the ability of democracy to address human security challenges.

This chapter first considers those situations in which the turn to democracy has not produced the socio-economic development that many advocates of transition had hoped would occur. The new system may be associated with rising inequalities among some segments of the population, leading to failures in service delivery, inequity in the distribution of public goods, or systematic socio-economic discrimination against elements of the population.

There are times when acute social crisis challenges both the social fabric and political order. When problems such as disease (HIV/AIDS) affect large numbers of people, stress economies, undermine social institutions/civil society, and deeply erode participation, democratic processes may falter. This is the subject of section 2 of this chapter.

The problem of 'façade' democracy—when powerful incumbent elites use democratic measures to generate legitimacy but in reality control political outcomes, fix elections, and disregard popular public attitudes or evade open accountability—is considered in section 3. Concerns about façade democracy arise in many countries where democratization processes are closely controlled by strong ruling government officials or the military and where true opposition is restricted or repressed—that is, there is 'liberalization'—an opening of political space—without genuine democratization. Allegations about façade democracy raise starkly the need to undertake clear assessments on all aspects of democracy and to build in capacities for monitoring, oversight, and response to non-compliance with international democracy norms.

Finally, many states, including 'established' Western democratic systems, such as the United States, the United Kingdom (UK), Canada, Australia and others within Europe, are under scrutiny for the way in which and whether they are preserving democratic governance, the balance of powers, the rule of law and guarantees of human rights in the light of both incidents that are deemed terrorist attacks and the imperative to formulate prevention-of-terrorism measures. Responses to the 2001 suicide attacks in the United States and the bombings of public transport systems in Madrid and London have introduced new limits on democratic norms and new behaviours in Western states.

> Concerns about façade democracy arise in many countries where democratization processes are closely controlled by strong ruling government officials or the military and where true opposition is restricted or repressed—where there is 'liberalization' without genuine democratization.

Like terrorist attacks, other forms of crises also have a deleterious effect on the practice of democracy. What are the appropriate balances between freedom, human rights, and the kind of intrusive and extensive power sought by the state's security forces in situations that are deemed to be a national emergency? These issues are the subject of section 4.

The chapter is followed by a set of guidelines for monitoring and evaluating the quality of democracy and its ability to manage the complexities of these varied situations. Through comprehensive democracy assessments, progress and problem areas can be identified, allegations of façade processes investigated, and strategies for improving democracy decided on the basis of the evaluative exercise. Those analysing democracy's quality in situations when it falters may assist with both agenda setting and action to address gaps, setbacks or reverses in national settings.

> What are the appropriate balances between freedom, human rights, and the kind of intrusive and extensive power sought by the state's security forces in situations that are deemed to be a national emergency?

For example, a 2005 UNESCO report entitled 'Promoting Human Security: Ethical, Normative and Educational Frameworks in the Arab States' highlights the issue of participation in public life and observes that the persisting 'democratic deficit' is itself a threat to human security in the Middle East, in addition to socio-economic underdevelopment. The author analyses carefully historical and context-specific reasons for this and points to sectors where change is needed or under way (Chourou 2005).

Box 4.2: Attitudes Towards Democracy in Jordan
- 91 per cent of Jordanians prefer democratic political systems over authoritarian alternatives, and support for democracy has risen compared with previous poll results.
- 49 per cent of Jordanians consider the Jordanian system democratic.
- A majority of Jordanians assess both the United States and Israel as having higher levels of democracy than their own country (they see Saudi Arabia, Syria, Palestine and Iraq as less democratic).

- 59 per cent of Jordanians believe the press is guaranteed freedom.
- 56 per cent believe they have freedom to hold their own opinions.
- 38 per cent believe they have freedom to belong to political parties and only one-third believe they have the right to peaceful demonstration.
- 80 per cent of the respondents fear that if they were to criticize the government publicly then they or their family members would be subjected to negative consequences.
- Some 80 per cent believe there would be negative consequences for themselves or their family members if they participated in peaceful political opposition activities.
- Nearly 50 per cent of respondents believe the Parliament is not executing its function of holding the government accountable, and only 39 per cent were pleased with the Parliament's overall performance.

Source: 'Democracy in Jordan 2004', Public Opinion Poll Unit, Center for Strategic Studies, University of Jordan, October 2004, <http://www.css-jordan. org/polls/index.html>.

1. When Democracy Disappoints: The Failure to Deliver

States in the Middle East that have experienced movement towards greater democracy find that there is broad support for the concept but, as in some states of the global North, there are concerns about issues such as representation, human rights (e.g. freedom of expression), and specific institutions such as legislatures or judiciaries. The Center for Strategic Studies at the University of Jordan has been conducting annual surveys on attitudes towards democracy since the turn to more open politics in 1989. The results of the most recent survey, conducted in 2004, are presented in box 4.2 as an example of public attitudes towards the idea of democracy and the quality of its practice.

Some countries have seen rapid improvement in development together with a democratization of the political system: in South Korea, for example, a turn away from authoritarian rule and rapid development following a comprehensive economic strategy have catapulted the country

> Democracy falters when anticipated, hoped-for and expected outcomes of the transition from authoritarian rule to open political competition fail to materialize.

into some of the highest categories in measures of wealth, prosperity and quality of life. Some scholars of the South Korean 'miracle' argue that the democratization and development processes have been mutually reinforcing (development created a middle class which then agitated for a more competitive democracy), aided by capable leaders such as the Nobel Peace Prize winner and president, Kim Daejung (see Oh 1999). Rapid economic growth and prosperous conditions in Korea have reinforced popular demands for greater participation, protection of human rights, a free press and access to the Internet (South Korea is now reportedly the most 'wired' society in the world).

The South Korean experience is perhaps unique. In many regions of the world, and especially in Latin America, transitions to democracy have not led to rapid economic growth. Indeed, poor economic performance under successive democratic regimes, combined with exceptional levels of socio-economic inequality, given the region's large gaps between rich and poor, has led to disappointment, social frustration, and at times rebellion and violence. In Bolivia, Brazil or Venezuela the lack of progress in socio-economic development has led to a backlash against democracy as it was practised in the immediate post-transition era (i.e. throughout the 1990s).

1.1. Democracy and Dissatisfaction: Poverty Reduction
The dissatisfaction with democracy in Latin America and the Caucasus is palpable.

In April 2004, the UNDP released a major report that sent shock waves through the world: headlines reported that, according to public opinion polls from 18 countries, only 43 per cent of Latin Americans fully supported democracy, 26.5 per cent held views that are 'non-democratic' and the remainder (30.5 per cent) were 'ambivalent' about democracy (UNDP 2004). More than half of Latin Americans (54.7 per cent), according to the report's findings, said they would prefer an authoritarian regime to a democracy if authoritarian rule would 'resolve' their economic problems (UNDP 2004). The key finding of the report is the close association between disaffection with democracy and socio-economic inequality: countries in the survey that experienced lower levels of inequality (such as Costa Rica) have a far greater level of satisfaction with democracy than those in which there is a yawning gap between rich and poor (as in Brazil).

Until recently, as a result of the region's historical situation, debate over the democratic performance of Latin America's political regimes basically focused on the minimal conditions for its political survival—the formal, electoral dimension. This went hand in hand with so-called 'first-generation' reforms involving adjustment policies and economic liberalization. Despite democratic continuity and a certain economic growth and opening up of trade, however, it is clear that the model of adjustment policies and economic liberalization could not respond to the region's social problems. As noted in *Democracies in Development: Politics and Reform in Latin America*, published by International IDEA and the Inter-American Development Bank (IDB), 'economic growth that is not backed by an improvement in the quality and coverage of institutions, as well as politics that functions better, will not necessarily lead to greater development; on the contrary, there is a risk that democracy will be undermined. Today's social deficits are also deficits of democracy' (International IDEA 2002).

In his extensive study of perspectives from Southern Africa in Volume II, Khabele Matlosa also touches on the notion of social deficit:

> Citizens are increasingly becoming disenchanted with politics, including democracy itself, given that they get mobilized during elections to elect politicians on the basis of political promises which are hardly ever realized after elections. This trend reduces

politics and democracy in the region to simple elite pacts and elite circulation at the state level, and in turn detaches the pursuit of democracy from the daily livelihoods of the citizenry—hence the high rates of voter apathy and declining public trust in political parties demonstrated graphically by the recent data from Afrobarometer Surveys . . . Even under the new democratic dispensation in Southern Africa today, which could be characterized as 'choiceless and voiceless democracies', evidence abounds that (a) both leaders and the electorate have little say in terms of choice of the democratic model in place, (b) people vote not so much for real national issues as for individuals or parties on the basis of 'pork-barrel' or patronage politics, and (c) the current democratization tends to amount to the regular circulation and self-reproduction of a small category of the political elite, thereby excluding the larger majority of the poor people who are remembered only at election time.

Moreover, when it comes to social and economic delivery, 'democracy' cannot can be viewed as a closed political system confined within state borders, but must rather be seen as part of the wider international system. Critics argue that the limitations of the new dominant democratization agenda may have their source in aspects of the Bretton Woods institutions and the US approach to democracy (Demmers et al. 2004). In US foreign policy, for instance, democracy may be seen as largely restricted to the political sphere. It is not always recognized as a channel through which political power is a means to transform unjust social–economic structures, nor that the social and cultural spheres may also have to be democratized (see also chapter 2). Instead, democracy is seen as a system in which a small group actually rules, and mass participation in decision making is confined to choosing leaders in elections that are carefully managed by competing elites.

In this view, civic and political rights are little valued beyond their instrumental role in electoral processes, while economic and socio-economic development is expected to be furthered by open markets and a subsidiary state. There is an implicit trust in the market itself, which is increasingly challenged. Good governance reform measures and standards are no doubt well intended, but do not always connect with social realities, particularly if they apply a minimalist view on the question of governing a (developing or industrializing) country, which is technocratic, non-political, and merely a rationalization of the remnants of the state.

Ilán Bizberg, of the Collegio de México challenges this view (see box 4.3).

Box 4.3: Democracy, Citizenship and Inequality in Latin America
The democratic regimes in Latin America have had to overcome the civil wars and military and authoritarian governments that have dominated the subcontinent. During the 1970s and 1980s most of the Latin American countries got rid of the military governments and ended most of the internal wars, especially in Central America. In the year 2000, the transition of the Mexican regime was achieved

with the election of a president who did not belong to the party that had governed the country for more than 70 years.

At the time of the authoritarian governments and civil wars the agenda of most of the democratic social and political forces and that of the population was clear: there was a consensus around the idea of changing the regime and ending the internal wars in order to institute a democratic regime. Paradoxically, nowadays the situation is more ambiguous because the agenda is not so clear. This has much to do with the diversity of the existing conceptions of democracy, as well as to the question of what democracy should imply.

We can identify four different positions with regard to this question.

1. There exists a minimalist definition of democracy that posits *equivalence to elections*.

2. Democracy does not only mean elections. More and more analysts consider that free and transparent elections do not suffice to define democracy, but what is needed for a democratic regime is a *well institutionalized and stable party system*.

3. An even more substantive conception of democracy considers that it exists only *when 'real' citizenship is implemented*, which implies that the relationship between the political system and the individuals is mediated by civil society organizations.

4. Finally, democracy has to *mean something to the people*—it has to 'deliver'. Democratic governments have to be effective in economic and social terms and increase the well-being of their populations.

The demand that democracy deliver and be effective in social and economic terms is especially important in Latin America, probably the most unequal region in the world, where important sectors of the population live below the poverty line... Only when the poor see that democracy translates into actual benefits in terms of better economic and social conditions will they value democracy over charismatic leaderships and revolutionary promises. As the United Nations Development Programme has stated, 'increasing frustration due to the lack of opportunities and of the high levels of inequality, poverty and social exclusion expresses itself in a lack of trust in the political system, radical actions and crisis of governance that question the stability of the democratic regime' (UNDP 2004: 127).

The sense of injustice of the poor population is reinforced by the fact that economic injustice is accompanied by social injustice. In Latin America, more than half of the prison population (54.8 per cent) are there without having stood trial.

For comparison, in the USA 18.8 per cent of those in prison are there without having stood trial (UNDP 2004: 115). This, among other reasons, explains why citizens in Latin America have such a poor conception of the judicial system. Only 32.5 per cent of the people interviewed by the UNDP said that the system was just and swift (UNDP 2004: 114).

This situation means two things. The first and most evident is that citizens expect their governments to solve some of the most severe problems in their countries, such as poverty, inequality and injustice. If the democratic governments cannot solve them, frustration with the government may arise which may eventually extend to democracy itself. This may make it possible for the populations of these countries to prefer an authoritarian regime if it solves these problems or if promises to do so.

Something similar is happening with the middle and upper classes with respect to another serious problem of our countries, which is violence. These classes may also prefer an authoritarian government that can fight violence. This is a real problem when we realize that, while in Europe there are 1.4 homicides per 100,000 habitants per year, in Brazil there are 23, in Mexico there are 14, in Colombia there are 70, and on average for Latin America there are 25 (UNDP 2004: 112).

Another factor in the socio-economic situation of most Latin American countries is *clientelism*. A lack of public support and trust is characteristic of many Latin American political party systems. This situation is further aggravated by the fact that in the last 20 years the capacity of most (if not all) of the Latin American governments to improve the situation of their populations has been strongly influenced by the neo-liberal economic model and by the receding state.

Democracy is defined by free elections, by the consolidation of a political party system, by institutionalized parties that represent the most relevant sectors of society, and by the belief that elections are the sole 'game in town'. Nevertheless, democracy also requires a certain level of organization of civil society in order to ensure the most ample representation of the political system and allow for the individuals to feel 'part' of the political system. Finally, citizens have to *perceive* that their governments are able to govern effectively and that their situation is improving.

Ilán Bizberg, Collegio de México: a personal view

A positive example of democratic practice in action may be found in Chile. Chile began the 21st century with poverty levels significantly reduced, the distribution of personal spending notably improved, and education, judicial and tariff systems substantially reformed. It was under a dictatorship that free market reforms were adopted, in a climate of severe repression and human rights abuse. This, however, did not result in economic growth which during the dictatorship was at historically low levels.

The question of how democratization may contribute to the realization of human security is key: the reduction of inequality, the advancement of rights, and the defence of free expression and freedom of movement. Development is about much more than economics. No two states will face identical challenges, as their geography, resource base, history, demography, cultural factors, and politics will always be unique. Chile, for example, has less poverty and a less divided society than its neighbour, Bolivia, as well as a political party system which transcends class lines and is broadly based. Its civil society is diverse with a wide range of interests and roles. Chilean policy choices of relevance to long-term human security needs have included measures to increase awareness and guarantees of human rights, judicial moves to lift the immunity from prosecution of former President Pinochet, and allowing increased voice and participation for the disaffected. Measures have included:

- improving access to and the quality and of public education, upgrading teacher training, increasing the number of hours for children in school, and modernizing curriculums:
- addressing both the quality and the efficiency of the judicial system through the creation of new criminal courts, faster handling of cases, improved transparency and fairness for trial processes and access of citizens to their court system; and
- crafting prudent measures for greater social security and an approach which combines conservative macroeconomic policies with progressive social measures.

The Chilean example has regional and wider relevance. In the IDEA Democracy Forum on Democracy and Poverty: a Missing Link, in 2000, four regional workshops representative of Latin America, South Asia, Africa and the former Soviet republics examined the link between participation and better democratic delivery: 'Change will occur when the government, private sector and civil society organizations in each country are convinced that they have to work together and move to do so, without directives or recommendations from donor agencies or other governments' (Kamal 2000).

Findings included the following.

- *Working together to set the development agenda would also mean reduced reliance on foreign donor agencies.* Their role as mediators between the government and NGOs, for example, would then become limited and their resources could go more readily to where they are more urgently needed—to disadvantaged groups and the poor.
- *There is a democracy–poverty nexus.* Economic growth without democracy leads to

greater degrees of inequality. Within democratic systems, where a greater proportion of people participate through political institutions in negotiations and debates, they can influence the economic system. The poor have at least the chance to try to bring about economic changes that can lead to the reduction of poverty and inequalities. The missing link between democracy and poverty must then surely be the political participation of the poor.

• *Participation by the poor is often constrained by 'the market',* by lobbying by powerful groups in the developed world, and by unelected authoritarian governments and elitist politics in the developing countries.

The IDEA forum also pointed to the essential link between democracy and development in South Asia through organizations of the poor and marginalized; the importance of women's participation as equal members of society in decision making, civic life and property rights; the use of affirmative action measures to strengthen the weaker sections of society; and the need to strengthen decentralization and local government's role in ensuring that services, such as compulsory education, access to primary health care, work and shelter are available.

1.2. Democracy and Delivery: When Are Democratic Governments Pro-poor?

There is a growing policy maker/practitioner consensus regarding the improvement of democratic delivery in poverty reduction. (For an overview of the scholarly findings, see Przeworski et al. 2000; and Diamond 1992.) Democratic governments are pro-poor:

• *when elections function in giving people a voice* for advocating their interests and needs; when in seeking to woo as many voters as possible in election contests, political leaders craft and implement policies that will gain the support of the poor. Failure to attend to the needs of the poor will see governments held accountable in elections;

• *when governments promote universal education, the flow of communications and the spread of knowledge.* The free flow of information and access can be linked to income generation; communications and infrastructure are necessary for economic markets to function effectively;

• *when governments prioritize public goods* such as education, health care, job training, a clean environment and, critically, the rule of law; and

• *when decision makers can anticipate and constructively deal (in negotiation) with the impact of foreign direct investment* or the terms of trade on poor sectors of the population, and craft policies which do not have adverse effects on poverty and inequality but have long-term benefits for poverty reduction. Trade policies matter. No longer are economies or democracies purely internal affairs.

However, despite this growing consensus, it is clear that not in all instances is democratization associated with tangible improvements in the conditions of the poor. Some scholars find no measurable effect of democratization on improvements in key indicators of poverty such as infant mortality rates. Country-specific conditions, global health trends (such as the HIV pandemic) and problems of access to information or to decision makers may all account for conditions in which democracy does not yield government whose intentions and actions are focused on alleviating the plight of the poorest citizens. University of California scholar Michael Ross argues that, while democracies provide public goods for middle and upper-middle income groups, there is less evidence of positive social or health outcomes for the poor. He builds on extensive research concerning democracies and redistribution, finding that:

> Democracy unquestionably produces non-economic benefits for people in poverty, endowing them with political rights and liberties. But for those in the bottom quintiles, these political rights produced few if any improvements in their material well-being. This troubling finding contradicts the claims made by a generation of scholars. ... This highlights the importance of understanding why democracies perform so badly for their poorest citizens, and what can be done to improve their record (Ross 2006: 27).

Arguably, then, democracy may serve as a conservative system in which entrenched socio-economic forces gain control of the reins of government to preserve an inequitable distribution of resources. In this view, democracy may have little to do with development. The countervailing argument would be that the agenda of poverty reduction must be put firmly forward as a priority for policy, with sharpened analysis of internal and external factors which contribute to keeping people poor.

If democracy fails to provide for justly distributed socio-economic development, human security is likely to be threatened. In situations of economic stress and acute poverty, the poor suffer disproportionately. Poor women are more likely to be subject to human rights abuses such as human trafficking or sexual violence; poverty and crime are closely linked, especially in areas where alternative livelihoods such as drug production and trafficking lead to organized criminal groups; and poorer countries are more likely to be at risk of violent conflict.

Better governance and pro-poor policies can be complementary. Democracy can both provide competitive politics and encourage civil society organizations, which in turn can contribute positively to poverty alleviation. The development of political capacities should be a key objective of anti-poverty policy since sustainable improvements to the position of poor people will depend on their collective capacity to defend and build on achievements. Domestic political mobilization and education, rather than conditionality imposed from outside, could make accomplishments in poverty reduction a criterion for the legitimacy of democratic parties and governments. Similarly, there is a need for a better understanding of what policies function as anti-poor in order to devise measures that are conducive to change.

Democracy may serve as a conservative system in which entrenched socio-economic forces gain control of the reins of government to preserve an inequitable distribution of resources.

Futures that include socially valued ends must be based on the understanding that human needs and human rights can best be served through the articulation of people-oriented participatory institutions at all levels of society. The state must be seen not only as a regulatory mechanism for diverse and sometimes conflictive interests . . . but also as an instrument for the achievement of socially desired collective goods and well-being of all of society's members. Such a state can only be built up from the grassroots level and thrive in a democratic environment. It is accountable at all levels and linked to the various other institutions of the civil society. These institutions, in turn, must become the countervailing power to state authority.

Democratization, decentralization, deregulation and devolution are all concepts linked to a socially responsible state. In this sense, the current emphasis on democratic elections may strengthen certain kinds of political regimes and the competition between political parties, but it does not guarantee state responses to collective needs, the participation of civil society in decision-making processes, or the social and political accountability of the ruling classes in developing and transitional societies (Stavenhagen 2003: 13–14).

Disappointment with faltering democracy finds its origins in the hopes that a political transition would lead to improved living conditions for the population through the realization of socio-economic development, mass popular participation and the protection of human rights. Instead, representation is inadequate or poorly managed, citizens are alienated from political life and do not participate, government officials abuse power without being held to account, elections are marred by fraud, and the state consistently performs poorly in delivering basic human security and human development objectives. There may be power grabs by dominant elites, continued underlying concentration of wealth in a few hands, endemic poverty, or informal structures that work against democracy through clientelism, patronage and exclusion.

But these factors in turn are linked to a greater paradox which affects both North and South. Whereas in theory liberal democracy is for freedom and against the concentration of power in just a few hands, whether political (as in a strong centralized state) or economic (monopolies, cartels), in practice, due to policies that favour open markets and extreme competition, market players have gained freedom at the cost of citizens' political influence, while economic inequalities have expanded. States have largely been unsuccessful in limiting the ongoing concentration of corporate power, while people are increasingly identified as consumers rather than citizens.

If, for example, as in the UK, essential services are increasingly contracted out to private companies, there is less reason to relate to elected representation. The danger of institutionalized liberalization is that it leads to the eclipsing of the state as an entity which

> Due to policies that favour open markets and extreme competition, market players have gained freedom at the cost of citizens' political influence, while economic inequalities have expanded. States have largely been unsuccessful in limiting the ongoing concentration of corporate power. If essential services are increasingly contracted out to private companies, there is less reason to relate to elected representation. The danger of institutionalized liberalization is that it leads to the eclipsing of the state as an entity which provides essential services and safety for citizens.

provides essential services and safety for citizens. Citizens in the United States may well ask why the Boeing (Air) Corporation now has contracts to run schools and prisons. Domestic politics and economics are not isolated or insulated from external forces and the realities of 'globalization'.

Box 4.4: Has the Spread of Neo-liberal Economics Undermined the Meaning of Democracy?

The political outcome of the international democracy agenda is . . . problematic. For people living in countries that were previously ruled by an authoritarian regime, democratization is a major step forward, although for those striving for more equal social and economic relations the new democracies can still be rather restrictive.

In addition, from a global point of view, the neo-liberal promotion of democracy has reduced (both theoretically and practically) the roles of the main intermediaries of political representation, political struggle and true consensus building. All in all, however, as Richard Falk also notes, globalisation so far has contributed to the decline in the quality as well as the significance of citizenship.

'The options offered to the citizen are becoming far less meaningful, especially for that bottom 80 percent of the citizenry that appears to be losing out as a consequence of economic globalisation' (Falk 1999: 159). Combined with the increasing international and national inequalities, this has produced a growing disinterest and distrust of formal political intermediaries.

Source: Demmers, Jolle, Fernández Jilberto, Alex E. and Hogenboom, Barbara, *Good Governance in the Era of Global Neoliberalism* (London: Routledge, 2004), pp. 11–12. See also Falk, Richard, *Predatory Globalisation: A Critique* (London: Polity Press, 1999).

Box 4.5: Democracy Assistance in the Caucasus and the Eclipse of the State

Since the early 1990s international interventions have been based on the assumption that the enlargement of the private sector, the free and unregulated market economy and the reduction of state intervention would lead to dynamics of development in both the economic and the political spheres; but not enough attention has been given to the state-building efforts of the newly independent republics. The support provided to NGOs and private business was not paralleled by the strengthening of national institutions, a culture of civic consciousness, responsibility and accountability. Foreign assistance to reform the political system and privatize the economy was often provided through a top–down approach based on Western instruments and models, without generating genuine public participation, debate and ownership regarding the underlying societal choices and changes. There is major inequality of access to resources and power between the majority of people and the oligarchs who monopolize financial and governance resources.

This, in addition to the undeveloped civic culture and civic self-organization, does not allow the development of democratic governance and genuine public participation. Most of the participatory processes undertaken by the authorities are purely formal since the power and civic culture elements are not targeted. Governance reform should also aim at empowering society by developing democratic norms and instruments for accountability. It is important to change the approach to governance reform and developing policy agendas to ensure that appropriate social policies are developed that ensure a human security approach to development in the region.

Armineh Arakelian
International IDEA Resident Representative and Head of Office
in Armenia: a personal view

In both North and South, 'globalization' in the sense of the rise of transnational and corporate actors, political and economic organizing principles, and the growing importance of decisions *made outside the state* has contributed to the decline in the quality as well as the significance of citizenship. This reality puts greater demands on democratic representation, elected legislators and social activists, so that they can better understand and deal with trade agreements, the possibilities of regional cooperation, better synergies between communities and the formulation of social policy.

In many developing states, poor governance and anti-poverty policies may stem from the lack of a tax-mediated social contract, since these governments are largely independent of their citizens for their revenue. There is a vicious circle of the poor having no money to pay in tax, the non-existent tax thus meaning non-provision of services, and the non-provision of services in itself being detrimental to access to education or jobs for the poor.

> Globalization in the sense of the rise of transnational and corporate actors and the growing importance of decisions made outside the state has contributed to the decline in the quality as well as the significance of citizenship.

Fragmented, unstable and personality-driven party systems tend to produce governments with lower commitments to the poor than governments where parties are stable, disciplined and programme-based. Civil society organizations can help increase the political capacity of the poor for either effective lobbying or creating new institutionalized political parties which are better able to shape public policy.

> Civil society organizations can contribute positively to poverty alleviation, mediate the relationship between the political system and the individual, and encourage real citizenship.

There are innovations which link populations to political decision making. An example of this is participatory budgeting for public expenditure policy-making processes. One of the most important findings of recent research is the value of providing opportunity for participation in public budgeting processes. Known as participatory budgeting, the process involves systematic consultations by state officials meeting with various stakeholder groups to consider public expenditures. Budgets are not just about spending money; instead the budgeting process is about defining priorities and balancing competing claims for scarce government resources. Participatory budgeting has seen success in Latin America, in land redistribution in Malaysia, in debating the terms of privatization in Bolivia, in providing credit opportunities for the poor in Fiji, in spending on vocational skills development in New Zealand, and in improving equity in housing allocations in Northern Ireland. This is an example of democratic practice in action insofar as it offers a bridge between people and policy. Scandinavian democracies have pursued progressive tax policies to address inequality in their societies—an example of consistent government and political party policy enjoying popular support.

2. Social Crisis and its Impact

Social crisis can drain and erode the human and institutional resources necessary for a functioning democracy. Such challenges may also galvanize participation and effective response when consensus on the need for action is high.

HIV/AIDS in Southern Africa is such a pressing example of a critical human security threat. A high incidence of HIV/AIDS in a given population leads to increased demand for health and social services over the medium to long term. This can be accompanied by growing, commensurate decline in public revenues due to lower productivity, increased formal and informal health expenditure, and a contraction of the skilled workforce. 'High-income nations were largely able to avoid such a situation in the early to mid-1980s due to massive public education campaigns and expensive intervention strategies to contain the epidemic within small groups, and spend money on costly treatment regimes for these groups out of generous public funds' ('Mapping the Future of HIV/AIDS, Security and Conflict in Africa', December 2005).

Whereas HIV/AIDS has achieved a high place on the international agenda, and visible sources for funding are on the increase, there is much to be done globally in terms of democratic practice in response. HIV/AIDS is a social crisis (at times seemingly silent but critical) in many parts of the world.

It is in Southern Africa that national governments have most vocally and demonstrably taken policy steps responding to popular need. Civil society groups are working closely with governments in clarifying key issue areas and in helping those with HIV to have a voice and access to medical and social support. There are orphans in unprecedented numbers to provide for, and long-term provision for children born with HIV imposes a massive demand for any people. The implications for a nation are huge, and the effects cross borders just as people do. One concern is the effect of high HIV rates on operational ability in African police and militaries, with an increased need for resources for recruitment and training to replace those who are sick. In the civil service, absenteeism increases, and chronic illness and medical confinement affect both operational effectiveness and general morale.

Women as a group, and especially poor and younger women, are more vulnerable to the effects of the spread of HIV/AIDS as they are more likely to become subject to human rights abuses such as human trafficking or sexual violence; poverty and drug abuse are also closely linked to HIV/AIDS. In addition, discrimination, stigma, lack of access to information and education, lack of access to property ownership rights, the risks of an affected pregnancy, and expectations in taking caring and nursing roles, are all contributing to making the effects of the spread of the disease worse generally for women than for men.

Another crucial related issue is that of refugees and displaced persons: 'The displacement crisis is arguably the greatest, and certainly the most visible, short-term threat to peace and security in the several African regions; notably West Africa. In addition, the position of refugees and Internally Displaced Persons (IDPs) in driving both the HIV/AIDS and in fuelling the social enmity that leads to conflict is central to understanding HIV/AIDS and violence in that particular sub-region, and has important implications elsewhere in Africa' ('Mapping the Future of HIV/AIDS' 2005).

Governments must make provision for the maintenance and protection of drug supplies and pharmaceutical assistance as international aid or donations, as well as their distribution and oversight. Finally, voter turnout itself is affected unless strategies are devised to enable those who have lost their mobility or are in the position of full-time providers of care, and constitutional guarantees are needed for HIV victims to guarantee their rights and inclusion within the democratic process.

> **Box 4.6: The HIV/AIDS Crisis and Democracy in South Africa**
>
> In a new research report, researcher Per Strand has found a close linkage between the HIV/AIDS crisis and the future of democracy in the Southern African region, especially South Africa. He argues that, while democracy should ostensibly help in managing the HIV crisis—open political competition will lead parties to advocate strategies for managing the disease and its effects, and voting should allow for government leaders to be held accountable in their response to the crisis—the harsh realities of the epidemic are such that it will undermine democracy in South Africa.
>
> In an Institute for Security Studies report, Strand presents a set of complex linkages between the pandemic and democratic performance, and argues that the

present and downstream effects of the disease (and its direct effects on educated, middle-class adults) will be to undermine electoral management capacities, inhibit parliamentary performance, complicate voter registration, limit direct citizen participation, and weaken local authorities and municipal councils.

Among the principal findings of the study are:

• The HIV/AIDS pandemic will undermine electoral governance as those sick with the disease and those caring for the ill will be effectively excluded from the electoral process (despite efforts to allow for special voting opportunities for the infirm).

• The disease will have a disproportionate effect on professional electoral administrators, undermining the capacity of the country to carry out core functions of election management.

• The choice of PR electoral systems, while useful for other reasons (see chapter 3), may be especially ill suited to the high HIV-prevalence environment because of the way members of parliament are replaced when they die while in office: the expected effect will be lower-quality representation.

The authors of another report conclude that 'as the effects of the HIV/AIDS epidemic become increasingly severe in Southern Africa, the prospect for an electoral process to be a constructive democratic remedy against the epidemic is being undermined' (Strand et al. 2005: 12).

See Strand, Per, 'AIDS and Elections in Southern Africa: Is the Epidemic Undermining its Democratic Remedy?', Institute for Security Studies Paper 110, Pretoria, July 2005. See also Strand, Per, Matlosa, K., Strode, A. and Chirambo, K., *HIV/AIDS and Democratic Governance in South Africa: Illustrating the Impact on Electoral Processes* (Pretoria: Institute for Democracy in Southern Africa, 2005).

The Treatment Action Campaign illustrates the *democratization of an issue area:* mobilization giving voice to the problem and need, direct engagement with local and national-level representatives and officials, and links to involved external actors— corporate, specialist or donor. The need for such substantive, multi-level work to enable effective 'local ownership' is echoed in early reports on the first year of response to the major tsunami crisis, relief and reconstruction during 2005, as in Sri Lanka and Aceh (Glasius et al. 2005).

Box 4.7: Advocacy for Addressing 21st Century Human Security Challenges: South Africa's Treatment Action Campaign

South Africa, a young democracy, has the highest number of people living with HIV/AIDS (*c.* 5 million) of any country on the globe. As the human security crisis of the AIDS pandemic in the country became more apparent, victims of the disease first formed a social movement, and have now formed a civil society organization, to mobilize for improved state support for the treatment, prevention and management of the extensive social effects of the disease. The movement, known as the Treatment Action Campaign (TAC), has gained international attention and acclaim—the TAC was nominated for the Nobel Peace Prize— for its dogged advocacy on behalf of those living with AIDS. In response to a perceived sluggish and ill-considered response to the AIDS pandemic from the South African Government, the TAC became a leading player in formulating and implementing the revised policies and programmes that came into effect in 2002. Yet the challenge of AIDS in that country has continued to increase.

According to an August 2005 report from the South African Ministry of Health, 6.2 million South Africans are infected with AIDS (meaning an overall prevalence rate of about 13.5 per cent)—an increase of 700,000 over 2004. All age groups saw increased prevalence rates but women in their mid-to-late 20s were the category most affected: nearly 40 per cent of women aged 25–29 are HIV-positive. The new report underscores a basic understanding about HIV/ AIDS in South Africa: prevalence rates overall have stabilized but there continues to be some growth in the overall number of people infected.

The Treatment Action Campaign called the new figures a 'disaster' for the country: 'This [report] is an indictment of the whole of South African society', according to the group, 'government, business, trade unions, ourselves'.

Among the activities that characterize the TAC's approach to popular mobilization and mass participation on HIV/AIDS policies and issues are demonstrations and protests; consultations and dialogue with local and national public health officials; litigation against and negotiation with international pharmaceutical corporations; close liaison with UNAIDS and international AIDS advocacy groups; and the implementation of direct assistance programmes to those afflicted with or suffering from the effects of the disease.

For further details see the TAC web site at <http://www.tac.org.za>.

3. Façade Democracy: Liberalization without Democratization?

Since the democratization wave of the 1990s, there have been a number of situations in which partial, misguided, 'captured' and incomplete transitions to democracy have occurred. As a result, any number of 'adjectives' have been applied to the democracy 'label', not so much to create new sub-types of democracy as to illustrate how it is practised differentially in a wide variety of settings. Thus, today democracy is often described 'with adjectives', such as 'authoritarian democracy', 'delegative democracy', 'neo-patrimonial democracy', 'military-dominated democracy', 'façade democracy' and 'pseudo-democracy' (see box 4.8).

These terms have arisen in efforts to classify differing forms and experiences of democratic systems and to provide a degree of analytical precision about the various types of democracy that occur. There are many adjectives that try to identify a particular attribute in the practice of democracy, such as the delegation of power to elites that occurs when citizen participation is restricted to occasional voting in the term 'delegative democracy' (O'Donnell 1994). These attributes are different from other types of descriptions which seek to describe certain characteristics or features of a particular democratic regime (such as consensual democracy, as described in chapter 3). Today, terms abound that seek to show that democracy has a bias against women's participation (such as 'male' or 'oligarchic' democracy) or that the people's access to government is somehow restricted by military 'guardianship'.

As the scholars David Collier and Steven Levitsky have commented, 'Although the new political regimes in Latin America, Africa, Asia and the former communist world share important attributes of democracy, many of them differ profoundly both from each other and from the democracies in advanced industrial countries. Indeed, many are not considered fully democratic' (Collier and Levitsky 1997: 430).

Box 4.8: 'Democracy with Adjectives'
In brief, the concerns about façade, 'delegative', 'guided' or 'controlled' democracy or other restrictions on democracy describe essentially absent or insufficiently realized attributes of democracy. Following Collier and Levitsky (1997: 440), these can be described as the following. The more recent term, 'façade democracy', might be seen as a combination or 'syndrome' that has many of the following characteristics.

Missing Attribute: Full Suffrage
• Limited democracy;
• male democracy; and
• oligarchic democracy.

Missing Attribute: Full Contestation
• Controlled democracy;
• de facto one-party democracy; and
• restrictive democracy.

Missing Attribute: Civil Liberties
• Electoral democracy;
• hard democracy; and
• illiberal democracy.

Missing Attribute: Elected Government has Effective Power to Govern
• Guarded democracy;
• protected democracy; and
• tutelary or guided democracy.

3.1. What is Façade Democracy?

Allegations of façade democracy can arise when liberalization measures are kept under tight rein by elites who fail to generate political inclusion. There is a declared opening up of the political space, allowing for electoral competition (sometimes with political parties, other times without), new freedoms for civil society, greater press openness, improved human rights performance, and greater representation of women. However, the processes of electoral competition are closely regulated by existing holders of power in order to ensure that opposition candidates do not have an opportunity to present an alternative vision and plan of governance. Allegations abound that democratic reforms are a show that masks the real exercise of power in a non-democratic way by incumbent elites. Democratic reforms are seen as manipulation to appease the international community, generate new legitimacy for existing power structures, or give the appearance of social change without disrupting existing (often unequal) power relationships.

> Allegations of façade democracy often occur when liberalization measures are kept under tight rein by elites who fail to generate political inclusion. There is a declared opening up of the political space, but processes for electoral competition are closely regulated by existing holders of power in order to ensure that opposition candidates do not have opportunity to present an alternative. Allegations abound that democratic reforms are a show that masks the real exercise of power in a non-democratic way by incumbent elites.

3.2. Concerns about Façade Democracy: Cases Considered

Concerns about façade democracy are best evaluated by analysing individual cases. Each situation has its own peculiarities, conditions and issues. At the same time, each set of concerns reveals a thread running through the debate about the quality of democracy. If democratic processes are manipulated by those in power to enable them to retain power, punish opponents and preserve the dominant social position of those they represent, what scope is there to redress such imbalance?

Belarus. The government of Alexander Lukashenko, first elected in 1994 to a five-year term, is seen as an example of the continual expansion of political power by the incumbent regime using electoral manipulation, the persecution of political opponents, manipulation of political party laws, and constitutional change to maintain political power. Consistently, OSCE monitoring teams have found that elections in Belarus have not met international standards for democratic practice. In efforts to prevent the overthrow of his government by popular revolts like those that occurred in Georgia and Ukraine, Lukashenko has conducted a widespread campaign to allege that Poland and the United States have conspired to unleash a pro-democracy movement to topple his regime.

Egypt. When 76-year old President Hosni Mubarak of Egypt announced in February 2005 that he would shepherd through Parliament a reform of the country's political laws allowing for multiple candidates to contest the presidency, many observers saw the move as the dramatic onset of democratic transition in this pivotal Middle Eastern state. Others, however, immediately criticized the move as a manipulation by Mubarak and his ruling National Democratic Party to retain power and possibly allow for Mubarak's son, Gamal, to succeed his father. Subsequently, Mubarak, who has ruled Egypt since 1981, announced that he would stand for another term of office. Civil society and opposition groups had been pressing for a liberalization of the electoral laws, as had close allies such as the United States. Mubarak won the presidential election in late 2005. In national elections in early 2006, members of the Muslim Brotherhood, which had long been banned, stood as independents and made a strong showing in the polls, indicating a major breakthrough in representation.

Paraguay. Before its transition to democracy in 1989, Paraguay had few traditions of democracy; on the contrary, the country had experienced 35 years of dictatorial rule under General Alfredo Stroessner and the promotion of a cult of personality. Following the most recent elections in 2003, Paraguay has made some progress towards democracy, although the ruling Colorado party (which has been in power for some 50 years) still has tight control over the reins of government. Peasants and the poor have been advocating land reform, the country is seen as a harbour for international criminal activity, and corruption is endemic.

Russia. In early 2006 internal and external observers expressed concern at new Russian legislation severely restricting NGO activity following severe restrictions on the media and the independent press and concern about human rights in the country. Outsiders remarked on the ease with which the bill strengthening government control over NGOs in Russia was passed in both houses of the Russian Parliament and failed to take fully into account recommendations made by the Council of Europe. The European Parliament, representing a regional body which receives appeals and communiqués from citizens also in neighbouring states, expressed concern in a debate on Russia, also observing serious human rights violations in the Chechen Republic, 'occurring on a large scale on both sides of the conflict and in a climate of almost complete impunity' (European Parliament 19 January 2006).

The European Parliament urged the Council of the European Union and the European Commission to confront their responsibilities in the face of the most serious human rights issues in the immediate neighbourhood of the EU. 'MEPs [members of the European Parliament] regret the fact that, during the preparation and conduct of the parliamentary elections in Chechnya, an opportunity for a truly political and democratic process involving all sections of Chechen society was missed. The House stresses that special emphasis must be placed on investigations into crimes against human rights activists, lawyers, prosecutors, judges and applicants to the European Court of Human Rights and their family members' (European Parliament 19 January 2006). Members of the European Parliament also urged the Commission to investigate whether the humanitarian aid it has provided for the North Caucasus region has in fact reached the people in need.

There is widespread unease about reports of administrative and judicial harassment of some NGOs active in Chechnya, which seems to be part of a more general process threatening freedom of expression and of association in the Russian Federation. The law limiting NGO activity followed similar measures which have effectively banned independent television, marginalized both the print media and the parliamentary opposition, and jailed or forced into exile perceived opponents among businessmen.

In this case, political space for democratic practice has been effectively and systematically eroded, often using the apparent instruments of democracy—elections, laws passed in the Parliament, judicial rulings—to effectively turn democracy into reverse.

Zimbabwe. A similar process may be observed in Zimbabwe, where one of the government's key vehicles for centralizing full control has been the introduction and use of restrictive legislation designed to suppress dissent and limit the rights of freedom of expression, association and peaceful assembly. Many provisions of these acts directly contravene Zimbabwe's constitution and international human rights standards which enshrine and guarantee the right to the freedoms of expression, association and assembly.

In February 2000 a referendum was held on whether to accept the government's proposed changes to the constitution. Following the government's unprecedented defeat, the political climate in Zimbabwe underwent a significant change. The government's defeat was met with surprise and alarm by the ruling party, the Zimbabwe African National Union–Patriotic Front (ZANU–PF) as it was the first time it had been defeated in a popular vote since independence. The government's surprise suggested that it was not used to opposition and was unaware of the extent to which Zimbabweans had grown dissatisfied with its many years of misrule and persistent human rights violations. The government had also underestimated the extent of support for the newly formed Movement for Democratic Change (MDC), particularly among the growing urban population, and the increasing strength of civil society, which had gained momentum in response to the drive for a new constitution (see e.g. Kagwanja 2005).

Gross domestic product (GDP) in Zimbabwe has fallen for each of the past seven years, and unemployment is rising every day. Inflation has now shot up (see box 4.9). The Zimbabwean dollar has plunged to an all-time low of 25,000 to the US dollar: it was 5,700 to 1 USD in December 2004; and, significantly, the black market rate shows an even heftier depreciation, to 45,000 to 1 USD. The government severed relations with the IMF at one stage, then turning to China for assistance. After a disappointing response, South Africa was asked for financial help, but the rescue package it offered was subject to serious concerns, including the need for political and economic reforms.

Box 4.9: When Democracy Falters: The Need for Multi-track Interventions in Zimbabwe

Zimbabwe currently faces a socio-economic crisis that threatens human security. The seriousness of the crisis has been described as unprecedented in a country that is not at war. Eighty per cent of Zimbabweans live below the poverty line. Over 70 per cent are unemployed. By March 2006, inflation had touched 914 per cent a year, at which rate prices would rise more than tenfold in 12 months. 'Experts agree that quadruple-digit inflation is now a certainty' (*New York Times* 2 May 2006). The local currency is now rated the weakest in the world. The health delivery system is on its knees, with 2,000 Zimbabweans dying of HIV/AIDS-related illnesses every week. Citizens have to devise survival strategies to cope with chronic shortages of basic commodities that include fuel, electricity, food, essential medicines, clean drinking water and so on. An estimated 2–3 million Zimbabweans have left the country, mostly for economic reasons.

While the current dire situation that Zimbabwe faces cannot be attributed to one factor alone, Zimbabwe's stunted transition to a democratic system of governance is a large part of the current crisis. In 1987 the Lancaster House constitution was amended to fundamentally change Zimbabwe's political system, resulting in the creation of an executive president endowed with far-reaching executive powers. The exercise of such powers in a partisan manner has precluded other contenders from attaining political power.

Meaningful contestation for political power is a key prerequisite for democracy, for it allows citizens to make a choice regarding who is to govern them. When in the late 1990s Zimbabweans increasingly called for changes to the manner in which they were governed, primarily in the form of constitutional reforms, the government responded with unmatched repression.

The serious and complex question is What could have been done to avoid this tragic situation? There are no easy answers to this question. Responses to the crisis and attempts to find a solution are needed at different levels:

• At the *national level* a vibrant and vigilant civil society which includes the media, human rights organizations, election monitoring groups, women's organizations, constitutional reform advocates and so on has played a vital role in keeping up the pressure with demands for a return to democracy. The innovative and sustainable provision of resources for civil society should be a priority in situations where the state is actively blocking democratic transition.

• *Sub-regional* groupings such as the Southern African Development Community (SADC) could show leadership and act in a manner which values the rights of citizens as much as the notion of national sovereignty.

• On a *regional level*, the African Union (AU) could find a mechanism for noting irrefutable evidence of the Zimbabwean Government's involvement in gross abuses of basic rights. Regional bodies are increasingly aware of their responsibilities in international law.

• The *international community's* response could be more consistent and coordinated. A number of ad hoc measures were put in place aimed at influencing the Zimbabwean Government to halt the repression of its citizens. The most visible of such measures are the so-called smart sanctions that were imposed by countries and regional bodies such as the European Union, the USA, Australia and New Zealand. While such sanctions cripple the economy and undermine the regime's ability to govern, it is ordinary citizens who are bearing the brunt of the current economic meltdown.

Ozias Tungwarara, Deputy Director, AfriMAP, Johannesburg,
South Africa: a personal view

It is important to note that it was the Public Order and Security Act (POSA), fast-tracked through the Parliament in December 2001, which apparently enabled the government to hamper the campaigning activities of the MDC in the run-up to the March 2002 presidential election. The intention was also to tighten restrictions on the independent media and give the police sweeping powers. Since its enactment in 2002, POSA has been used by the authorities to target opposition supporters, independent media and human rights activists and specifically restrict their rights to freely assemble, criticize the government and president, and engage in, advocate or organize acts of peaceful civil disobedience. The police have used POSA to arbitrarily arrest hundreds of Zimbabweans, mainly opposition supporters, since its enactment. Many of those arrested have had the charges against them dropped or dismissed in court due to lack of evidence. However, the legislation has provided the police with a pretext to intimidate, harass and brutally torture real or perceived supporters and members of the opposition.

The government contends that the restrictive elements of POSA are necessary to enable the police to deal with alleged threats to public safety, including 'terrorist' threats following the attacks of 11 September 2001 in the USA. The official line from the Ministry of Justice, Legal and Parliamentary Affairs is that the legislation ensures that Zimbabweans can move about peacefully and enjoy their freedoms. The evidence points to the contrary.

4. The Question of Special Powers

Special powers are often invoked in time of crisis, and there are varieties of constitutional provision for this. Concerted acts of violence (or threats of such acts) are a challenge that demands steady, painstaking response lest the state compromise its very legitimacy through the measures enacted and the loss of public confidence. Democracies face acute dilemmas when confronting acts of violence which fall under the rubric of terrorism. Overreaction can alienate the population, damaging government legitimacy as much as (or more than) the actions of small terrorist groups. At the same time, if government, the judiciary, the police and the military prove incapable of upholding the law and protecting life and property, then their credibility and authority will be undermined.

4.1. States of Emergency

As Aziz Huq argues in Volume II, states of emergency raise unique questions of institutional design—the architecture of legislature, executive and judiciary—because of the risk that temporary suspensions of democratic rules and rights may become a gateway to permanent usurpation of political power and curtailment of human rights. Paradoxically, emergencies can facilitate the destruction of the democratic values which democratic institutions exist to preserve. Deepening the paradox, frequently it is the executive branch, unencumbered by the need for consensus or voting, that is both optimally tailored to respond quickly to crisis and the branch most at risk of overreaching and entrenching its powers due to its unitary decision-making power and its control of administrative and military resources.

- First, the singular dilemma of emergencies is the question how to constrain the executive branch, whereas much political theory has focused on the problem of domineering legislative majorities.
- Second, legislatures and judiciaries may acquiesce in their own marginalisation, although on rare occasions they may change the way in which an emergency is handled. Of special importance is the role of these other branches prior to an emergency. At this earlier moment, courts and legislatures either facilitate or hinder executive overreach. Facing naked claims of executive authority, though, courts and legislatures are unlikely to defeat the executive—although Huq's case study of India in Volume II gives a counter-example of an electoral process, and hence a legislative body, upending an abusive emergency regime.
- Third, the actions of legislatures and courts over time, before an emergency develops, shape the political culture—the presumptions, inclinations and values of the elite who occupy positions in the legislature, the judiciary and the executive. Since these branches of government are stocked from the same class of people, the shared culture of this elite influences the likely use of emergency powers.

Recent events in Nepal provide a vivid example. In 1990, Nepal underwent transition from an absolute monarchy to a democratic, constitutional monarchy. From 1996 onward, a succession of coalition governments floundered in the face of a rural Maoist insurgency. Failing to counter the rebels either politically or militarily, these governments relied increasingly on the palace for authority. In 2002, a prime minister suspended elections, with royal support, only to be dismissed by the king and replaced by a royal appointee. February 2005 saw further entrenchment of royal power, with an outright coup, a new overtly monarchist dispensation and an explicit state of emergency. During this state of emergency, 'preventive' detention and torture of political opponents and independent journalists spread widely. In short, as the emergency deepened, one political faction entrenched itself and eliminated political competition (see box 4.10).

> Paradoxically, emergencies can facilitate the destruction of democratic values. Frequently it is the executive branch, unencumbered by the need for consensus or voting, that is both optimally tailored to respond quickly to crisis and the branch most at risk of overreaching and entrenching its powers due to its unitary decision-making power and its control of administrative and military resources.

Box 4.10: When Democracy Falters: Strategies to Resolve the Constitutional Impasse in Nepal

Not only were the royal interventions in Nepal in October 2002 and February 2005, ostensibly to fill the vacuum of the failed leadership of the political parties, against the constitution (which assigns the king a role of constitutional monarch and gives a pre-eminent role to the political parties as the engines of democratic government); they also went against all norms of democracy as understood globally.

The political and constitutional impasse requires impartial initiatives to:

• *create spaces for dialogue within and between the parties* engaged in this conflict (i.e. the political parties, the Maoists and the conservative forces aligned with the palace);
• *review the constitutional process* which has enabled an ambiguous role for the monarchy while perpetuating the social, economic and political exclusion of a wide group of citizens;
• *identify ways of ensuring a participatory and inclusive constitutional process*: what substantive issues should be considered to ensure the protection of human rights, minority and gender rights and the foundations of a democratic order? and
• *build trust among the major political actors and trust in the democratic process* as a way of ensuring peaceful political participation and the resolving of political disagreements.

Initiatives by both national and international actors in the contexts of armed conflicts usually tend to focus on the main warring parties and on solving the problems at elite level, and thus to exclude citizens' perceptions. In Nepal, surveys and opinion polls have been carried out to fill this vacuum. One such countrywide qualitative sample survey of opinion, citizens' attitudes and values was carried out by Krishna Hacchethu from the Tribhuvan University in 2004.

The main messages of the survey were:

• Despite almost ten years of the Maoist insurgency, disappointment with the political parties, a worsening security situation and rampant corruption, *a clear majority of Nepali citizens still prefer democracy to any other system of governance.*
• *Two-thirds of the respondents disapprove of the king's intervention since 4 October 2002.*
• To bring the armed conflict to a negotiated settlement, the majority of those who responded recommended convening a *round table conference*, the formation of an *interim government* that included the Maoists, and a *constituent assembly.*
• *A majority of those who favoured convening a constituent assembly were expecting 'peace and stability' from this initiative.*

Even if the major actors—the political parties, the Maoists and the government (the palace)—did agree on reviewing the current constitution, legitimate concern on the part of the excluded communities would remain. Initiatives to ensure a participatory and inclusive constitutional process have been discussed by civil society: the National Coalition Against Racial Discrimination (NCARD) which is an alliance of Nepal's many discriminated groups and minorities was founded as a follow-up for the UN Summit in Durban in 2001. NCARD has initiated a process of nationwide consultations on constitutional topics. The consultation process is aiming at:

• discussing and reaching a consensus on basic *constitutional principles* which would guide the constitution-drafting process;
• *informing and educating marginalized groups* on the content and the process of inclusive constitution building; and
• *establishing channels of communication* between the civil society groups and the political parties so as to ensure that these voices will be heard.

A senior Nepali journalist, Kanak Mani Dixit, has written that once a people's rather than the king's government is in place it will be important for those in the saddle not to forget the pressing constitutional, political, economic and social issues that must be tackled in order to ensure that the fruits of democracy are finally delivered to the people of Nepal. Unless at least a proper attempt is made to address these 'promises of democracy', Nepal remains vulnerable to authoritarian and violent rebounds.

On the positive side, Nepalese society has many critical elements enabling it to address these issues:

• the existence of vibrant media;
• the existence of an active civil society and academia;

- a second-tier political party leadership that is open to change;
- the interest of the international partners; and
- continued support for democracy as a form of governance by the Nepalese population. The survey finding 'hope over experience' tells about the huge social capital Nepal has and can still build on.

Leena Rikkila, Nepal Project Manager, International IDEA

To date most international attention to states of emergency has focused on the establishment of a baseline below which human rights cannot be reduced. Accountability issues during the application of special powers are not always clear in national constitutions.

The 1966 International Covenant on Civil and Political Rights (article 4), the 1950 European Convention on Human Rights (article 15) and the 1969 American Convention on Human Rights (article 27) all stipulate rights from which no derogation is possible. But, as there is no supranational agency capable of real-time enforcement (and the International Criminal Court poses no threat of playing this role for the time being), some domestic institution is needed to protect rights. The 1984 Paris Minimum Standards of Human Rights Norms in a State of Emergency, drafted by the International Law Association, reflect the importance of basic rights and add important institutional checks.

The study by Aziz Huq presented in Volume II suggests that problems raised by emergencies should also be seen as issues of institutional design. Huq builds on the Paris Minimum Standards by surveying recent innovative thinking in constitutional engineering. Box 4.11 summarizes his findings.

Box 4.11: Special Powers
- History shows that emergency powers, even when necessary, bring destabilizing hazards.
- States of emergency can facilitate transformation of the constitutional political order.
- During an emergency, checks upon and monitoring of the executive branch fall away.
- In the absence of inter-branch constraints, a temporary majority may seek to entrench itself in political power.
- There is a creeping logic of escalation that afflicts emergency powers. This logic arises because of the difficulty of anticipating clear boundaries to necessary emergency powers, either in time or in terms of subject matter. Initially, the public may see the suspension of a handful of rights as acceptable, but as an emergency wears on and public nerves fray, or as subsequent emergencies arise, the initial suspension of rights or curtailment of democratic process may appear mundane,

even unobjectionable. Public demand for more substantial measures may grow, with the executive only too keen to oblige.

• A political culture in which sustained commitment to the rule of law remains paramount, and where legislatures and judiciaries play active roles in channelling invocation of emergency powers, is far less vulnerable to the executive branch overreaching itself in an emergency.

• Even if neither the courts nor the parliament can resist the executive branch in perilous times, preserving their ability to provide oversight at other times shores up a political culture in which overreaching is resisted, and assists in eventual challenges to emergency powers.

• Emergencies can impinge deeply on minorities' rights. Specific constitutional provisions for their protection, to guarantee equality of rights, need to be in place and reviewed by the judiciary or considered in terms of constitutional overview and review of measures. Recent events prompt significant concerns for non-citizens, who have been targeted in the United States and the UK following terrorist attacks and whose rights require protection by the constitution.

• Courts have a crucial role in reviewing the factual justification for individual detention determinations and ensuring that detainees are treated humanely.

Source: Based on the study by Aziz Z. Huq in Volume II.

In short, emergency powers tend to grow as executives find new reasons to claim ever more dramatic authority. The events surrounding the terrorist attacks of July 2005 in the United Kingdom illustrate this dynamic. A previous, stringent set of restrictions on human liberty, which the British Parliament had enacted in the immediate wake of the September 2001 attacks on New York and Washington, was presumed inadequate in the light of the London bombings. Within days of the second wave of bombings, the British Government pressed for new detention and deportation powers, new curtailments of asylum rights, more stringent immigration rules, and expanded proscription of certain religious organizations. Although the case for any given security measure may be weak, public pressure for visible change combines with executive desire for power to extinguish hesitations (see the case study by Huq in Volume II).

The British example is one in which the Parliament was slow to debate or challenge decisions of the executive branch (possibly because of the implicit need for national unity in times of threat, particularly in the light of the London bombings of July 2005) and where the judicial system has been a testing ground for the interpretation and application of measures. It is also a case where there is a trend towards executive challenge of the universality of human rights. This in itself is contentious in the country and for the international community. It raises a serious spectre of double standards which has wide ramifications.

Box 4.12: The Danger of Double Standards

Democracy may be said to falter seriously if and when the norms of international human rights are flouted, and it is of concern when there are high-level suggestions that rights apply only to some and not to others. Thus there were repercussions from the US presidential directive (denounced by the American Association of Law Schools in early 2002) that neither the Taliban nor al Qaeda members were entitled to protection under the Geneva conventions; 'taking the gloves off' was advocated for interrogation techniques used on prisoners at Guantanamo Bay, resulting in such techniques as 'sleep adjustment' and sleep deprivation, solitary confinement, 'forced grooming', stress positioning, sensory deprivation and removal of clothing. Rendition policies have placed prisoner groupings out of the reach of the International Committee of the Red Cross (ICRC); international law is held non-enforceable in US courts. And yet the USA is a party to the 1984 UN Convention Against Torture.

Democracy is defined by the fact that its political institutions treat all citizens equally, but the force of law is only as strong as the underlying moral consensus, and the cultivation of fear is undermining this consensus. The true costs to democratic society of legitimating torture are so high that their consequences invalidate democracy itself. (Non-citizens also have rights but currently fall through legal 'loopholes' in terms of legal protection and access to assistance.)

Good legislation may not be rushed, and requires review—for example, legislation for search warrants which require no judicial oversight or involvement. The issuing of a warrant can come to be treated as a matter between the executive and the police only, which lends itself to abuse over time. It undermines checks and balances and the separation of powers while diminishing police accountability. In fact, accountability is being compromised at the same time as executive powers are being increased. There is a need for public-interest monitoring of police powers, for democratic accountability. Special search or detention measures require 'sunset' clauses giving a clear time limit and a specified process for examination before renewal.

For new democracies there is also a 'modelling effect' through the behaviour of so-called mature democracies. If an established democratic power utilizes military tribunals in non-war settings, claims 'exception' from the Geneva conventions or international law, or advocates 'targeted assassination' or the use of torture, this sets a precedent and an example for others. Indeed, some current policies may be counterproductive to the promotion and cultivation of democracy worldwide.

Source: Based on the study by Judith Large in Volume II.

Experience in Northern Ireland (UK), Nepal, Spain, Indonesia, the Philippines and the Commonwealth of Independent States (CIS) countries indicates that the label 'terrorist' has policy implications that are detrimental to political solutions based on structural or negotiated outcomes. It has been argued that the fragile peace process in Mindanao was set back by anti-terrorist support for the Philippine military which used US attack helicopters against Moro Islamic Liberation Front (MILF) camps in 2003, thus renewing hostility, displacing thousands, and further alienating a civilian population in one of the poorest provinces of the country, where rebel demands have included calls for constitutional reform and agreement on a federal structure.

In cases of foreign or international acts that are deemed terrorism, public feelings and consensus may veer towards xenophobia, racial or ethnic intolerance and division. The fact is that many minorities now feel 'labelled' or victims of stereotyping in settings from the UK to the Philippines, and there is increasing danger that local conflicts involving Muslim populations will become immediately internationalized, as has happened with media attention to Nigeria or Thailand (see the contribution by Judith Large in Volume II). Governments are thus faced with having to set international realities or security needs against very individual social perceptions and the need for social cohesion—that is, having to consider human security in its very widest sense when contemplating measures in response to perceived threat.

A new IDEA State of Democracy Study for South Asia, based on extensive surveys and dialogues in Bangladesh, India, Nepal, Pakistan and Sri Lanka, echoes this:

> In each of these countries, the recent years have witnessed a proliferation of new internal security laws, a strengthening of the security apparatus and an escalating expenditure on law and order. Much of this has been occasioned by an increasing threat perception arising out of the growth of terrorism. What is inadequately appreciated is that unlike the perception of security experts, citizens are more concerned about everyday issues of threats to life, liberty and property than fear of external aggression (International IDEA 2007, chapter 8 on 'Freedom from Fear').

In the past, the national and international dimensions of terrorism were known issue areas, but the recent focus on global/international concerns is having an unprecedented impact on national-level policy, with implications for both mature and emergent democracies. Some international aid flows from the developed to the less developed world now come with 'anti-terrorist' conditionalities attached which are open to wide interpretation as regards internal opposition or dissent. There is a danger that development itself is becoming 'securitized'—that is, linked and bound to security measures and military defence rather than need, rights, poverty, and the cultivation of democratic governance and reform. In this case democratization is put 'on hold' and 'faltering' virtually guaranteed. Aid expenditure for military and police budgets is potentially outpacing that dedicated to poverty reduction or health measures. A 2004 survey of Caribbean, African and Asian experience states that 'For many, the fight against terrorism in the Commonwealth has meant that justification has been found to further limit their existing freedoms' (Bascombe 2004: 20).

Spain underwent the transition from the regime of Franco to a new democracy while dealing with the frequently violent expressions of Basque nationalism. When in March 2004 Madrid experienced train bombings which took civilian lives and caused international outrage, the Spanish public took to the streets in mass demonstrations against the bombings and in resistance to 'knee-jerk' reactions which made allegations of blame with no evidence or proof. Spanish authorities proceeded to use police, forensic experts and links between security services to investigate, but did not suspend existing civil liberties.

One year later, on the anniversary of the 11 March bombings, the Spanish public, in another nationwide civil act, came to a standstill for five minutes at noon. Trains stopped running, drivers stopped their cars, workers stopped working, children stopped studying and playing, to commemorate the victims. In the days prior to this, the Club de Madrid, formed by former heads of state, held the International Summit on Democracy, Terrorism and Security, which was supported by the local government and attended by both the Spanish prime minister and UN Secretary-General Kofi Annan. Leading up to the official proceedings were international on-line debates, public meetings and awareness-raising events on the theme of democracy and terrorism. The official publication resulting from the summit devoted a special volume to 'Towards a Democratic Response' in which it was stressed that:

> Governments are thus faced with having to set international realities or security needs against very individual social perceptions and the need for social cohesion—that is, to consider human security in its very widest sense when contemplating measures in response to perceived threat. In the past, the national and international dimensions of terrorism were known issue areas, but the recent focus on global/international concerns is having an unprecedented impact on national-level policy.

> It is important to note that terrorist attacks do not occur because of gaps in the substantive law. All acts of terrorism are already criminalized under existing national penal offences and under international law. Closed systems of governance, lack of accountability and failure to resolve conflicts lie behind much of the political unrest and motivation for terrorism. The focus of governmental machinery must shift from short-term tactical measures to long-term policy designs in the pursuit of a global vision for security. Respect for human rights and fundamental freedoms must be central to such an endeavour (Club de Madrid 2005: 28).

To effectively undercut the basis of support for terrorist activity, any liberal democratic response must rest on one overriding principle—a commitment to uphold and maintain constitutional systems of legal authority. In instances where the state fails to abide by this fundamental dictum, counter-terrorist responses run the very grave risk of posing even more of a danger to underlying liberal and democratic norms and institutions than extremist political violence itself.

5. Conclusion

The wide variety of ways in which democracies are challenged—outlined in this chapter—reflects a diverse set of concerns. In older democracies facing the need for special measures or response to risks of political violence, many consider that perceived immediate or short-term vulnerabilities (transparency, accountability, human rights and due process of law) are in fact long-term strengths.

For states in transition from other forms of government, from war or collapse, the liberal democracy model will seem a tall order. Support must be given to the long-term and difficult processes of change to enable and to reinforce moderate and proportional measures, rather than to bolster overly repressive ones. When democracy falters, it may be reoriented through 'bottom–up' and inclusive processes; increased institutional accountability; support for constitutional checks and balances on the national level; and scrutiny of the programmes and policies of international financial and economic institutions and their impact on society's vulnerable groups.

What is consistent throughout the analysis of democracy's faltering is the relevance and utility of *democratic practice*, that is, a broader understanding of democracy that goes beyond simple electoralism. This is true in those cases of Northern societies where 'faltering' may be seen in low voter turnout or apathy towards government and parties, or in the global South where 'faltering' is often associated with the failure of democratically elected governments to deliver. The *quality of democratic process is critical,* including transparent and accountable government and equality before the law.

This consideration of the faltering of democracy evokes the need for systematic tools of evaluation in specific contexts, to yield findings that point to ways of moving beyond the analysis of shortcomings and towards recommendations for improvement. The annex to this chapter introduces the IDEA democracy assessment approach and methods, highlighting again that no democracy is perfect, and that systematic analysis across the broad range of democratic practice can help yield insights into its betterment and reform.

Annex: The IDEA State of Democracy Methodology

Public views can be measured in various ways, and not all surveys or polls will be reliable. But conducted in a responsible manner with clear samples of the population and transparent methodology they add a vital dimension to social–political diagnosis. Public opinion surveys may in themselves be tools of democratic process, in situations of trust and if they give legitimate, documented voice to public views otherwise lacking means for expression. More in-depth views may be obtained by democracy assessment.

IDEA's understanding of democracy is that of a system of political governance whose decision-making power is subject to the controlling influence of citizens who are considered political equals. A democratic political system is inclusive, participatory, representative, accountable, transparent and responsive to citizens' aspirations and expectations.

Democracy is not an all-or-nothing affair. It is a question of the degree to which citizens exercise control over political decision making and are treated as equals. These values of democracy are realized through political institutions and practices. There is no universal model of democracy. A country's political institutions and practices are often shaped by its history, culture, social and economic factors. Democratization is not a linear process that moves from an authoritarian to a democratic regime. It is a multi-faceted, multidisciplinary process that moves back and forth, where some institutions are more developed than others. A functioning democracy therefore requires many interdependent elements and processes that are based on a culture of citizen participation in public affairs (IDEA, 'Democracy Assessment', <http://www.idea.int/democracy/index.cfm>).

The International IDEA Guidelines for Democracy Assessment

Democracy is usually defined as a set of governmental institutions or processes, but people rarely stop to think what it is that makes these institutions democratic. Thus, when these institutions are used, as they frequently are, for undemocratic purposes, the automatic association of them with democracy simply results in democracy itself being given a bad name. The assessment framework used by International IDEA starts from the proposition that democracy should be defined in the first instance by its basic principles or values. It is these that make particular institutional arrangements democratic, and they provide the litmus test of how democratic they are in practice.

What are these principles? They are twofold: popular control over public decision making and decision makers; and equality between citizens in the exercise of that control. Insofar as these principles are embodied in governing arrangements we can call them 'democratic'. These are the principles that democrats at all times and in all places have struggled for: to make popular control over public decisions both more effective and more inclusive; to remove an elite monopoly over decision making and its benefits; and to overcome obstacles such as those of gender, ethnicity, religion, language, class, wealth and so on to the equal exercise of the rights of citizenship. Democracy is thus not an all-or-nothing affair, but a matter of degree—of the degree to which the people can exercise a controlling influence over public policy and policy makers, enjoy equal treatment at their hands, and have their voices heard equally.

These principles are broad and strong ones, but they require to be specified more precisely in the context of a system of representative government, in which the people assign to others the right to decide public policy on their behalf. So we need to identify a set of mediating values, through which these two principles are realized in practice. These are the values of participation, authorization, representativeness, accountability, transparency, responsiveness and solidarity. It is from these values that the familiar

147

institutions of representative government derive their democratic character, and it is these values that can in turn be used to assess how democratically they actually work in practice.

It is this two-way relationship between values and institutions that gives the democracy assessment process its intellectual foundation and validity. The relationship is illustrated diagrammatically in the accompanying table. The first column of the table lists the main mediating values that derive from our two democratic principles. The second column sets out what is required for these values to be made effective. The third column lists the typical institutions through which these requirements can be met in a system of representative government. Together they build up the main features of what is to be assessed, and the criteria by which that assessment is to be made.

The democracy assessment framework below with its search questions begins with the rights of the citizen, then deals with the representativeness and accountability of government and the different aspects of civil society, and concludes with the international dimensions of democracy. The questions for investigation would be framed in the comparative mode (How much? How far? etc.), in line with our conviction that democracy is a question of degree, not an all-or-nothing situation, which you either have or do not have. (For the full list of search questions and further information see Beetham, Bracking, Kearton and Weir 2002. See also <http://www.idea.int/ publications/sod/democracy_assessment.cfm).

Table 4.1: The IDEA Democracy Assessment Framework: Search Questions

Mediating Values	Requirements	Initial Means of Realisation
Participation	• rights to participate • capacities/resoures to participate • agencies for participation • participatory culture	• civil and political rights system • economic and social rights • elections, parties, NGOs
Authorisation	• validation of constitution • choice of office holders/ programmes • control of elected over non-elected executive personnel	• referendums • free and fair elections • systems of subordination to elected officials
Representation	• legislature representative of main currents of popular opinion • all political institutions representative of social composition of electorate	• electoral and party system • anti-discrimination laws • affirmative action policies
Accountability	• clear lines of accountability, legal, financial, political, to ensure effective and honest performance civil service and judicial integrity	• rule of law, separation of powers • independent auditing process • legally enforceable standards • strong parliamentary powers of scrutiny
Transparency	• government open to legislative and public scrutiny	• freedom of information legislation • independent media
Responsiveness	• accessibility of government to electorates and different sections of public opinion in policy formation, implementation and service delivery	• systematic and open procedures of public consultation • effective legal redress • local government close to the people
Solidarity	• tolerance of diversity at home • support for democratic governments and popular democratic struggles abroad	• civic and human rights education • international human rights law • UN and other agencies • International NGOs

References and Further Reading

Bascombe, Dominic, 'An Update of Anti-Terror Legislation in the Commonwealth', July 2004, <http://www.humanrightsinitiative.org/ new/anti_terror_legislation_cw2004.pdf>

Beetham, David, Bracking, Sarah, Kearton, Iain and Weir, Stuart, *Handbook on Democracy Assessment* (The Hague: Kluwer Law International for International IDEA, 2002) (for a summary see the IDEA web site at <http://www.idea.int/publications/sod/democracy_assessment.cfm>)

Chourou, Bechir, 'Promoting Human Security: Ethical, Normative and Educational Frameworks in the Arab States', United Nations Educational, Scientific and Cultural Organization (UNESCO), Paris, 2005, <http://unesdoc.unesco.org/images/0014/001405/140513e.pdf>

Club de Madrid, 'Towards a Democratic Response', Madrid Summit Working Paper Series, Vol. III, Madrid, 2005, <http://summit.clubmadrid.org/responses/>

Collier, David and Levitsky, Steven, 'Democracy with Adjectives: Conceptual Innovation in Comparative Research', *World Politics*, 49 (April 1997), pp. 430–51

Demmers, Jolle, Fernández Jilberto, Alex E. and Hogenboom, Barbara, *Good Governance in the Era of Global Neoliberalism* (London and New York: Routledge, 2004)

Diamond, Larry, 'Economic Development and Democracy Reconsidered', *American Behavioral Scientist*, 35 (4/5) (1992), pp. 450–99

European Parliament, 'Chechnya After the Elections and Civil Society in Russia', Press release, 19 January 2006, <http://www.europarl.europa.eu/news/expert/infopress_page/030-4347-018-01-03-903-20060113IPR04289-18-01-2006-2006-false/default_sv.htm>

Glasius, Marlies et al., *Human Security, EU Policy and the Response to the Tsunami* (Stockholm and London: Swedish Ministry for Foreign Affairs and Centre for the Study of Global Governance, November 2005)

International Institute for Democracy and Electoral Assistance (IDEA), 'Democracy Assessment', <http://www.idea.int/democracy/index.cfm>

International Institute for Democracy and Electoral Assistance (IDEA), 'State of Democracy Study for South Asia', forthcoming 2007

International Institute for Democracy and Electoral Assistance (IDEA), Latin America Office, Discussion Paper for 'Strategy on Political Parties and the Promotion of Poverty Reduction and Social Cohesion', 2005 (internal document)

International Institute for Democracy and Electoral Assistance (IDEA) and Inter-American Development Bank (IDB), *Democracies in Development: Politics and Reform in Latin America*, published by IDEA and the IDB, 2002, <http://www.idea.int/publications/dem_dev/index.cfm>

Kagwanja, Peter, 'When the Locusts Ate Zimbabwe's March 2005 Elections', Electoral Institute of Southern Africa, Occasional Paper no. 32, May 2005, <http://www.eisa.org.za/PDF/OP32.pdf>

Kamal, Simi, Paper presented at the International IDEA 2000 Democracy Forum on Democracy and Poverty: A Missing Link?, Stockholm, 8–9 June 2000

'Losing Faith in Democracy: A Warning from Latin America', UN Wire, <http://www.unwire.org>, 26 April 2004

'Mapping the Future of HIV/AIDS, Security and Conflict in Africa', Concept Note for the Joint Academic/NGO Seminar, King's College London, 6 December 2005, <http://www.justiceafrica.org>

New York Times, 2 May 2006, <http://www.nytimes.com/2006/05/02/world/africa/02zimbabwe.html>

O'Donnell, Guillermo, 'Delegative Democracy', *Journal of Democracy*, 5 (January 1994), pp. 56–69

Oh, John Kie-chiang, *Korean Politics: The Quest for Democratization and Economic Development* (Ithaca, N.Y. and London: Cornell University Press, 1999)

Przeworski, Adam, Alvarez, Michael E., Cheibub, Jose Antonio and Limongi, Fernando, *Democracy and Development: Political Institutions and Well-Being in the World, 1950–1990* (New York: Cambridge University Press, 2000)

Radio Free Europe/Radio Liberty, 'Russia: Council Of Europe Condemns Human Rights Violations In Chechnya', 25 January 2006, <http://www.rferl.org/featuresarticle/2006/01/db6660d3-511a-407b-a489-f3c8e833a6c6.html?napage=2>

Ross, Michael, 'Does Demoracy Reduce Infant Mortality?', Paper for the University of California Department of Political Science, January 2006, p. 27, <http://www.polisci.ucla.edu/faculty/ross/>

— 'Is Democracy Good for the Poor?', Stanford Center on Democracy, Development and the Rule of Law Research Papers no. 37, February 2005

Stavenhagen, Rodolfo, 'Needs, Rights and Social Development', Overarching Concerns Paper No. 2, United Nations Research Institute for Social Development, July 2003

Strand, Per, 'AIDS and Elections in Southern Africa: Is the Epidemic Undermining its Democratic Remedy?', Institute for Security Studies Paper 110, Pretoria, July 2005

—, Matlosa, K., Strode, A. and Chirambo, K., *HIV/AIDS and Democratic Governance in South Africa: Illustrating the Impact on Electoral Processes* (Pretoria: Institute for Democracy in Southern Africa, 2005)

United Nations Development Project (UNDP), *Democracy in Latin America: Towards a Citizen's Democracy* (New York: UNDP, 2004), available at <http://www.democracia.undp.org>

CHAPTER 5

5. Democracy in War-torn Societies

The challenges to democracy as a solution to conflict include lack of trust among the protagonists; the influence of elites who may continue to mobilize on divisive nationalist, ethnic or racial lines in their quest for power; and the weakness or fragmentation of the state, the political parties and civil society. When a settlement can be negotiated, it is critical that former combatants be demobilized and reintegrated into society, and that a new and viable security sector is developed. There is also today an increased appreciation of the essential role that a human rights agenda plays in the pursuit of conflict management. Failure to integrate human rights concerns into the peace process and the settlements it results in will adversely impact on the credibility of the process and agreements.

The realization of a settlement or 'peace process' depends on public trust and participation. Peace agreements imposed from above invariably encounter obstacles to implementation. They must include stakeholders and the main political actors. In a context of political competition, the exclusion of key political actors robs the process of the acceptance and legitimacy it requires for momentum and progress to a final settlement. Power sharing is an approach to crafting democratic political institutions that assure all major interests in society of a place in the structures and decision-making processes of governance; but in a post-war environment, consensus does not often reflect shared visions or objectives. It is rather a kind of lowest common denominator. Integrative power-sharing solutions have an inherent advantage if they can be achieved.

Central to the debate on democracy's relationship to conflict management is the challenge of electoral processes in societies that are prone to, involved in, or emerging from violent conflict. Elections and their outcomes can be a stimulant for violence by those who expect to lose. Among practitioners of international peacemaking and peace building, there is widespread concern about the nature, timing and administration of electoral processes as an instrument for conflict management.

Democratic practice at local level is as important as general elections. Informal structures and even traditional structures of authority or customary law can be important: sometimes they have functioned and proved resilient right through periods of conflict.

With the principal form of armed conflict today occurring within countries and not between them (see chapter 1), the evaluation of how democracy contributes to peace has been re-framed since the end of the cold war. Democratic solutions to armed conflicts have helped bring relative peace to many societies that were torn by war during the superpower conflict that characterized the second half of the 20th century. In Namibia, Mozambique, El Salvador and Cambodia, for example, the early 1990s saw war-to-democracy transition pursued as a way to build foundations for peace. Subsequently similar directions were forged following wars in Bosnia, Timor-Leste, Liberia and Sierra Leone, and for Sudan and the Democratic Republic of the Congo (DRC).

Today, there is an appreciation that democracy in war-torn societies encompasses a much broader range of concerns than previously considered. Notably, democracy and war can often unfold side by side, as has been the case in Colombia and Indonesia. Similarly, some armed conflicts have been stabilized by ceasefires but agreement on a fully inclusive democratic solution as a pathway from violence remains elusive, as in Azerbaijan or Sri Lanka. The fact that democratic countries may themselves be war-torn raises questions about democracy and negotiated peace agreements, as hardened public attitudes may limit the ability of elected governments to make concessions in negotiations with rebel forces. Relevant factors will include popular grievances not met within the political framework, geopolitics and regional factors, and the way in which the political machinery relates to the conduct of war or negotiations on a ceasefire or comprehensive peace agreement.

For example, the Ugandan democratic framework is still severely tested by ongoing violence in the north, where local populations have suffered for over a decade, caught between Lord's Resistance Army raids (over the border from Sudan) and the national military response, with people being housed by the thousands in 'protected villages' where they are unable to till their land or have access to health care or education. Colombia prides itself on a democratic constitutional history, but must deal with ongoing internal war and non-state actors with wide-reaching links in the region and beyond. Sri Lanka's history is an example of missed opportunities for offering inclusive political measures to the Tamil minority, and is fraught with problems over the functioning of its majoritarian democracy. Israel has political elections and a parliamentary system, while being territorially based on priority for a single religious identity, with severe restrictions on citizenship for minorities. This policy is rationalized by Israelis themselves as being due to their own minority status in a complex region.

Historically, a fuller democracy can, ironically, emerge from war. When the United States fought its own bitter civil war in the mid-19th century, democratic notions of citizenship and rights were far from developed or universal. As in many early settings, there was a legacy of suffrage being granted only to white male landowners; subsequently this was extended in response to social mobilization for change over time. Mobilization for war itself will generally be a last resort and, as the US experience would bear out, historically, 20th century findings indicate that it is 'semi-democracies' and transitional regimes that have the highest incidence of civil wars.

Critically at stake is *what kind of democracy* is to be established. 'Democratic governance has tended to be a structural preventor of conflict over the long term, but the democratization process has been a short-term contributor to armed conflicts. Imposed or dissimulated democratization may do little to avert violent conflicts, but democratic institutions that develop *strong social roots* do appear to have a preventative effect' (Miall 2003: 68, emphasis added).

Democracy in war-torn societies is fraught with dilemmas and apparent contradictions. States with democratic frameworks find that political forces polarize around the armed conflict, just as the violence itself is an extension of politics. There are several levels of paradox which may operate simultaneously. One is that elections can become referendums on a given stance in negotiation or strategy, thus inhibiting or influencing political leadership at critical junctures (for better or worse). National crisis may be used to justify restrictions on mobility or travel, press reporting or communications, precisely when citizens' expectations and need of opportunities to travel and for information are high. Finally, whereas elite 'track one' and highly sensitive political negotiation may require confidentiality, the actual realization of a settlement or 'peace process' is linked entirely to public trust and participation. Ironically, public voice in a democracy that is in civil war may be detrimental to progress on the peacemaking front—unless stages in political developments are made clear and varied constituencies are brought on board to ensure ownership of agreements made. Democracy and conflict management may work at cross purposes.

This chapter begins with a consideration of these dilemmas, with specific reference to the case of Sri Lanka, which is instructive in several ways. While every civil war is painful and unique in its history, features and suffering, the Sri Lankan experience is illustrative of peacemaking taken to electoral politics; of the gaps between elites, political parties and broadly-based constituencies; and of their implications for viable ceasefires, negotiations, settlements and peace processes or peace building. It also offers examples of the crucial question of 'who represents whom' when warring parties are at the negotiating table, and of the diverse roles of external actors in war-torn societies.

> Democracy in war-torn societies is fraught with dilemmas and apparent contradictions. States with democratic frameworks find that political forces polarize around the armed conflict itself, just as the violence itself is an extension of politics. Public voice in a democracy that is in civil war may be detrimental to progress on the peacemaking front—unless stages in political developments are made clear and varied constituencies are brought on board to ensure ownership of agreements made.

The chapter then reviews post-settlement democratization processes in settings with collapsed or destroyed governance structures, including cases where the international community has taken a role in interim peacekeeping and state-building measures. It considers specifically human rights and peacemaking; negotiated agreements and power sharing; the functions of elections after violence and their role and meaning for recovery; and the need for local-level democratic practice during post-war recovery.

1. The Politics of War in a Democracy: The Case of Sri Lanka

Sri Lanka is an example of a society in which a majoritarian democracy (of then Ceylon), sequential constitutions and a presidential system (in which president and prime minister are elected separately) have been severely tested. Early legislation, such as the 1948 Citizenship Act (citizenship was no longer to be conferred by birth in the country but by 'descent' or 'registration') meant that the Tamil immigrant minority did not qualify. The following year further legislation combined to effectively disenfranchise those who failed to get citizenship, reducing overall Tamil representation in the Parliament by one-third.

The passing of the Official Language Act in 1956 (often referred to as 'Sinhala Only') confirmed the pre-independence fears of the Tamil minority that they would lose out in representation and voice in the new state. A new republican constitution in 1972 ushered in the new Republic of Sri Lanka and confirmed the inferior status of Tamil, declaring Sinhala the only official language (Coomaraswamy 1983).

Language policy is sensitive when it reflects and reinforces deeper inequalities in society—'second-class' or inferior status for some and privilege and control mechanisms for others, leading to deepening division and mistrust. Those without language as an entry point to the economy, jobs and training become increasingly marginalized. As one response to growing frustration, the Liberation Tigers of Tamil Eelam (LTTE) made themselves known with attacks on Sinhalese politicians and police officers. Increasing militancy brought about backlashes and spirals of violence, as in severe anti-Tamil riots in the south of the country in 1983.

The study by Paikiasothy Saravanamuttu in Volume II addresses the practical democratic dilemmas experienced in Sri Lanka, where conservative estimates put casualties in the war between the government and the LTTE since the civil war began in 1983 at well over 60,000.

The Indo-Sri Lanka Accord (1987) paved the way for a system of limited devolution through provincial councils via constitutional amendment. Despite the government of the day enjoying a five-sixths majority in the legislature, the necessary legislation had to be passed with legislators and Parliament under armed guard and amid demonstrations in the streets. Leading armed protagonists representing the Tamil community were not signatories to this agreement (which was signed by the government of Sri Lanka and the intervening government of India), and in the space of three months they had reverted to hostilities—now against Indian forces themselves. More recently, in 2002, the government of Sri Lanka and the LTTE signed the Cease Fire Agreement (CFA). It also raised questions of representation and inclusiveness, the Tamil homeland in question also being home to other groups, including a substantial Muslim community whose agreement is crucial for a durable settlement. By the end of 2005 the CFA was itself under severe threat owing to the escalation of hostilities.

There were special features in the political context of the ceasefire which are important when considering participation and peace processes. The Sri Lankan constitution of 1977 enshrines the office of the executive president as the highest in the land with a vast array of powers. The December 2001 parliamentary election resulted in the defeat of the president's party and a president and a prime minister from two different parties. Although the president is the commander in chief of the armed forces and chief executive, she was not part of negotiations, and the CFA was signed by the prime minister. The prime minister and his party argued that the electorate's verdict was a repudiation of the president's policies. With an open rift in government, the president subsequently took over three key ministries (Defence, Media and Internal Security), citing the threat to national security as grounds, as a prelude to the dissolution of Parliament and new elections. Subsequently the president's party won the parliamentary election in coalition with the vociferously anti-LTTE Janatha Vimukthi Peramuna (JVP), in April 2004.

The persistence of a zero-sum culture of political competition should be noted here. The coalition with the JVP, given the differences between the president and that party on the peace process, was not based on a policy consensus but rather on . . . the desire for a parliamentary majority and the logic of the electoral arithmetic to achieve this . . . The alliance collapsed when the president went ahead and signed an agreement with the LTTE over tsunami relief in 2005.

The foregoing raises the question of the inclusion of stakeholders at the Track One level and the danger of 'spoilers'. In a democratic context, the impact of spoilers extends beyond the political office they may hold to their whole political constituency. The exclusion of a key political actor is also the exclusion of that actor's constituency, and in a context of political competition this exclusion robs the process of the widespread acceptance and legitimacy it requires for momentum and progress to a final settlement (see the study by Saravanamuttu in Volume II).

This issue of inclusiveness is mirrored in the Eastern Province, where the population includes Tamils, Muslims and Sinhalese. Tamil political representation claims the Eastern Province together with the Northern Province as constituting the traditional homeland of the Tamils of Sri Lanka. But this claim has given rise to demands for separate Muslim political representation and aroused fears that the concerns of the Muslim community will be sacrificed in a peace agreement between a predominantly Sinhalese state and the LTTE. Muslim political leaders have therefore insisted on being a party to peace negotiations and on separate arrangements to deal with their concerns in a peace settlement. There has been strong opposition to a redefinition of negotiations as tripartite in composition.

> Ultimately, peace settlements need all-party or at least bipartisan support, especially those that require constitutional change.

Failure to include such key stakeholders, in Saravanamuttu's view, 'runs the risk of greater militancy within the community and the likelihood that it would follow the same trajectory of political evolution as the Tamil community did in the late 1970s and 1980s'.

Box 5.1: Democratization and the Peace Process in Sri Lanka: Lessons Learned

1. *Elite-level peacemaking without the groundwork of public awareness and acceptance will suffer as a consequence in the implementation phase.* This in turn will reinforce suspicion, mistrust and frustration between the negotiating partners.

2. *Following from this, peace settlements invariably (in Sri Lanka) entail fundamental change of the constitution, of the polity, and of political attitudes and culture. Public education and information are therefore of primary importance with regard to the nature and consequences of the change required.* However, if they are seen to be partisan, public education and awareness raising will significantly detract from the overall success of the exercise.

3. *In a democratic context of political party competition, it is crucially important that there be a minimum consensus among the political parties or at least the two main parties regarding the overarching importance of peace through a negotiated settlement.* Political parties are the principal vehicles of political mobilization and are critical to public participation. Ultimately, peace settlements need all-party or at least bipartisan support, especially those that require constitutional change. This does not entail 'taking the question of peace out of the political fray' but it does entail minimum consensus on its overarching importance.

Political competition can continue to be possible on the basis of differing approaches, emphases and tactics, rather than on the strategic objective of a peace settlement through talks. In the case of the agreements signed by the Federal Party in 1957 and 1966, it was the mobilization of opposition against the agreements by the principal opposition party which made them inoperable, thus *institutionalizing the bad practice of subjecting ethnic harmony and peace to the dynamics of zero-sum political party competition.*

4. *Failure to integrate human rights concerns into the peace process and the settlements it results in will adversely impact on the credibility of the process and agreements.* This is a primary concern in respect of the CFA. Continued violations cast doubt on the commitment of the parties to a political settlement and on the viability of a negotiating process.

5. Peace agreements imposed from above which last, though challenged at inception, invariably encounter obstacles to implementation which in turn reinforce suspicion and frustration. Furthermore, such agreements have to be re-worked, and it is likely that, as in the case of the Indo-Sri Lanka Accord, the grievances and demands that have to be addressed at a later date will be greater than those at the time of the original agreement.

6. Public support for and the legitimacy of the peace process are conditioned by the nature of the democracy and the health of its democratic institutions and processes. ... At the time of the signing of the Indo-Sri Lanka Accord, the government of Sri Lanka faced an insurgency in the south on the grounds that it was autocratic and had postponed elections through a dubious referendum. The JVP, which mounted the armed challenge against the state in the south of the country, was able to add to charges of bankruptcy and authoritarianism the charge ... of a sellout to a foreign power.

7. The fundamental change of attitude and political culture required to effect and animate a new and federal constitutional architecture of the state necessary for a democratic peace in Sri Lanka hinges crucially upon public participation in peacemaking and peace building.

Source: Extracts from the study by Paikiasothy Saravanamuttu in Volume II.

1.1. 'Top–Down' and 'Bottom–Up' Spheres of Action: The Realm of Public Participation

At the opposite end of the spectrum from the high electoral politics of national government are the public realms of 'civil society' and local-level or grass-roots constituencies. A Sri Lankan study of 'track two' initiatives highlights interventions that were meant to surmount social divisions and enhance reconciliation among the population, in tandem with track one negotiations. Numerous activities are documented—inter-community exchanges, multi-stakeholder dialogues, peace committees, conflict resolution training, reconciliation media programmes and so on—and the authors cite hundreds of community conflict resolution training workshops since the 2002 CFA. Some communities in the North and the East boast multiple peace committees, with as many as five or six committees set up by different organizations servicing the same target population.

> Peace agreements imposed from above invariably encounter obstacles to implementation which in turn reinforce suspicion and frustration.

In contrast there has been little done in the realm of restorative interventions, and many of the activities remain largely confined to the psychosocial sector and then only to a handful of individuals and organizations that operate with innovation and sensitivity to the local context. Secondly, there has been very little in the way of agenda-setting, option-generating, capacity-building, public mobilization and political lobbying on reconciliation by Track 2 actors. Thirdly, many of the interventions have been one-off activities lacking the sustainability required for restoring fractured relationships over time. Fourthly, a good majority of them appear to work within comfortable circles of like-minded intermediaries, and have little access and outreach to those who fall outside of the circles mentioned earlier. Finally, most interventions appear to suffer from a creativity block and are unable to move away from textbook interventions to more strategic and context-specific ones (Ramiah and Fonseka 2006).

The Sri Lankan experience illustrates vertical and horizontal fractures which go far beyond the open political confrontation between the LTTE and the government of Sri Lanka. Communities will have differing experience of war according to geographic and social or class positioning. There are divisions between and within Sinhala, Tamil and Muslim groupings: 'The fault-lines between the three major communities are non-linear (they periodically exacerbate and ameliorate) and are fashioned by other factors such as geographic proximity, religion, gender, age, lived memory, and of course individual and group experience' (Ramiah and Fonseka 2006). For many the current debate on the divisions within Sri Lanka 'leans less on the rhetoric of historical and deep-rooted ethnic differences and more on the systematic failure of the political elite to deliver on a resolution to the problem. To that end, the interpersonal relationships between the different groups are to a large extent conciliatory and turn antagonistic only when they intersect with the political' (Ramiah and Fonseka 2006). This was also the case in Slovenia and Croatia during the dissolution of the former Yugoslavia, when the culture of 'anti-politics' was proclaimed by anti-war activists.

There are significant multiple and simultaneous spheres of action if support for a negotiated settlement and its legitimacy are to be secured in conflicted democracies. Among them are:

- *mistrust* of non-representative political elites;
- *identity-based constituencies* that are 'locked in' to political or familial patronage;
- *zero-sum electoral politics,* or underdeveloped cross-party consensus on national futures;
- *political inequality*—embedded class and caste barriers or functional barriers to political participation;
- *civil–military relations*—who decides on tactics and strategy and where does accountability lie?;
- *the role and behaviour of the national police and the national military*;
- *press freedom*—to what extent may correspondents publish and investigate?;
- knowledge and application of the *Geneva conventions*—what rights for combatants?;
- *access to information and justice*—what will families of the missing and dead know

of their fate? Are there rights to compensation or restitution?;

• *national education*—what narrative of events is presented in schooling?;

• *the costs of war*—spending implications for health, shelter, infrastructure; gendered experience in deaths, disability and widowhood; single-headed households and patterns of poverty; and

• *the management of additional resources introduced by external actors*—where and how is money used? Is delivery among groups equitable or biased, thus influencing or inducing additional competition?

All these factors have implications for human security and democratization. They intersect and cumulatively contribute to the possibility of public momentum in support of a negotiated settlement and its legitimacy. They are determinants of the 'fundamental change of attitude and political culture required to effect and animate a new and federal constitutional architecture of the state necessary for a democratic peace' (see box 5.1). Sri Lanka's war is bitter and protracted, a secessionist struggle based on a territorial claim in the name of minority rights. But the internal locations of struggle and change listed above would also apply in the very different settings of Nepal, Uganda in relation to its war in the north, Sierra Leone in its intervals of war and peace, and Northern Ireland.

> There are significant multiple and simultaneous spheres of action if support for a negotiated settlement and its legitimacy are to be secured in conflicted democracies.

From yet another region, an extensive comparative study of peace processes in Nicaragua, Guatemala, Chiapas (Mexico), Colombia, Peru and El Salvador documents how war itself can generate pressures for peace 'from below', lending legitimacy to settlements, and demonstrating a positive correlation between democratic transitions and the end of guerrilla war.

> Even if war initially serves as a pretext for the destruction of democratic space and the suppression of normal politics, war itself can generate pressures to devise or expand mechanisms of participation and inclusion. 'From above' these mechanisms may be designed to provide a political alternative to the guerrillas in the context of counterinsurgency. 'From below', however, they represent the expression of civil society's disenchantment with the fighting and an insistence on an alternative to a military solution (Arnson 1999: 447).

2. Democracy in War-Torn Societies: Varieties of Experience

Democracies waging war against other states is a theme that is receiving new attention; but democracies which are themselves war-torn would appear to be under-studied. Although each situation is unique, there are four broad categories of situations in which democracy and democratization operate in societies torn by internal and regional conflict:

• when democratic processes such as elections are in place, but the country is engaged in *internal armed conflict or civil war*. In situations such as Colombia or Russia, elections have occurred when the country is engaged in an armed struggle against rebel forces;

• when democratic processes such as elections occur in *countries that are situated between war and peace*, with perhaps a ceasefire in place but no comprehensive peace agreement that settles the underlying causes of conflict, such as a bid for secession. Azerbaijan and Sri Lanka both find themselves in this category today;

• when a country has experienced war that led to a *clear military victory* of one side over others, and that country moves towards democratization on the heels of such a unilateral victory. In Rwanda, following the civil war that culminated in the 1994 genocide, the victorious Rwandan Patriotic Front sought to cautiously and carefully democratize the government through local elections, national elections, reconciliation processes and a constitution-making process; and

• when democratization is the overall theme of a *comprehensive peace settlement*, often brokered or backed by the international community; in some instances, such as United Nations transitional administrations or other multidimensional peace operations, the transition is guided initially by the international community as democracy is gradually introduced. From Namibia in 1990 to Liberia in 2005, this form of democratization has become known as war-to-democracy transitions.

2.1. Negotiated Settlements and 'Post-war' Democratization

It can be argued that one effect of globalization and the expansion of multi-level international engagement is a higher likelihood of negotiated outcomes to internal wars. This is a contested issue, as the same tendency to increased intervention may also, by reducing tactics for 'total victory' (increased access for humanitarian aid, development assistance, reports on human rights abuse and the presence of UN or international NGO actors in war zones), prolong a grey area of 'not war, not peace'.

Internationally assisted efforts to democratize after bitter internal conflicts have featured prominently in Angola, Bosnia, Croatia, Timor-Leste, El Salvador, Ethiopia, Guatemala, Nicaragua, Northern Ireland, Sierra Leone, South Africa and Zimbabwe, to name but a few. Hopes are pinned on the ballot box replacing the battlefield as the principal way in which social conflicts are waged. The greater willingness of international actors to intervene in today's conflicts has the effect of putting all parties to the conflict on a more level playing field. The prevailing view today is that negotiated solutions are more desirable than military victory by one side because definitive defeat of an opponent in internal conflict may lead to genocide, 'ethnic cleansing' or forced migration. International intervention through peacemaking (mediation) or peacekeeping (military intervention) can induce more of a balance of power among competing forces, thereby making negotiation more attractive—because the war is really not winnable—and the pursuit of military victory more costly and perhaps futile.

Barbara Walter undertook a comprehensive analysis and concluded that between 1940 and 1990 only 20 per cent of civil wars ended in negotiations (Walter 1997). Times have changed, however. Recent evidence suggests that today's wars are much more likely to end at the peace table than on the battlefield. Wallensteen and Sollenberg report that, of the 116 conflicts since 1989, 75 had ended by 1998. 'Of these', they write, '21 were ended by peace agreements, whereas 24 ended in victory for one of the sides and 30 had other outcomes (cease-fire agreements or activity below the level for inclusion). Many new peace agreements were signed in the middle and late parts of the period, particularly 1995–96' (Wallensteen and Sollenberg 1999: 597). In sum, today some 50 per cent of wars end at the peace table, a dramatic increase over the broad historical average.

At the same time there are unusual and unresolved situations, such as that of Somaliland, which broke away from Somalia in 1991 and has undertaken democratization without official recognition or support from the international community. A breakaway state challenges notions of sovereignty and territoriality in any region, and may be seen as a threat to the status quo. (Some would argue that rapid European recognition of Slovenia contributed to the bitter and progressive dissolution of the former Yugoslavia.) Somaliland's self-directed and peaceful adaptation of democracy stands in sharp contrast with the situation in Somalia and international efforts there to forge a transitional federal government from outside. Somaliland's constitutional plebiscite, three peaceful elections to date, and work in adapting traditional structures and clan organization to promote the evolution of political parties also demonstrate what could be possible for wider Somalia. 'They also provide inspiration for civil activists advocating democratic change elsewhere in the region, such as Djibouti and Eritrea' (Aboko et al. 2005).

Many observers hope for a long-term influence from Somaliland in the Somali region, where the resort to arms is still a frequent occurrence. As Baker has observed, 'Conflict managers tend to concentrate on short-term solutions that address the precipitous events that sparked the conflict; above all they seek a swift and expedient end to the violence. Democratizers tend to concentrate on long-term solutions that address the root causes of the conflict; they search for enduring democratic stability. The former see peace as a precondition for democracy; the latter see democracy as a precondition for peace' (Baker 1996: 568).

2.2. Challenges for Democracy After War

If a peace settlement is to succeed, both in ending armed violence and in promoting reconciliation, the terms of a new, just and mutually beneficial post-war order must be established through collaboration and dialogue. For a negotiated agreement to have meaning 'on the ground', civil wars need a peace process, or step-by-step reciprocal moves to build confidence, resolve issues such as disarmament and physical recovery, and carefully define the future. Challenges will include:

Lack of trust. The lack of trust among parties who were at war is a principal peril for democracy as a post-war system of conflict management. The meaning and logic of war can overtake the desirability and logic of peace; there is a wariness of the ballot box. The conduct of war itself generates a powerful set of incentives that can prevent

163

parties from taking the usually risky steps towards a negotiated end to their struggle, or towards accepting the likely uncertainties of elections in a post-war democracy.

Persistence of deep divisions. 'Them and Us' divisions may remain, whether along class or along ideological lines, or as the product of extreme nationalisms or the bitter politicization of ethnicity or religion. When absolute claims for self-determination and independence clash with inflexible positions on territorial integrity, as in Russia/ Chechnya, there is little room for compromise on basic principles.

Factions and frictions. It is as important to look *within* protagonist organizations in civil wars as at the relationship between the adversaries. What are the factions and frictions within a party at the table? What happens inside organizations like governments and rebel groups influences whether moderates can rise to the level of leadership and 'deliver' for their constituencies in post-war politics. The balance of power between moderates and hard-liners (those who will fight to the bitter end) is an important factor in the viability of a peace process.

Lack of credible commitment and external support. Although there are many variables involved in successful mediation in civil wars, credible external commitment, providing the parties with the resources and personnel for a long-term commitment to assist a country on the path to accepting the inherent uncertainties of democracy, is crucial.

Building legitimacy for new institutions and governance. The 'peace' agreed must be a legitimate one which deals with the grievances underlying previous violence; this can mean reorienting the relationship between political authority and the citizenry. Similarly, demilitarization is more than demobilization and disarmament; attitudes and mindsets may have been geared for years to armed struggle, and people's expectations of political leaders will be coloured by experience from the past.

Critical for peace building, then, is the crafting of post-war democratic institutions to foster the legitimacy and inclusion which create conditions for reconciliation. For the international community, the question is how to enable the protagonists in civil wars to design a democratic system that will help manage and ameliorate the underlying causes of conflict over the long term. Such a settlement should also avoid winner-take-all outcomes in elections: it should be designed as a self-sustaining system of conflict management for the long shadow of the future. Appropriate trust-building political systems in divided societies will be key in healing social wounds and to preventing new wars from emerging.

> Lack of trust among parties who were at war is a principal peril for democracy as a post-war system of conflict management. The meaning and logic of war can overtake the desirability and logic of peace. The conduct of war itself generates a powerful set of incentives that can prevent parties from taking the usually risky steps towards a negotiated end to their struggle, or accepting the likely uncertainties of elections in a post-war democracy. 'Them and Us' divisions may remain. Critical for peace building is the crafting of post-war democratic institutions to foster the legitimacy and inclusion which create conditions for reconciliation.

2.3. Human Rights and the Peace Process

As Saravanamuttu argues in box 5.1, 'failure to integrate human rights concerns into the peace process and the settlements it results in will adversely impact on the credibility of the

164

process and agreements'. Today, there is a greater appreciation of the essential role that a human rights agenda plays in the pursuit of conflict management. From the conflicts of the 1990s, there is growing consensus that the promotion of human rights must be part of an overall strategy for the creation of multiple rule-of-law mechanisms (judicial institutions, and community access to justice, ad hoc commissions or conciliation forums).

Christine Bell has evaluated the role of human rights protection in peace processes and finds that early in the negotiations and through the implementation phase there is a window of opportunity to create new institutions, to define and shape transitional and forward-looking agreements on human rights, and to emphasize safeguards under a future regime. She notes that 'individual human rights provisions... are crucially shaped by the deal at the heart of the peace agreement ... The protection and promotion of individual human rights are part of a bigger constitutional picture' (Bell 2003: 172).

In El Salvador the UN Secretariat consciously developed a human rights component to the negotiated settlement and effectively integrated it into the peacekeeping operation that implemented the agreements. The strategy was premised on the belief that impunity for previous human rights violations was a core cause of the conflict, as were the underlying socio-economic inequalities that could equally be considered a human rights issue. Effective conflict management beyond a ceasefire demanded immediate and sustained attention to stem human rights abuses, promote judicial independence, end a cycle of impunity, and address structural issues such as the inequitable distribution of land. Eventually, all the parties in the conflict agreed on these points through a process that allowed for a general amnesty for the Farabundo Marti National Liberation Front (Frente Farabundo Marti de Liberacion Nacional, FMLN) rebels in the 1992 National Reconciliation Law and the establishment of an Ad Hoc Commission that would evaluate the military, which had been widely seen as responsible for many human rights abuses. In Volume II Enrique ter Horst examines in depth the El Salvador Peace Agreement of January 1992, which put an end to the 11-year-long conflict that caused over 100,000 deaths.

In cases such as that of East Timor (now Timor-Leste), the sheer scale of sudden violence, the extent of destruction of infrastructure, the sudden departure or loss of the majority of the civil service, acute logistical problems for access to outlying regions and the almost total dislocation of the population pose daunting challenges. There is not so much as a peace process as an emergency response followed by nation and state building. The flow of people over porous borders, through difficult terrain, and the remoteness of peripheral regions from the capital make it difficult to track, record and monitor human rights. In these cases there are no judiciary, no courthouse, no prison, and little data. The mandates and the means to build up capacity take time.

In the vast area of south Sudan (New Sudan), 'traditional' authority and local customary law formed an important part of the administrative and legal structure, continuing to function even during prolonged and devastating civil war. In some areas chiefs were regarded as the most responsive and accountable structures of authority, living amid the population and under scrutiny if they did not act in their interests. This is particularly the case in Upper Nile, where chiefs have four-year elected terms. During the war their relations with the Sudan People's Liberation Movement (SPLM) and the Sudan People's Liberation Army (SPLA) were often strained. A challenge for the peace—and democracy—will be the negotiation of viable structures and understandings of civil and legal authority. It is noteworthy that in Sudan in July 1995

> ... the SPLM/A [Sudan People's Liberation Movement and Sudan People's Liberation Army] signed the Ground Rules of Operation Lifeline Sudan and thereby recognised international standards of humanitarian principles and human rights, expressing official support for the Geneva Conventions and Additional Protocols and the Convention on the Rights of the Child. By signing the Ground Rules, the armed movements nominally committed themselves to the protection of the rights of civilians and support for human rights norms. The Ground Rules provided a leverage mechanism for the Movement's civilian component who wanted reform, and were reportedly used by Sudanese non- governmental organisations (SINGOs) to protect operations from SPLM/A abuse. Although hard to separate the impact of the Ground Rules from the SPLM/A's internal reforms, the effects of the dynamic between civil pressure from below for internal reform and external commitments to humanitarian principles and human rights was to further an incremental process of reform (Bradbury et al. 2000: 21).

It is frequently the case in war zones that women assume de facto leadership roles, taking part in armed struggle, and more often heading households in the absence of men who are away or dead as a result of fighting. Their roles as equal or sole agents can be diminished when the formal-level agreement takes place, and care must be taken to build in protective measures which help guarantee their place as citizens with rights in the new polity. Similarly it is not uncommom for domestic or sexual violence to increase in 'peacetime', when highly militarized men return home, often to a degree of disillusionment or uncertainty in the aftermath of war. Civil provisions for responding to violence or abuse, training for police and legal safeguards are vital components in the new social and institutional framework: 'The true story of the peace programmes can not be read in the statistics. The accounts of female combatants indicate that we need to study the daily problems that female beneficiaries confront, if we are to comprehend the situation of women in the peace process. If we listen to what these women have to say, the crucial difference between formal and substantive equality is impossible to ignore' (Luciak 2001: 228).

Ultimately the most immediate link between peacemaking at the negotiating table and human rights 'on the ground' will be the creation of conditions for the provision of rule of law, freedom from fear, and safety in movement and expression.

Box 5.2: The Human Rights Agenda: Core Concerns for Conflict Management and Challenges for a Democratic Framework

Freedom of speech and advocacy. When does freedom of speech allow for the spread of divisive and conflict-causing, mobilizing ideologies, such as hate speech, intolerance, ethnic or racial stereotyping, or radical world views such as fascism?

Freedom of religion and belief; protection from intolerance. Are there limits to the freedom of religion and belief if such creeds may lead to social violence? For example, should states enact legislation that prevents the emergence of radical politicized faith groups if their beliefs provide a justification for violence?

The right to associate, form political parties and advance a platform. The right to associate in political parties is a cornerstone of the freedom of association, but when should some political parties be made illegal or not be allowed to form? For example, in many post-war situations local 'warlords' or criminal networks control territory. Should parties with power bases in local criminal networks be allowed to compete for office? Should parties that represent exclusive communities or that espouse exclusive ideologies, such as extreme racism, be allowed to form political parties and contest elections?

Citizenship. Access to justice is often defined by legal citizenship, yet in many conflict situations today citizenship is contested and is often the basis for underlying grievances. How do citizenship laws and access to justice contribute to conflict, and how can review, revision or reconsideration of basic citizenship laws contribute to conflict management?

Criminal justice: prisons, torture, denial of due process, and collective punishment. Today, in every major conflict setting, the criminal justice system is weak in capacity, often biased, and ill suited to the social conflict it should be designed to address. Poor criminal justice systems are a significant root cause of many internal conflicts today. How can criminal justice reform to ensure fairness, due process and access to justice be at the forefront of conflict management strategies today?

Judicial composition and administration. In divided societies that have experienced a long history of dominance by a particular group and systematic exclusion of minority or disadvantaged groups, as in Sri Lanka or South Africa, the composition of the judiciary is a key concern for conflict management. The judiciary must reflect in a balanced and careful way the society it is intended to regulate. Similarly, judicial administration—the legal system, courts, prisons and legal community—must be well balanced for the rule of law to been seen as legitimate and effective.

2.4. Demobilization and Security Sector Reform

In acute humanitarian emergencies where human security is threatened by armed violence, the restoration of security—especially at the community level—becomes a paramount concern and a precondition for democratic state building. Restoring security is a critical first step in post-conflict state building, and security is also necessary for moving beyond immediate humanitarian relief to reconstruction and development. This involves disarmament, demobilization and reintegration (known as DDR) as well as the building of legitimate, inclusive national, regional and local-level security forces. Experiences with disarmament processes in recent civil wars reinforce the imperative of action to address threats to human security as an essential step in the creation of conditions in which democratic processes can be effective.

- *Demobilization without disarmament will be ineffective,* as seen in seen in Angola, Cambodia, Burundi and Rwanda. In situations where no or insufficient collection of issued weapons took place before demobilization, this created conditions under which communities fear that ex-soldiers will threaten their security.
- *The fears of middle-level military and militia leaders must be addressed.* Middle-level military commanders face highly uncertain prospects in demobilization. For them, loss of status, fear of reprisals, loss of income flows and profit, and fear of prosecution can mean non-cooperation or a return to arms.
- *At the level of the individual soldier, given the risks of reprisals or revenge and the uncertainties surrounding the loss of their previous role and of employment, the security concerns of ex-combatants warrant attention.* Successful approaches combine poverty alleviation and training programmes which allow ex-soldiers to associate for their collective interest in self-help development projects. The spectre of unemployment looms large for people who have known nothing but fighting for an extended period.
- *Women former combatants will have particular needs, often facing stigma or social sanction for having departed from prescribed gender roles.* 'Re-entry' to society will have specific problems, and the need for training and employment options will be acute. The same applies to under-aged ex-combatants who may have killed on command in the same community that they are expected to return to. These groups may not even come forward as ex-combatants to benefit from formal demobilization programmes (e.g. in Aceh in 2006), which calls for sensitive community outreach and long-term work on women's rights, instead.
- *Basic policing and community security will need to be reconstituted on the basis of a service rather than militaristic behaviour.* Probably the only way in which the interests of these key participants in the war can be met is to ensure them a fairly similar role in a reconstructed army or police. Vetting procedures are essential. Demobilization of the middle-level military elite should be considered in conjunction with an overall strategy for transitional justice (such as amnesty-for-truth deals) before new roles are considered.

J. 'Kayode Fayemi (see the study in Volume II) argues that, if post-conflict security sector reconstruction is to be effective and sustainable, it should be part of a multidimensional approach, with linkages from humanitarian relief through transitional measures for rehabilitation to long-term development. He points to factors which appear to be central to securing peace in the aftermath of conflicts: an effective and sustainable ceasefire-cum-peace agreement; transitional, political and constitutional arrangements with capacity to reorder power relations and guarantee inclusion and access to the wider population (mechanisms for addressing grievances that

could reignite conflict); functioning public-sector institutions that are capable of providing citizens with their basic needs, especially safety and security; economic development aimed at addressing the grievances that produced or exacerbated conflict in the first place; and post-conflict mechanisms to address human rights violations.

Fayemi's study, based specifically on Liberia and Sierra Leone, gives graphic insights into the practical and social dilemmas in demobilization and security sector reform. For example, the UN Mission in Liberia (UNMIL) originally calculated that there were 38,000 fighters to be disarmed, but the disarmament and demobilization phase dealt with 103,019 ex-combatants. Prospects for 'reintegration' hinge on access to training and jobs, uncertainties about opportunity and resettlement, and the state of flux-as civil–military relations reconfigure after a negotiated settlement. In addition to this, Fayemi argues that the implementation of peace agreements is often complicated by 'the facts that civil–military relations are in a state of flux rather than in a post-bellum phase (ceasefire agreements notwithstanding) and that changes are occurring in varied political contexts, with their own local dynamics and challenges, and incorporating different prospects of utilizing peace agreements as the basis for the development of democratic norms and controls'.

2.5. Power Sharing After War

From Macedonia to Sri Lanka, from Bosnia to Burundi, from Cambodia to the DRC, it is difficult to envisage a post-war political settlement today that does not in some way offer guarantees to all the major elements of society that they will be assured some permanent political representation, decision-making power, or autonomous territory in post-war governance. Power sharing is an approach to crafting democratic political institutions that assure all major interests in society—such as ethnic, national or religious groups—of a place in the structures and decision-making processes of governance. Ostensibly, power-sharing solutions are designed to marry principles of democracy with the need for conflict management in deeply divided societies. Power sharing involves a wide array of political arrangements—usually embodied in the constitution—in which the principal segments of society are guaranteed a place, and influence, in governance.

Comprehensive peace agreements in war-torn societies often include power sharing as an essential element of a strategy to create the institutional arrangements for future conflict to be peacefully managed through democratic institutions.

> It is difficult to envisage a post-war political settlement today that does not in some way offer guarantees to all the major elements of society that they will be assured some permanent political representation, decision-making power, or autonomous territory in post-war governance. Power sharing is an approach to crafting democratic political institutions that assure all major interests in society of a place in the structures and decision-making processes of governance.

• *Negotiation for conflict management.* First, peace agreements are the product of negotiation. Settlements in internal conflicts reflect the convergence point of the parties at the negotiating table among their preferences for new rules, structures or institutions, to constitute the post-war peace. Waterman (1993: 292) argues that 'civil wars are conflicts over political order' and settlements in them entail the 're-creation of the conditions for a viable, common political order'. Importantly, settlements do not end conflict; they are simply agreements to continue bargaining under consensually defined rules of interaction.

• *Interests and expectations.* Second, power-sharing settlements reflect the interests and expectations of the parties, not an abstract idea of what the 'best' form of power sharing may be. In negotiations, parties formulate their positions based on their expectations of how the structure of the new institutions will serve their interests; they exercise 'analytical imagination' about the costs and benefits of alternative institutions, such as the electoral system. (For more on this approach to analysing the origins of power-sharing agreements, see Sisk 1995 and du Toit 2001.) Therefore, settlements do not end conflicts; they are *promises* to end conflicts by creating new rules of the game to which all parties at the table can agree. The operative concept here is that the parties engage in 'institutional choice'.

• *Temporary or permanent?* Third, power-sharing settlements in internal conflicts can be either 'interim' or 'final'. In interim settlements, parties are able to arrive at some basis for reconstituting normal politics but cannot agree on, or prefer to defer, highly sensitive or unresolved issues. Interim settlements are usually partial agreements, whereas final settlements purport to be comprehensive in scope. One example of an interim agreement which has not seen a happy period of implementation is the 1993 Declaration of Principles on Interim Self-Government Arrangements (the Oslo Agreement) in the Israeli–Palestinian dispute. In contrast, the 1995 Dayton agreement (the General Framework Agreement for Peace in Bosnia and Herzegovina) is wide-ranging, but it is so final in its terms that it is widely criticized as too inflexible and insufficiently dynamic.

• *Systems of incentives.* Fourth, institutions establish systems of incentives. All settlements seek to formalize patterns of interaction and in this respect they seek to establish new incentive structures in their own right, resolving some of the uncertainty about the new rules of the game that characterize earlier phases of the peace process. In many cases, they are package proposals that resolve multiple issues simultaneously by linking them. Similarly, many of the more celebrated settlements in recent years have featured 'democratization as conflict resolution', explicitly marrying the goals of conflict amelioration with the introduction of competitive, multiparty politics.

Fayemi in Volume II examines the Lomé Peace Agreement for Sierra Leone (1999) and the Accra Peace Agreement for Liberia (2003) with an eye to representation and implementation, not unlike the factors considered in relation to Sri Lanka above (see box 5.1). He considers that the Accra agreement took account of previous experience (Sierra Leone 1996 and Liberia 1997) in which elections had served as conflict triggers for those excluded from the process. The Accra agreement thus pursued a transitional government option.

The 1999 Lomé agreement for Sierra Leone has been widely criticized as having set aside grave concerns about human rights violations by the rebel Revolutionary United Front (RUF), which had perpetrated extreme atrocities in the civil war. For example, the United Nations did not accept the amnesty provisions of the accord, especially the concessions provided to RUF leader Foday Sankoh. Eventually, both Sankoh (who passed away in prison) and former Liberian President Charles Taylor whose government signed the Accra Agreement were indicted by a United Nations Special Court for gross violations of human rights and crimes against humanity.

> **Wholly foreign-brokered peace processes, as an approach to building stable and democratic civil–security relations, remain inherently problematic.**

Box 5.3: Peacemaking in West Africa: Comparing Settlement Terms

The Lomé Peace Agreement, Sierra Leone, 1999	The Accra Peace Agreement, Liberia, 2003
• Signed between the government of Sierra Leone and the RUF; witnessed by select civil society organization (the Inter-Religion Council)	• Signed between the government of Liberia, LURD, MODEL, political parties and civil society representatives
• Power-sharing agreement between major parties to conflict: 4 cabinets positions and 4 non-cabinet positions to each; chairmanship of Strategic Mineral Commission to RUF	• Power-sharing agreement: 5 cabinet positions each to the government of Liberia, LURD and MODEL; 6 cabinet positions to political parties and civil society
• Elected president continues in office with vice-president to rebel leader, Foday Sankoh	• Elected president replaced with an independent chairman of transitional government and no key positions for rebel leaders
• Existing legislature remains in office	

The Lomé Peace Agreement, Sierra Leone, 1999	The Accra Peace Agreement, Liberia, 2003
• Amnesty provision • Vague agenda for security sector reform • Transitional justice provisions • No timetable for implementation RUF = Revolutionary United Front	• New Transitional Legislative Assembly with 76 members: 12 seats for each faction and 18 seats to political parties and civil society • No amnesty provision • Detailed provisions for security sector reforms • Similar transitional justice provisions • Timetable for implementation LURD = Liberians United for Reconciliation and Democracy MODEL = Movement for Democracy in Liberia

Unlike Sierra Leone (1996) and Liberia (1997), where elections served as conflict triggers for those excluded from the process, the Accra agreement also took account of this and decided to pursue a transitional-government option.

The difference is that the Accra Peace Agreement was driven largely by Liberians and the regional body, ECOWAS [the Economic Community of West African States]. This is a pertinent lesson: wholly foreign-brokered peace processes, as an approach to building stable and democratic civil-security relations, remain inherently problematic. ... The assumption that every post-conflict situation must produce agreements that follow a set pattern of actions—humanitarian relief, elections, disinvestment of state-sector companies and a reduction in security expenditures—or a shift from the military to policing is too generic.

Source: Extracts from the study by J. 'Kayode Fayemi in Volume II.

The Accra Peace Agreement of 2003 is unusual in that both political parties and civil society representatives took part in the signing. The power-sharing arrangement included cabinet positions for these parties, and no key positions went to former rebel leaders. This stands in sharp contrast with more conventional practice of negotiations (and outcomes in political power holding) being confined to the main 'belligerent' parties. While 'Who speaks for civil society?' is a valid question, the pattern of the agreement reached will be considerably influenced by those immediately around the table.

In application, however, a *power-sharing arrangement functions on the basis of consensus.* Needless to say, in a post-war environment that is characterized, almost by definition, by low levels of democratic culture and practice and by high levels of mutual mistrust of stakeholders at different levels of governance, consensus does not often reflect shared visions or objectives, but is rather a kind of lowest common denominator—what remains as common ground when all mutual safeguards have been applied. Thereafter, governance is more 'reactive' than 'proactive', often reduced to applying vetoes to measures proposed by the 'other entity' or 'constituent people'.

For Liberia, a trusteeship under ECOWAS and the UN was considered, as was a UN trusteeship, but the transitional government was the option chosen. Every war, every agreement will be unique and must be seen in context. The very different war in Bosnia and Herzegovina resulted in an international administration with no clear exit date, and the institutionalization of a new territorial 'status quo' reflecting forced migration and ethnic delineations. Vital decisions taken at national level have consistently been the result of international pressure, rather than the manifestation of any genuine consensus among the leaderships of the two entities of which Bosnia and Herzegovina is now made up (see box 5.4 and the annex). This is also true of the 2002 constitutional amendments aimed at ensuring that all three constituent ethnic groups are represented in the governments and parliaments of both entities.

In the long run, particularly if peace is maintained, if the resurgence of conflict becomes unlikely and if fear and mutual mistrust among ordinary people are gradually replaced by the acceptance of coexistence and of some level of cooperation, the multiple safeguards built in to the power-sharing agreement will appear unnecessarily rigid, burdensome and even undemocratic in as much as they emphasize collective, ethnic rather than individual rights.

No one denies that the Dayton accords have been highly effective in achieving their main purpose in 1995, that is, in stopping the war and preventing its resurgence. They have offered the belligerent ethnic leaderships and their traumatized communities some assurance that their autonomy and their collective rights will be protected. On the other hand, ten years after the peace was signed, the complicated tripartite power-sharing structure of governance is increasingly seen as ineffective, economically counterproductive, fiscally unsustainable and even, by some, at odds with the European Charter of Human Rights given the fact that it prevents citizens from enjoying full civic and political rights on the entire territory of the country.

The annex to this chapter summarizes the features of the two main forms of power sharing—consociationalism and the integrative approach.

> **Box 5.4: Ten Years After Dayton: Overview of the Effects of the Power-sharing Arrangements of the Bosnian Constitution**
>
> The signing on 14 December 1995 of the General Framework Agreement for Peace in Bosnia and Herzegovina marked the end of the extremely violent conflict that had ravaged the country for more than three years. The document, also referred to

as the Dayton agreement, is more than a simple peace accord since it also contains in its annex 4 the constitution of the Republic of Bosnia-Herzegovina.

Based on the Dayton constitution, Bosnia and Herzegovina has three 'constituent peoples'—Bosniacs, Croats and Serbs. The constitution also mentions 'Others' as well as 'citizens of Bosnia and Herzegovina', but the latter two categories are not included as such in any of the multiple and exclusively ethnic balances that define the country's intricate institutional make-up at national, intermediary and local level.

In terms of governance structure, Bosnia and Herzegovina is an 'asymmetrical' federal republic composed of two highly autonomous entities: the Federation of Bosnia and Herzegovina, being the entity of the Bosniacs and Croats, and the Republika Srpska, being the entity of the Serbs. Both entities have municipalities as first-level local institutions. Furthermore, the Federation is composed of ten cantons as intermediate governance institutions between the municipalities and the entity level.

On the other hand, the Republika Srpska is highly centralized without any intermediate governance institution between the municipal council and the entity government. The state and the two entities have their respective presidencies, governments, and legislative bodies composed of two chambers. At the level of the Republic of Bosnia and Herzegovina, the presidency is a tripartite rotating body whose members, of course, belong each to one of the three main constituent peoples.

The political system is also different in the two entities: while the Federation has a parliamentary system, the Republika Srpska has a presidential one. There are also three types of citizenship: the citizenship of Bosnia and Herzegovina and the citizenships of each of the two entities.

In terms of responsibilities, 'all governmental functions not expressly assigned . . . to the institutions of Bosnia and Herzegovina shall be those of the entities'. Yet in some domains responsibilities overlap. For example, although foreign policy, foreign trade policy and customs policy are said to be responsibilities of the institutions of Bosnia and Herzegovina (federal level), the entities are nevertheless explicitly authorized to 'establish parallel relationships with neighbouring states' and to 'enter into agreement with other states and international organizations'.

The Dayton agreement, as often observed, satisfied the minimum requirements of each party to the conflict while giving full satisfaction to none. As a rather extreme example of post-conflict power sharing, it highlights the virtues, the limits and the negative side effects of such solutions.

The Effects of Power Sharing as Enshrined in the Dayton Accords
Critics of the Dayton-based power-sharing constitution see its detrimental effects in the following in particular.

- It has 'frozen' a highly dysfunctional system of governance.
- It promotes ethnic and local allegiances and clientelism rather than accountability.
- It prevents the establishment and consolidation of a responsible and professional public administration.
- It has detrimental effects on economic reform and discourages foreign investors.
- It has become an obstacle to the reconciliation process since the power-sharing elites tend to perceive all cross-ethnic or non-ethnic initiatives as a direct threat to their power.
- Finally, it has 'depoliticized' and 'demoralized' a significant part of the citizenry: people are losing faith in democracy and the hope that the current situation can be changed through elections.

Bosnia, according to these critics, should be called a 'tripartite ethnocracy' rather than a democracy.

The 'democratic deficit' of the Dayton process is further enhanced by the extensive powers of the High Representative of the International Community. His office can veto candidates for ministerial positions, impose legislation and create new institutions.

If such a strong authority was seen to be indispensable in the early years of the implementation of the Dayton accords in order to discipline the spoilers and fight their systematic obstructionism, today it is also seen as having seriously undermined local ownership of the process and the accountability of elected representatives at different levels.

Voices demanding constitutional change are becoming stronger both within the country and in the international community. Strengthening the viability and effectiveness of the state in Bosnia and Herzegovina has become a key objective of the international community and a strong demand addressed to local decision makers. The outcome of the process is still highly uncertain. Yet it seems quite evident already that the ten years of peace have made the kind of pure and rigid power-sharing agreement that is incarnated in the Dayton accords quite obsolete—an obstacle to rather than a catalyst of the further democratization of society.

Goran Fejic and Kajsa Eriksson, International IDEA

Lessons for Power Sharing

Ideally, power sharing will work best when it can, over time, wither away. Whether in South Africa, Northern Ireland, Bosnia or Lebanon, in the immediate term formal power sharing has been a necessary confidence-building device to ensure that all groups with the capacity to spoil a peace settlement are included in the institutions and given influence in decision making. Over time, however, post-war societies need to move beyond the mutual hostage-taking that a guaranteed place at the decision-making table implies, the immobilism it inevitably creates, and the construction of post-war societies around fixed and unyielding social boundaries such as heavily politicized ethnicity, religion or language. *Integrative* power-sharing solutions have an inherent advantage if they can be achieved. Putting it simply, when successful, they engineer a moderation-seeking centripetal 'spin' to the political system, one that allows for ethnicity but encourages political alliances that transcend identity differences and promote fluid coalitions.

One method for achieving a subtle but steady move towards a more integrative power sharing is to keep the process of constitution making going well into the post-war order. Peace agreements cannot freeze in time the conditions that prevailed at the end of the war. Peace settlements need to end the war with certainty, but they also need to be imbued with a certain set of provisions for flexibility, continued bargaining, and opportunity for amendment. They need an incentive structure that encourages ongoing bargaining, moderation and conflict management (Rothchild 1997). A second practical way to begin is to purposefully manipulate the electoral system to provide new incentives for moderates to coalesce across group lines, as suggested in chapter 3. Electoral systems should be designed to give politicians real incentives to motivate moving beyond a perhaps natural instinct to play the 'communal' card in order to attain power (Human Rights Watch 1995). Yet a third method is to engender cooperation by designing territorial divisions of power within a country, eschewing territorial boundaries arranged around lines of identity such as ethnicity or religion.

None of these methods will ensure success. Institutional choice and design, no matter how careful, cannot resolve some of the inherent commitment problems that occur in post-war societies; rules on paper cannot address the deep-seated fear that opponents will win in elections or in parliament what they had not won on the battlefield or in the streets. But with a willingness to escape from violence,

> A power-sharing arrangement functions on the basis of consensus. In a post-war environment that is characterized, almost by definition, by low levels of democratic culture and practice and by high levels of mutual mistrust of stakeholders at different levels of governance, consensus does not often reflect shared visions or objectives, but is rather a kind of lowest common denominator and risks 'freezing' divisive allegiances. Ideally, power sharing will work best when it can, over time, wither away.

> One method for achieving a subtle but steady move towards a more integrative power sharing is to keep the process of constitution making going well into the post-war order. The electoral system can be used to purposefully manipulate the electoral system to provide new incentives to moderates to coalesce across group lines; and cooperation can be engendered by designing multi-ethnic territorial divisions of power within a country, eschewing practices of 'ethnic federalism'.

the right set of power-sharing institutions—one that carefully matches problems to solutions—can provide incentives to tip the balance from war to peace, from rigid political divisions to a more fluid democracy in which moderation trumps extremism.

2.6. Creating a Democratic Framework: Credible Election Processes and Their Meaning

Whether in war-torn Bosnia following the Dayton agreement, in fragile, newly emergent states such as Timor-Leste, or following protracted wars such as Sierra Leone's, elections are used as highly visible arenas in which to restore some semblance of legitimate governance. In El Salvador between 1984 and 1987 debate revolved around whether negotiations should precede elections or whether elections themselves would be the vehicle for a political outcome, with the FMLN participating as a political party. This was in contrast to the course of events in Guatemala, where Torres-Rivas observed that 'efforts towards peace turned out to be a consequence of the process of democratization' (quoted in Azpuru 1999: 99).

As described in chapter 2, one of the most vexing challenges facing policy makers in the international community, and protagonists in societies deeply divided by internal conflict, is the nature of immediate post-war elections. From Namibia in 1989 to Afghanistan in late 2004, there have been many instances in which after a civil war a new government is inaugurated in first-ever elections. Although each situation is unique, it is possible to anticipate factors which will influence whether elections may be relatively successful as a turning point to peace, and when they might serve instead to stimulate new fears, provoke new violence, and set back a peace process rather than advancing it. Among the common challenges are the following.

- *Trust among the protagonists for power is likely to be low* because often there is no external force (such as UN peace operation) capable of enforcing the outcome of elections: parties lack a sense of credible commitment by their opponents to the peace deal and fear cheating or rejection of legitimate election results.
- *Post-war elections feature high stakes for the winners*, particularly in situations where there are 'lootable' commodities or rents: loss of power may endanger economic fortunes.
- Post-war environments may be vulnerable to the *emergence of wily elites* who will mobilize on divisive nationalist, ethnic or racial themes in their quest for power.
- *After civil wars, political parties are often weak* and the political party system is either underdeveloped or untested: there is a high degree of uncertainty regarding the relative strengths of the factions, which heightens tensions and fears about winning and losing.
- *Civil society is weak and populations are traumatized* by the effects of war: weak civil society and affected populations are less able to stand up to political forces led by extremists or ideologues, and displaced persons and refugees are often uncertain as to positions and procedures.
- *Basic state capacities are weak*, with governments often unable to ensure proper preparation for elections or to meet other higher-level human needs, rendering

elections somewhat surreal as voters vote in conditions that are otherwise fraught with insecurity and amid destitution.

Box 5.5: Post-war Elections: Three Types

Elections under UN Security Council-legitimated transitional administrations—Namibia (1990), Bosnia (1996) and Kosovo (October 2004), and the Cyprus referendums (May 2004).

Elections under other international occupation—Iraq (2005), 'Démocratie au bout des bayonettes!'.

Elections under negotiated settlements—South Africa (1994), Northern Ireland (1998). Both feature pre-election power-sharing pacts. As South African negotiator Kader Asmal said of the 1994 vote, 'We knew the results before the vote was counted'.

Experiences with post-war elections lead to an appreciation of three key areas of concern about these types of processes.

• *Sequencing.* When, following the end of fighting, should elections be held? Most observers agree that the November 1996 elections in Bosnia, just a year after the guns fell silent, were held too soon. But waiting too long can also be problematic as interim or transitional administrations inherently lack legitimacy. It might also make sense to consider local elections first, and then move to national elections, rather than the now somewhat standard practice of sequencing national elections first and having local elections thereafter. In other situations, however, local elections might have deleterious results for peacemaking; each situation needs to be carefully considered for how the sequencing of elections in the post-war environment may affect the prospects for peace and for subsequent democratization.

• *Electoral dispute resolution.* Procedures for handling electoral disputes through impartial, efficient, legally valid and widely accepted mechanisms are crucial even in the most advanced democracies. Accidents happen, mistakes are made, and trust is low: the institutions and procedures for dispute resolution need to be established and tested early in the electoral process, such that by the time voting day arrives there is trust in the fairness of the mediation and arbitration process. Without such institutions and mechanisms for dispute resolution, parties may well turn to violent means to press their interests in an election dispute, as happened in Ethiopia in 2005.

• *Engendering trust: election observation and verification.* Election observation means evaluations by internal and external neutral organizations of all aspects of the electoral process. Verification is more extensive and occurs when such organizations actually oversee and verify that the electoral management body has run the election fairly. The role of international observers has emerged in the 1990s and 2000s as an essential element in post-war elections precisely because domestic observer capacities are weak. Extensive electoral observation in post-war elections is a necessary component if the results are to be accepted both internally and externally as the result of a process that is free and fair in both procedural and substantive terms.

Central to the debate on democracy's relationship to conflict management is the challenge of electoral processes in societies that are prone to, involved in, or emerging from violent conflict. In many instances—such as the 1992 presidential elections in Angola, or in the run-up to post-intervention elections in Iraq in 2005—elections and their outcomes can be a strong stimulant for violence by those who expect to lose. Likewise, for incumbents in office who seek to maintain a grip on power, the use of violence and intimidation to ensure a win at the polls is an all-too-common practice; in the run-up to the parliamentary elections of March 2005 in Zimbabwe, opposition leaders were arrested and tortured, the press was intimidated and international observers were kept away. It is for this reason that, in the community of practitioners promoting international peacemaking and peace building, there is widespread concern about the nature, timing and administration of electoral processes as an instrument for conflict management.

Surveying developments in the context of Southern Africa, Khabele Matlosa (Volume II) argues that post-conflict elections must only be held if parties have signed a peace agreement and have devised an achievable peace, harmony and reconciliation programme. 'This peace and reconciliation programme must also be accompanied by the signing of a . . . code of conduct for all the key actors especially political parties. It is a gamble to hold elections under conditions of violent conflict when parties have not agreed to peaceful conduct of politics and a process of reconciliation and have not signed some form of a code of conduct . . . as the Angolan situation so amply demonstrates. There is a dire need to provide adequate time for preparations for elections after armed conflict.'

> There is widespread concern about the nature, timing and administration of electoral processes as an instrument for conflict management. In many instances elections and their outcomes can be a strong stimulant for violence by those who expect to lose or are seeking to maintain a grip on power.

National elections after war are not a symbolic completion of a process and an exit strategy for international actors. Rather, they are the beginning for a national framework with implications for all of the war-affected population. They may be formal exercises to construct new leadership in high office, but also hold practical meaning in terms of the population census, legal registration and entitlements for civilians whose lives have been severely disrupted.

> Post-conflict elections must only be held if parties have signed a peace agreement and have devised an achievable peace, harmony and reconciliation programme. There must be a functional state structure before elections are conducted after armed conflict. Demobilization of troops or warring factions and the integration of militias into a national army and/or police force, as well as peacekeeping operations, are vital before elections can be held.

Box 5.6: Elections and Conflict in Southern Africa: Key Points

There are multivariate preconditions if elections are to successfully anchor and sustain democracy and peace after armed conflict.

1. *All belligerent parties must commit themselves to peace, harmony and reconciliation.* To this end a peace accord and a clearly defined reconciliation and political healing programme are required, as both the Mozambican and the South African situations vividly illustrate.

2. *Post-conflict elections must be held only if the parties have signed a peace agreement and have devised an achievable peace, harmony and reconciliation programme.* This peace and reconciliation programme must also be accompanied by the signing of a code of conduct for all the key actors, especially political parties.

3. *There must be a functional state structure before elections are conducted after armed conflict.* If the very existence of the state is in doubt, as is the case with many failed states such as Somalia, international assistance probably cannot fill the gap, and elections cannot bring political stability or resolve conflicts.

4. *International assistance and external democracy promotion are highly valuable in post-conflict elections.* War-torn countries such as Angola and the DRC have severely ravaged economies and a constrained resource and production base from which to finance electoral processes. The involvement of international observers contributes immensely to the credibility of the elections and the acceptance of their outcomes by the political parties concerned and the electorate at large. Moreover, it reduces the probability of large-scale fraud and cheating.

5. *Demobilization of troops or warring factions and the integration of militias into a national army and/or police force, as well as peacekeeping operations, are vital before elections can be held.* This process of demilitarization of politics is crucial in transforming the culture of politics of violence and coercion and embracing the politics of dialogue and consensus.

Although the demilitarization and integration of armed formations has been relatively successful in Namibia, South Africa, Zimbabwe and Mozambique, it has not been successful in Angola and the DRC. This in part explains why elections have not really deepened and consolidated political stability and democratic governance in Angola, and this pattern is likely to be repeated in the DRC after its election of 2006.

6. *Prior to elections which follow violent conflict, returning refugees and displaced persons must be settled and allowed sufficient time to register as electors.* Refugees

and displaced persons are often the worst victims of civil wars. Their active participation in elections is needed to strengthen the peace process.

7. *The clearing of landmines and the banning of military supplies from external sources are also important preconditions for elections after armed conflict.* This was very important in the cases of Angola and Mozambique, two countries whose opposing factions have received massive amounts of external military supplies and which are also heavily mined.

Landmines harm the population years and years after hostilities have ceased and make life miserable for ordinary people in the villages. The intense fear of landmines among rural people triggers migration to the urban areas. The population pressure in Luanda in Angola and Maputo in Mozambique has been caused more by war than by normal rural–urban migration.

8. *Elections after violent conflict must be run and administered by credible, autonomous and competent institutions that are not in any way linked to any of the belligerent parties in a partisan fashion.* To this end, the establishment of independent electoral commissions is essential.

It is also crucial that the rules of state administration and electoral administration are agreed upon as a basis for all parties to accept the outcome of the elections. In this manner, the view of politics as a zero-sum game is likely to be replaced by one that conceives of it as a positive-sum process. 'It must be recognized that in a democracy winners and losers are partners and not enemies who must destroy each other'... .

9. *The institutionalization of intra-party democracy is also crucial, so that the democratic practices and cultures within parties will help them to see the value of dialogue and politics of consensus when dealing with their adversaries.* It has been found that in the majority of African states the political parties lack internal democracy, and this in part accounts for the current disintegration and fragmentation of opposition parties.

Although the incumbent rulers work hard to undermine and weaken the opposition and the electoral system, weak opposition parties are also hindered by the First Past The Post (FPTP) system and internal leadership squabbles, not necessarily based on ideological or policy differences. All these factors have wreaked havoc upon the opposition parties in Southern Africa.

10. *There is a need for constitutional reform in countries that have experienced a violent conflict before elections are held* so that belligerent parties engage in dialogue and negotiation around a new social contract regarding the form of state,

Finally, election processes carry diverse meanings and implications for the human security of populations who have suffered during protracted war, devastation and displacement. The right to vote may represent a shift in demonstrable rights, voice or participation, as in Afghanistan in 2004, or an affirmation of a new era in political leadership, as in post-Suharto Indonesia since 1999 or Liberia in 2006. Elections may be an opportunity to send a message to the international community and to the immediate national leadership, as in both Palestine and Haiti in 2006.

Ter Horst (Volume II) relates how post-war 1992 Salvadorian legislation regulating political parties did not cover the essential, basic needs of a modern, democratic state; a large part of the population was excluded from the electoral register, particularly in the regions formerly controlled by the opposition. The armed forces, directly and through their security apparatus, had previously influenced the preparation and outcome of elections, and access to the media was restricted. 'Intolerance was the norm among political adversaries, and politically-motivated assassinations increased during electoral campaigns.' Changes in electoral oversight structures and regulations, a new election code and extensive voter registration extended the right to vote to those who had previously been excluded.

Currently in Sudan and the DRC, negotiated power-sharing agreements and interim governments are aiming for elections to validate new political consolidation and democratization processes. Sudan's Comprehensive Peace Agreement is between the national government in Khartoum and the south Sudan government, following extended civil war. In the DRC, after what has been referred to as Africa's 'world war' (due to the extensive involvement of neighbouring states and numbers dead—an estimated 4 million), the president shares power with vice-presidents representing former rebel opposition groups. Massive population transfers are under way in and between the DRC and south Sudan as thousands return after being uprooted by war. Voter registration for many means official recognition of existence and validity, entitlement to food aid or assistance, and permission to travel freely and gain the rights of a citizen.

Box 5.7: What Elections Mean: Identities, Return and Reintegration in the DRC

A strongly-held conventional wisdom holds that the purpose of elections is for people to vote for the person or party who they think will furnish them with a brighter future. Yet in some post-conflict situations the process of getting registered to vote may be as important as the voting itself when it comes to assuring or re-establishing people's day-to-day access to security and services.

In the DRC, for example, national identity cards had last been issued by the state in the early 1990s; the best most people were subsequently able to obtain was an 'attestation of loss of identity document' written by their local administrator. In the conflict zones of eastern DRC this route to an identity as a Congolese citizen was seen as being open to abuse by factions bringing in fighters from neighbouring countries from the late 1990s onwards, and these attestations were widely viewed as of dubious standing.

When voter registration cards were issued in a whirlwind registration campaign from mid-2005 onwards, applicants had several possible ways by which to prove their identity. For those who succeeded in doing so, the cards also doubled as legally recognized temporary identity documents, and thus quickly became the most valid and legitimate means of establishing juridical identity and citizenship.

Those who were unable to register to vote, however, were substantially disadvantaged, as was evident in Kinshasa where, within weeks of registration closing, there were reports of people without a voter card finding themselves being severely harassed by the authorities. In some eastern parts of the DRC, with roadblocks to be negotiated every few kilometres, the lack of a voter registration card risked becoming even more of an ongoing liability.

There were, though, many reasons for people failing to register: the registration campaign allowed only three weeks per province—and many of DRC's provinces are larger than Rwanda, Burundi and Uganda combined; the DRC's several million internally displaced were likely to have lost their documentation at the time of flight; many who had suffered multiple displacements over the years were unlikely to be able to find five witnesses from their host population; and for the hundreds of thousands of refugees in nine neighbouring countries, the three-week registration period was an impossibly small window of opportunity within which to organize to return home after years in exile. Thus the registration process risked excluding some of the very people whose return and participation in the elections would be a key indicator of a successful post-conflict transition.

The DRC case thus highlights that elections, and the prior registration process, both of which appear to be very specific, time-bound and forward-looking events, are in reality also key indicators of success or failure in re-establishing the claim to citizenship—and its concomitant minimum guarantees of security—of those displaced by conflict.

Chris Dolan,
Director, Refugee Law Centre, University of Makerere,
Kampala, Uganda

2.7. Democratic Practice and Peace Building

This chapter opened with a consideration of democracies and civil war, citing the case of Sri Lanka where the Indo-Sri Lanka Accord of 1987 was intended to pave the way for limited devolution through provincial councils via constitutional amendment. With insufficient public information and a widespread perception of foreign interference, a rational measure was badly received and never took root fully. The gap between centralized power and outlying populations, between high politics and the local level, remains wide. The 'top–down and bottom–up' spheres are both determinants of eventual substantive democratization. Khabele Matlosa points out in his survey of Southern Africa that local government elections are as important as general elections and, in much the same way, are as conflict-ridden.

Whereas much of the conflict around general elections is primarily among political parties, the principal conflict in local government elections revolves around the power struggle between modern and traditional institutions of governance, although inter-party strife also marks local-level conflicts. Matlosa points out that, although many of the Southern African Development Community (SADC) countries have embraced the idea and practice of holding legislative and presidential elections on a fairly regular basis (bar three—Angola, the DRC and Swaziland), almost all of them exhibit a poor record in terms of regular local government elections. 'Devolution of power to local areas in the form of democratic local government is yet to be institutionalized in the SADC region. This still remains one of the major challenges of democratic consolidation in the region and the entire African continent' (Matlosa, Volume II).

The reconstruction of local politics as an integral part of reconstructing the state, and interdependence between local and central authority, will impact on the viability of the state, its governance and its capacity for delivery to the population. In reality, for many post-war settings there is no culture of representative accountability for elected legislators, who may not visit constituents until campaign time. There are no systems for conveying information or accessing resources; basic infrastructure is non-existent or under reconstruction; and new formal democratic institutions may sit uneasily alongside other informal structures of power or authority.

There is increasing interest in systems of local governance that have functioned during war and are respected and responsive to the needs of the people. Such strengths may be built upon and not undermined. An example would be the experience of local wartime democracy in the Nuba mountains. SPLA 'democratization' can be traced back to 1992 when a Nuba commander convened an Advisory Council with 200 delegates. This became the Regional Liberation Council and met annually to decide policy, developing civic structures and a civil administration.

Jarat Chopra and Tanja Hohe argue that the 'front line for international interventions that exercise any degree of political authority in transition has proved to be at the level of local administration. Here, the Western-style paradigm of state building, which is preoccupied with forming a national executive, legislature, and judiciary, confronts resilient traditional structures, socially legitimate powerholders, abusive warlords out to win, or coping mechanisms communities rely on under conflict conditions. Options for the establishment or reconstruction of governing institutions seem stark: either reinforce the status quo and build on it, further empowering the already strong; or replace altogether what exists with a new administrative order':

> In the past, in Somalia and Cambodia, and later in Kosovo and East Timor, interveners invariably followed the line of least resistance, rendering themselves irrelevant in terms of the impact they had where the overwhelming majority of the population lives. The result was a social and political reality that developed by itself, regardless of the size of the international presence or the scope of the mission's mandate. ... Instead, what may be feasible is a longer-term transition in which space is provided for local voices to be expressed and for communities to get directly involved in the evolution of their own cultural or political foundations, as part of a gradual integration into the national state apparatus (Chopra and Hohe 2004: 289).

This argument calls for a more in-depth understanding of local perceptions and human security realities. It implies a need for more understanding of the meaning and possible limitations of elections, in order to find ways to make them more relevant. Individuals may turn out to vote but still have other sources of moral and/or political authority, quite different from those that the ballot gives them.

> A democratically elected powerholder may be recognized internationally though not locally, since the voting process was unrelated to beliefs regarding sources of political legitimacy. The problem is more acute when voting for distant national representatives than for more familiar local leaders. The result can be a recycled conflict between what the people and the rest of the world understand as the rightful powerholder (Chopra and Hohe 2004: 289).

Many international participants in peace-building missions are wary of 'traditional structures' due to restrictions on the roles and rights of women which they may carry over from previous times. But cultural forms are not fixed, and societies can be encouraged to adapt and change in keeping with what women as part of the local population want. Sceptics voiced misgivings about the Loya Jirga set in place by the

Bonn Agreement of 2001, which created an interim administration in Afghanistan and a timetable for setting up a future, elected government. In the time-honoured manner, representatives were chosen at the local level, by *shuras*—groups of elders considered to represent the respected or powerful families in the region. Given the fragile and unique circumstances of Afghanistan, this was considered to be the only way to give legitimacy to any kind of the post-war process. Provision was made for political, gender-based and ethnic inequalities to be dealt with by a commission which allocated seats for civil society leaders, women, university faculty, religious scholars, trade groups and other professionals.

IDEA's 2005 study on *Democracy and United Nations Peace-building at the Local Level: Lessons Learned* points to the importance of informal structures, such as peace committees which take a major role in providing resilience and leadership during war (see box 5.8).

Box 5.8: Key Questions on Local Security and Democracy

1. What has been the experience on the establishment of security at the local level? Who has been the responsible agent for the legitimate use of force at the local level?

2. Has there been a (spoiler) challenge to military authority emanating from a local context (e.g. a local warlord, gang or aggrieved party)? How were the challenges dealt with?

3. What are the principal challenges to human security for local communities? (e.g., who are the most vulnerable populations and how have their needs/vulnerabilities been addressed?). What outlets and futures are there for young people and ex-combatants?

4. Where are the sources of moral authority and leadership to be found, within religious or social settings not included within the scope of conventional politics?

5. How was the DDR process handled and by whom? Which agents—international peacekeepers, national authorities, local communities—have been most effective in the DDR process?

6. Have there been other sources of threats to human security at the local level? For example, has any given community seen significant violations of human rights in the peace-building period?

7. What has been the experience with the creation of security by the post-war state (government), both military and in terms of policing, at the local level? Which approach has been most or least successful in establishing post-war security?

---

8. To what extent have measures to promote human rights—monitoring, assessment, responses—been put into place? Which approaches have been most effective? What lessons learned are there to involve the local community in the provision of basic human security? (e.g. is there local oversight or involvement on security issues?).

9. What are the options for improving human security and human rights in this particular case? What needs to be done urgently, in the medium term, and over the long term?

Source: Adapted from the International IDEA study on *Democracy and United Nations Peace-building at the Local Level: Lessons Learned* (Sisk and Risley 2005).

Democratic practice at local level—indeed, democratization in war-torn societies—entails a rebuilding of the state in such a way that citizens are linked to governments and local level to central level, if it is to be meaningful exercise in building the peace.

This is a crucial issue area for the international community, and one which will also call for self-examination. Just as there are various ongoing sites in any context (as in the case of Sri Lanka above) for democratization, there are opportunities for laying the foundations for participation, representation and accountability. Any influx of external agencies dealing with human needs must be wary of functioning for too long as a stratum between people and the government that is meant to answer to them. Humanitarian aid and development assistance beyond the phase of immediate emergency should be examined carefully for their implications for the newly evolving (or non-existent) political order.

Peace building, then, could also more consciously embody democratic practices at earlier, post-emergency stages of development. Democracy would be seen more clearly as not equal only to elections, nor an 'add-on' at some unforeseen future date, but as a process that is started at different levels in the course of recovery after war.

> Any influx of external agencies dealing with human needs must be wary of functioning for too long as a stratum between people and the government that is meant to answer to them. Humanitarian aid and development assistance beyond the phase of immediate emergency should be examined carefully for their implications for the newly evolving (or non-existent) political order.

Annex. Power-Sharing Practices: An Overview

As discussed also in chapter 3, the power-sharing debate is relevant not only to post-war transition settings, but to states and societies as diverse as Belgium, Switzerland, Fiji, Cyprus, and others.

A long-standing misconception of power-sharing institutions is that they are all of a specific type, which for many years has been called 'consociationalism' (Lijphart 1977). The elements of this approach to power sharing are well known: grand coalitions, proportional representation, cultural autonomy or federalism, and the mutual veto. Representation is determined by success in proportional representation elections, generally waged by parties that campaign on an identity basis.

In contrast, the *integrative approach* eschews ethnic groups as the building blocks of a common society. The integrative approach seeks to build multi-ethnic political coalitions (again, usually political parties), to create incentives for political leaders to be moderate on divisive ethnic themes, and to enhance minority influence in majority decision making (Horowitz 1985).

The elements of an integrative approach include electoral systems that encourage pre-election pacts across ethnic lines, non-ethnic federalism that diffuses points of power, and public policies that promote political allegiances that transcend groups. Some suggest that integrative power sharing is superior in theory in that it seeks to foster ethnic accommodation by promoting cross-cutting interests. Others, however, argue that the use of incentives to promote conciliation will run aground when faced with deep-seated enmities that underlie ethnic disputes hardened during the course of a brutal civil war.

Table 5.a: Consociational Power Sharing

Principles	Practices	Problems
Broadly-based coalitions among ethnic political parties	Grand coalition governments	Elites may initiate conflict to bolster their power at the centre
Minority or mutual veto on matters of importance to the group	Group rights defined in constitutional terms for named ethnic, racial, religious, or cultural groups; cabinet or executive decision making may require a consensus or so-called 'concurrent majority'	Can reify ethnicity, reinforcing the divisions in society rather than promoting cross-cultural understanding
Proportionality	Proportional representation (PR) electoral system and the proposed proportional allocation of jobs, spending, representation, and participation by ethnic group leaders	PR may reflect well the divisions in society but does not provide incentives for building bridges across community lines
Group autonomy	Federalism, territorial or 'corporate'	May contain disincentives for contending groups to live peacefully together

Table 5.b: Integrative Power Sharing

Principles	Practices	Problems
Incentives for elite and mass moderation on divisive ethnic or racial themes	A president who stands for all groups and who emphasizes moderation and reconciliation (such as a Nelson Mandela)	Leaders who can rise above the fray of inter-group enmity are hard to find; they cannot be simply invented
Intra-group contestation and inter-group moderation in electoral contests	The use of vote-pooling electoral systems, such as the Single Transferable Vote (STV) or the Alternative Vote (AV)	People may be unwilling to vote for candidates which are not from their community
Minority influence, not just representation	Federalism is a way to give all minority groups access to power in various regions; the regions serve as a training ground for national-level moderates,	Political leaders and key publics may not be willing to respond to the incentives for moderation, preferring that minority representation remains token or symbolic

Although this typology presents two conceptually distinct approaches, it is clear that power-sharing options can be pieced together in a number of ways. Like any menu, levers of democratic influence can be combined to suit individual tastes. In deciding which power-sharing institutions and practices might work, there is no substitute for intimate knowledge of any given country.

In multi-ethnic Fiji, for example, a four-year expert review of the country's political system produced a set of recommendations for a recently adopted constitution that combines measures to guarantee a minimum level of traditional Fijian (as opposed to Indo-Fijian) representation in Parliament (a group building-block option) with measures to promote the formation of political alliances across group lines (an integrative option). The Fijian case is instructive precisely because the efforts of spoilers to disrupt integration along ethnic lines were only temporarily successful; as Fiji recovers from the attempted *coup d'état* of 2000, it has returned to an integrationist formula for resolving its ethnic tensions.

A glance at the power-sharing structure for Bosnia and Herzegovina, shown in table 5.c, will reveal built-in factors meaning a problematic legacy.

Table 5.c: The Republic of Bosnia and Herzegovina: An Overview of Power Sharing

- **Form of government: federal republic**
- **2 entities:**
    - the Federation of Bosnia and Herzegovina; and
    - the Republika Srpska.
- **3 constituent peoples;**
    - Bosniacs;
    - Croats; and
    - Serbs.
- **3 constitutions;**
    - 1 state constitution (annex 4 to the peace accord, the General Framework Agreement for Peace in Bosnia and Herzegovina);
    - 1 entity constitution for the Federation of Bosnia and Herzegovina; and
    - 1 entity constitution for the Republika Srpska.
- **5 presidents;**
    - 3 members in the state presidency (2 from the Federation of Bosnia and Herzegovina and 1 from the Republika Srpska);
    - 1 president in the Federation of Bosnia and Herzegovina; and
    - 1 president in the Republika Srpska.
- **13 prime ministers;**
    - 1 on state level;
    - 1 in the Federation of Bosnia and Herzegovina;
    - 1 in the Republika Srpska; and
    - 1 in each canton in the Federation of Bosnia and Herzegovina (10).

References and Further Reading

Aboko, Adan Yusuf, Kibble, Steve, Bradbury, Mark, Yusuf, Haroon Ahmed and Barrett, Georgina, 'Further Steps to Democracy: The Somaliland Parliamentary Elections September 2005', Progressio Report, London, 2005

Arnson, Cynthia, 'Conclusion: Lessons Learned in Comparative Perspective', in C. Arnson (ed.), *Comparative Peace Processes in Latin America* (Stanford, Calif.: Stanford University Press, 1999)

Azpuru, Dinorah, 'Peace and Democratization in Guatemala: Two Parallel Processes', in C. Arnson (ed.), *Comparative Peace Processes in Latin America* (Stanford, Calif.: Stanford University Press, 1999)

Baker, Pauline, 'Conflict Resolution versus Democratic Governance', in Chester A. Crocker, Fen O. Hampson and Pamela Aall (eds), *Managing Global Chaos: Sources of and Responses to International Conflict* (Washington, DC: United States Institute of Peace, 1996)

Bell, Christine, 'Human Rights and Minority Protection', in John Darby and Roger MacGinty (eds), *Contemporary Peacemaking: Conflict, Violence and Peace Processes* (Basingstoke: Palgrave Macmillan, 2003)

Bradbury, Mark et al., 'The Agreement on Ground Rules in South Sudan', London, Overseas Development Institute, 2000

Chopra, Jarat and Hohe, Tanja, 'Participatory Intervention', *Global Governance,* 10 (2004)

Coomaraswamy, Radkhika, *Sri Lanka: The Crisis of the Anglo-American Constitutional Traditions in a Developing Society* (Delhi: Vikas Ltd., 1983)

du Toit, Pierre, *South Africa's Brittle Peace* (Basingstoke: Palgrave Macmillan, 2001)

Horowitz, Donald, *Ethnic Groups in Conflict* (Berkeley and Los Angeles, Calif.: University of California Press, 1985)

Human Rights Watch, 'Playing the Communal Card: Communal Violence and Human Rights', New York, 1995

Lijphart, Arend, *Democracy in Plural Societies: A Comparative Exploration* (New Haven, Conn.: Yale University Press, 1977)

Luciak, Ilja A., *After the Revolution: Gender and Democracy in El Salvador, Nicaragua, and Guatemala* (Baltimore, Md. and London: Johns Hopkins University Press, 2001)

Miall, Hugh, 'Global Governance and Conflict Prevention', in F. Cochrane, R. Duffy and J. Selby (eds), *Global Governance, Conflict and Resistance* (Basingstoke: Palgrave Macmillan, 2003)

Ramiah, Dev Anand and Fonseka, Dilrukshi, 'Reconciliation and the Peace Process in Sri Lanka' [provisional title], International IDEA, forthcoming 2006

Rothchild, Donald, *Managing Ethnic Conflict in Africa: Pressures and Incentives for Cooperation* (Washington, DC: Brookings Institution Press, 1997)

Sisk, Timothy, *Democratization in South Africa: The Elusive Social Contract* (Princeton, N.J.: Princeton University Press, 1995)

— and Risley, Paul, *Democracy and Peacebuilding at the Local Level: Lessons Learned* (Stockholm: IDEA, 2005), <http://www.idea.int>

Wallensteen, Peter and Sollenberg, Margareta, 'Armed Conflict 1989–1998', *Journal of Peace Research,* 36/5 (September 1999), pp. 593–606

Walter, Barbara, 'The Critical Barrier to Civil War Settlement', *International Organization,* 51/3 (summer 1997), pp. 335–64

Waterman, Harvey, 'Political Order and the "Settlement" of Civil Wars', in Roy Licklider (ed.), *Stopping the Killing: How Civil Wars End* (New York: New York University Press, 1993), pp. 292–302

CHAPTER 6

CHAPTER 6

6. International Democracy Building: Pursuing Peace in the 21st Century

This chapter addresses a fundamental question: How can international efforts to build democracy be strengthened to address challenges to human security? The answer requires a fresh approach and innovative thinking. The rationale for democracy assistance needs to be reclaimed. In recent years there has a been a trend towards severely compromising the cause of democracy building on the part of powerful actors such as the United States under the Bush administration, with narrow national-interest aims and ill-considered approaches (Carothers 2006; Diamond 2005). There is a need to re-evaluate the ways in which democratization is supported and sustained. Global democracy building involves a wide range of approaches at various levels, beginning with community-level and civil society, fostering democratic institutions and mechanisms of accountability at national levels, improving regional norms and cooperation across borders, and improving and reforming the international system's architecture and processes.

In sum, 21st century human security challenges require the promotion of a broader definition of democracy that includes concerns of human rights, capacity for social and economic development, accountability, building consensus in settings of high diversity, improving electoral processes, and promoting public involvement. If there is an emergent global democracy-building 'network', there is also concern with how to support domestic advocates for democratic governance in situations where countries are undergoing crisis or difficult and uncertain transitions. At the same time, there is a need for increased emphasis on democratic governance as a means to foster sustainable human development. Linking democratic governance with human security needs will be key to the viability of peace-building processes, and indeed to broader conflict prevention in many societies undergoing rapid change and dislocation.

> Democratic governance must be responsive to local conditions and needs. At the same time, building the institutions of democracy alone will be insufficient. Free and fair elections are not a solution in and of themselves. The concept of democracy must be broadened beyond elections and technical support.

1. Evolving Rationales for Democracy Building

The findings which emerge from examining the linkages between democracy, conflict and human security suggest evolving rationales for democracy building.

First, the root causes of conflict cannot go ignored; the world cannot afford a business-as-usual approach to growing inequality and demographic, environmental and health insecurities.

Second, the building of democracy must itself be legitimate and based on local realities. For democratic practice to flourish over time it should not be introduced or imposed by fundamentally undemocratic means, either by authoritarian governments practising 'façade democracy', or by international actors that lack legal or de facto legitimacy of action in guiding war-shattered countries from violence to democracy.

Third, progress towards democracy can be enhanced even when national realities limit the functioning of a fully-fledged, complete system of democracy at all levels of society; in transitional processes, at local levels, in interim ways, or through dialogue processes, practices based on the fundamental values of democracy can lay the foundation for a more extensive, meaningful and stable system to emerge over time.

Box 6.1: Reclaiming Democracy: The Nexus between Democracy, Conflict and Human Security

- *Democracy worldwide is 'under fire'*: contrary to the end-of-the-cold-war predictions concerning the triumph of democracy as a political system, there are glaring 'challenges of delivery' and new questions of legitimacy and viability for the state.
- *Democratization has to be linked to meeting human needs*: many current challenges relate to improved development and the reduction of inequality.
- *Violent conflicts may have their origins in human insecurity*: insecurity is linked to *exclusion and lack of access to resources and power.*
- *There is a need for democratic practice*: democratic systems must move from formal to broadly-based democracy, including devolution of power and giving voice to those who feel marginalized.
- *Democracy building is highly political and not just a technical exercise*: respect for the dignity of citizens, local ownership and effective public policy dialogues are essential, with visible results in improved delivery.
- *Questions and determinants of future viability include legitimacy and ownership*: clear accountability, 'checks and balances' and the devolution of power are essential for effective response to human security needs.

1.1. Emerging Links between Democracy, Peace and Development Rationales

The case for the international community linking democracy, peace and development rationales is increasingly articulated, with differences in rationale and interpretation. It is not uncontested, and there are valid questions regarding motivation and ownership.

The UNDP 2005 *Human Development Report* confirms the worst fears of the international development policy and practitioner community: in 2003, 18 countries with a combined population of 460 million people registered lower scores on the human development index than in 1990; the world's richest 500 individuals have a combined income greater than the poorest 416 million; and more than 1 billion people in abject poverty survive on less than 1 USD a day. The World Bank's *World Development Report 2006: Equity and Development* states that inequality of opportunity, both within and among nations, sustains extreme deprivation, results in wasted human potential and often weakens prospects for overall prosperity and economic growth. For more effective poverty reduction, *Equity and Development* recommends ensuring more equitable access by the poor to health care, education, jobs, capital and secure land rights, among other things. It also calls for greater equality of access to political freedoms and political power, breaking down stereotyping and discrimination, and improving access by the marginalized and poor to justice systems and infrastructure.

Underdevelopment and maldevelopment, such as growth that deepens inequality, are consistently seen as contributing factors in contemporary violent conflict (see chapter 1). Development studies and practice have shifted from emphasis on large-scale infrastructure and national capacity-building projects to participation, 'empowerment' and poverty reduction. As the discussion in chapter 1 of the conflict in Bolivia and the cases of South Africa, Sri Lanka or Nepal illustrate, the nature of the state is contested in direct relation to the human security needs of the most vulnerable. Inclusion and effective response are thus essential to the viability of a state, and to the peace within states.

There are glaring omissions, however, if poverty is analysed only internally because globalization is accelerating powerful external forces which also impact on the poor and on the state itself. Charles Ukeje has observed, 'This is where the irony about globalisation and (the) African security problematic most reveals itself: at the same time that globalisation is undermining the capacity of the state—and the state itself is reeking [*sic*] under the weight of its own internal contradictions—it is still expected to be a major force for stability and security in contemporary Africa' (Ukeje 2005: 6–7). Here, as in other regions, externally influenced factors such as the nature of aid and conditionality, disadvantageous terms of trade, and the provision of small arms and weapons, weigh heavily. The discussion on the need for donor coherence will return to this theme, below.

Ukeje and others (Willett 2004: 101) also express concern for the 'securitization of development' which 'is leading to a shift from development/humanitarianism to a category of risk/fear/threat; and shown by the gradual shift in policy initiatives' from foreign to defence ministries. Ukeje expresses a widely held critique that the war on poverty is fast becoming synonymous with the war on terror. In other words, 'whose security' is at stake? There is no doubt that the question of motivation will colour relationships, transactions and outcomes. This highlights the importance of legitimacy and local ownership for development processes themselves.

At the same time, there is recognition that current contradictions and rising inequality call into question which type of state is best able to enhance human security. As Ukeje also observes, if contemporary limitations on state sovereignty, the rise of international civil society and global norms, and the sharing of power between state and non-state actors in a globalizing world leave a clear message that the state is no longer able to monopolize the concept and practice of security,

> Where then should the state acceptably belong since it is impossible to exclude it in any way from the process of reconstructing the security landscape in the [African] continent to accommodate human security? The answer to this is that no project of human security can be accomplished without the presence and active participation of the state. Since the state cannot be excluded, then, a human security approach means providing within the state an environment that allows for the well-being and safety of the population as an equally important goal (Ukeje 2005: 13).

The call for 'an environment that allows for the well-being and safety of the population as an equally important goal' brings us to the need for democracy building from local perspectives and needs, and to the relevance of democratic practice. Increasingly democratization strategies go beyond procedural or technical approaches, to enabling broad engagement for the realization of human development.

Within the UN system the UNDP has pioneered practical interventions which involve communities in determining development needs and initiatives, as avenues out of violent confrontation. A 2006 UNDP report states that 'building democratic governance means ensuring that the poor have a real political voice, alongside access to justice and basic services, including health and education' (UNDP 2006). Donor agencies of states created to distribute official development assistance increasingly articulate the links between conflict, development and democracy. Their efforts have included strengthening election programmes; promoting civic engagement and funding NGOs at the global, regional and domestic levels; promoting constitutional reform, civic education, legal assistance, gender programmes and local governance; general support for a wide range of civil society organizations; and promoting democratically-oriented civil–military relations.

1.2. Democracy and Post-war Peace Building

Democratization, together with state building, has also emerged as a key strategy of peace building after civil war. Kofi Annan, the seventh secretary-general of the United Nations, succinctly described the connection between democracy and peace:

At the centre of virtually every conflict is the State and its power—who controls it and how it is used. No conflict can be resolved without answering those questions, and nowadays the answers almost always have to be democratic ones, at least in form... . Democracy is practised in many ways, and none of them is perfect. But at its best it provides a means for managing and resolving disputes peacefully, in an atmosphere of mutual trust (Annan 2001).

Peace-building strategies have recognized the need for post-war democratization (see chapter 5). 'Democratic validation' of peace agreements reached by political leaders—government officials and rebels, for example—is appreciated as a necessary step, and a critical turning point, in the process. Ensuing tasks include the creation of electoral administration institutions, registering new voters, training election officers, helping draft political party laws, assessing the security situation in relation to polling, managing election day(s), counting ballot papers and certifying outcomes. There is a need for additional efforts to build national capacity for conducting and monitoring elections, assistance to constitutional processes, and demonstrable links between the elected and their constituents.

Approaches to democracy building in post-war contexts have thus also been extended to the local level, as presented in IDEA's 2005 report on *Democracy and UN Peace-building at Local Level* (International IDEA 2005). Participation

> The rationale for democracy building in post-war peace building has been extended to the local level.

cannot be limited to electoral processes such as voting, but must also mean having a voice about what matters for the realization of development and social cohesion, as illustrated above in such cases as the current implosion and critical agenda-setting in Bolivia, in the ongoing failure of democratic governance in Sri Lanka with regard to the peace settlement, and in Olayinka Creighton-Randall's exploration of building the democratic peace in Sierra Leone presented in Volume II of this publication (see below). Growth of civil society and enhanced decentralization are two avenues. The issue of inclusiveness, with participation by ethnic minorities, other identity groups, socio-economic groups, women and young people throughout society, is critical.

Olayinka Creighton-Randall addresses the issue of 'the role of the international community in supporting democratization processes and why it matters', from the standpoint of experience in Sierra Leone. She describes how during civil war 'All the institutions which should have acted as a check on the government were destroyed and there were no avenues left for critical thinking—one of the main tenets of democracy'. It is precisely those avenues for informed engagement with the political process that must be established on a local level if democracy is to be meaningful and strengthened from inside and below for improved and sustained delivery. This is further demonstrated in box 6.2.

Box 6.2: Post-war Democratization and Human Security in Sierra Leone

The [pre-war] over-centralization of political authority had the consequence of stifling local initiatives and alienating society from the state. It left the majority of the citizens marginalized and it also had the further consequence of making the presidency the target of all struggles for power ...

It stands to reason therefore that the voice of ordinary citizens, as represented by civil society organizations, also now plays a hitherto unprecedented role in setting the security agendas and policies. In Sierra Leone, as people move to the centre of the security debate, a Security Sector Working Group consisting of members from across government and non-governmental agencies was set up by the Office of National Security in order to carry out a security sector review. One of the main conclusions of this review was that the internal threats to people's security in Sierra Leone were perceived as being greater than the external threats. External threats were very low on the list whilst internal threats ranked highly and were mainly structural in nature. Examples of these [all threats to democratic principles and practice as well] were:

- corruption;
- lack of political will;
- an over-centralized political and administrative system; and
- lack of monitoring and effective implementation of government policies.

The Local Government and Decentralisation Act devotes a whole chapter to issues of accountability and transparency. This chapter marks a watershed in the history of Sierra Leone as it legally and specifically mandates councils to be as transparent as possible with the publishing of minutes of meetings and council budgets put on notice boards for all to see. It also mandates all councillors to declare their assets. However, if civil society and the local communities do not have the capacity or know-how to monitor and hold the councils to account then the spirit of the act will remain unfulfilled. In addition, if at the central level these moves to incorporate accountability and transparency are not required or enforced, problems will ensue. The majority of councillors have not declared their assets and when asked why not they respond that if members of Parliament are not required to, then why should they?

Source: Extracts from the study by Olayinka Creighton-Randall in Volume II.

1.3. The Legitimacy of International Action

In recent years, democracy building has faced an increasing crisis of legitimacy as geopolitical realities have eroded an otherwise broad international consensus about democracy promotion as a pathway to human development and human security. The

2003 invasion of Iraq by the US- and UK-led multinational coalition was originally justified in terms of pre-empting the regime of Saddam Hussein from deploying weapons of mass destruction that could be sold, bartered, or transferred to the soldiers of global jihad personified by the al-Qaeda network. Over time, however, as it became clear that 'smoking gun' evidence of nuclear, biological or chemical weapons would not be found, the rationale for the intervention changed to one of promoting democracy in the Middle East as a way to address the underlying frustrations that give rise to jihadist orientations. Simply put, many see the efforts of the Bush administration in the USA as an imperialist power 'imposing' a political solution on another state using rhetoric disguised as democracy assistance (Ignatieff 2005; Carothers 2006).

In UN Security Council Resolution 1546, adopted by the Security Council in June 2004, there is ostensibly international support for Iraq's transition, yet international assistance to the process has by and large been limited by the ongoing lack of de facto legitimacy of the continued US–UK occupation of the country and the escalating violence between the coalition forces and an emboldened insurgency. Although in international legal terms Resolution 1546 makes democracy assistance in Iraq 'legitimate', it is clear that the efforts to build a post-Saddam democracy suffer *deficits of de facto legitimacy* in the international community and from key segments in the Iraqi community whose participation or acquiescence is required if the transition towards a new order is to be sustainable and violence is to de-escalate.

> For democratic practice to flourish over time it should not be introduced or imposed by fundamentally undemocratic means.

The imposition of democracy through the barrel of a gun has prompted a deep, divisive debate in the international community not only about the rationale of democracy building but also about the legitimacy of international action to end dictatorships or civil war, form transitional governments, launch constitution-making processes, and address the thorny issues of transitional justice. In the words of a citizen in neighbouring Iran, 'The fact is not that we do not like democracy; the fact is that we do not believe that you bring us democracy' (Arabi 2005). (For a statement of the Bush Administration's position on democracy promotion, see Dobriansky 2004.)

An intervention which is considered legitimate may lose credibility if the resulting implementation and actions are perceived by the local population as ineffective. Credibility in the eyes of the recipient population will be closely linked to effectiveness and approach. Whereas major strides have been made in attempts at concerted donor action or better coordination in approach, efforts to plan assistance with a better understanding of its functioning 'on the ground' and of the viewpoints and experience of affected populations need to be further refined. The example in box 6.3 from Sierra Leone is a reminder that 'how' something is done is as important as 'what' when it comes to implementation.

> An intervention which is considered legitimate may lose credibility if the resulting implementation and actions are perceived by the local population as ineffective.

Box 6.3: An 'Inside–Out' View of Donor Coherence and Implementation, from Sierra Leone

In having practically no guidance from the (failed) state, international supporters were at liberty to choose the areas their support would be channelled into, and in doing this to choose the issues that would be addressed. This happened at both the macro and micro levels and resulted in a certain amount of duplication of effort and neglect of certain areas. Donor governments and agencies have only very recently started consulting each other and collaborating with each other in an attempt to provide holistic support with little duplication. There are still serious challenges in this area, however, and one instance of support for the decentralization process can be taken as an example.

A number of the major development partners involved in Sierra Leone, such as the World Bank, the UNDP and the British [Department for International Development] DFID, are all providing support to decentralization, and yet it is still not entirely clear just how much support is being given and in which precise areas. The governmental institution which should be best placed to provide direction to interventions in this area is the Ministry of Local Government and Community Development. As the ministry seriously lacks capacity, a secretariat was formed with funding from the World Bank to provide support to it. As regards local ownership, though, this secretariat is housed in a completely different building quite a few miles away, together with other institution-strengthening' projects. Staff employed there earn much better salaries than those civil servants working in the ministry so that it is very difficult to imagine any sort of capacity transfer in such a situation. This has the effect of undermining local ownership.

Source: Extract from the study by Olayinka Creighton-Randall in Volume II.

> Donor coherence involves much more than coordination. It implies complementary actions within shared national vision, such that initiatives are not contradictory or at cross purposes but rather mutually supportive.

1.4. Unintended Consequences of International Action

In addition to legitimacy questions concerning international action, there are equally concerns about the effects—intended or unintended—of international engagement. 'Good governance' programmes intended to assist with shaping state institutions to high standards of performance, management and accountability do not always take into account the process dimensions of how institutions interact with or deliver to populations, or how the elected interact with or deliver to their constituents. In the name of both peace building and development, agencies including the World Bank, the UNDP and the US Agency for International Development (USAID) have employed various 'bottom–up approaches' in a whole range of interventions. There are abundant efforts to strengthen civil society and to improve capacity building for 'governance' according to multiple definitions.

The word 'governance' is used in a narrow sense to mean efficient and effective public management, or more broadly to encompass the mechanisms and institutions through which constituencies articulate their interests through 'participation'. Chopra and Hohe argue that development agencies have treated 'participation' in a universal sense (Chopra and Hohe 2004). If this is the case, it can still too often imply a technical requirement, rather than engaged and effective involvement.

The international financial institutions (IFIs) also now advocate participatory approaches, but these have not been free of controversy. For example, there are contrasting views of this feature of the Poverty Reduction Strategy Paper (PRSP). PRSPs were developed to replace structural adjustment programmes and are intended to be country-led documents. They are required by the IMF and the World Bank before a country can be considered for debt relief under the Heavily Indebted Poor Country Initiative. Some see the PRSP as a 'potentially transformative vision of pro-poor reform, covering both national governments and donors'; others claim that 'instead of transforming what governments do, PRSPs run the risk of overriding or derailing domestic political and policymaking processes by international priorities and undermining local level political accountability' (Piron and Evans 2004: 34).[1]

Rethinking PRSP policy implies linking poverty reduction with notions of inclusion and citizenship—if a poverty reduction strategy introduces new social disparities or stratification, it will not ultimately contribute to increased human security. Democratic practice would mean a further attempt at reaching the poor themselves for needs definition ('power sharing' in terms of setting the agenda) and mechanisms for accountability in the receipt and use of funds. An unintended consequence of PRSP implementation can be a widening of the gap within the recipient society between those who have technical expertise and can speak/reproduce donor language, and those who have needs but no vocabulary or access to external *or national* resources or power (see box 6.4).

> **Box 6.4: Rethinking Poverty Reduction Strategy Papers**
> Participation is . . . open to manipulation by relatively powerful international actors, including NGOs, so that the process strengthens their influence as they build new local and international 'reform coalitions'. From this perspective, PRSPs can be understood as having been designed by and for groups capable of expressing their project in the language of logical planning matrices and poverty discourse. But here there is a problem. Few such groups exist, and few are likely to emerge from domestic social processes in developing countries. PRSPs thus inevitably fail to engage with the identities and priorities driving the 'civil society' that exists in reality.
>
> Instead international NGOs seem desperate to find and build the capacity of 'pro-poor' organisations despite the fact that most recognise the difficulty of finding groups both able to claim some legitimate representative function in

poor communities, and willing to construct their arguments in the technocratic form required to 'participate' effectively in a PRSP. Bi-lateral donors and NGOs are thus encouraging 'local civil society' to fill the political space provided by the PRSP process by providing advice, training and funding to ensure that more and more civil society groups emerge, and that those willing and able to engage do so.

The PRSP is then in some senses a joint project of the international financial institutions, bi-lateral donors and Northern NGOs, all of whom collaborated to design the process, all of whom expect their interests to be served by it, and all of whom understand that the process cannot 'perform' without the active engagement of all the others. Northern NGOs have welcomed PRSPs because they believe it opens up political spaces in developing countries in which their discourse and priorities will be privileged. The World Bank and IMF are relatively comfortable helping to open those spaces because they understand that 'reasonable' voices are being supported to ensure they dominate the process. PRSPs are thus being used to legitimate the increasingly intrusive supervision of developing country political communities. At the same time existing local political identities, institutions and representatives are undermined, and democracy weakened.

See Alistair Fraser, Ontrac no. 21, 31 September 2005, <http://www.intrac.org>

2. Global Democracy Building: A Network Approach?

In other areas of managing global interdependences—such as trade, the environment, weapons proliferation, or even the management of global sport—there is an increasing awareness of the importance of global networks that constitute the sum total of international action. (For an overview of 16 different global networks, see Simmons and de Jonge Oudraat 2001, or the study on 'global public policy networks' conducted for the UN, entitled *Critical Choices* (Benner et al. 2000).) In the evolution of the democracy-building network, there is clearly a supply side aspect—the international community's interest in the spread of democracy—and a clear demand side that stems from the desire of people around the world not be to ruled by authoritarian, corrupt regimes that do not provide for basic safety or facilitate prosperity. Some argue that the practical learning by the wider democracy promotion network is slow in coming and in dire need of improvement (Carothers 2004).

The UN's Electoral Assistance Division (see below) within the Department of Political Affairs and the newly established United Nations Democracy Fund (UNDEF) both function in response to democratization challenges in complex settings. The newly established Peacebuilding Commission will be another point of reference in the shared concern for assistance to transitional processes. This represents an acceleration in the interest in and priority given to democracy support, in contrast to the situation in 1995 when IDEA was founded as a multilateral initiative.

2.1. Bottom–Up Democracy Building: Communities and Civil Society

The last decade has seen increased provision of financial resources for democracy promotion NGOs in transition countries. Sectoral work has included electoral administration and monitoring, civic education, human rights and security sector reform, anti-corruption work, promotion of the freedom of the press, and political party development. The external actors providing this function include donor states, multilateral aid agencies, international organizations and philanthropic foundations. Issues in the direct, external funding of opposition-related NGOs or community-based organizations include degrees of recipient autonomy, potential intrusion into internal affairs, ways in which to genuinely assist capacity building, sustainability over time, transparency, and the legitimacy (or potential dependence) of local actors when they receive external financial support.

There are positive examples of local actors achieving reform from the bottom up in national democratization experiences. The study by Arifah Rahmawati and Najib Azca in Volume II describes the case of work with the Indonesian police from below as part of the transition to democracy. 'From below' means 'an approach which assumes that police reform will be most effective and valuable if it is conducted with not only a "top–down" but also a "bottom–up" strategy. This approach is complementary in character rather than exclusively opposed to "police reform from above". The word "below" means two things: first, from lower (and middle) levels of the police force; and, second, from societal actors, particularly civil society' (Rahmawati and Azca, Volume II). While specific reasons will lie in Indonesian history and context, the authors maintain that security sector reform is a critical item on the agenda for newly democratic countries, since the core of the security sector, particularly the military, is usually the backbone of the old authoritarian regime. In the case of Indonesia, 'the outbreak of communal violence can be seen as a symptom, and simultaneously a consequence, of the poor performance of the security sector during the transition period. The lack of capacity and the unprofessional attitude and behaviour of the security forces in dealing with social unrest led to the eruption of social or communal violence in some areas in the archipelago'.

> **Box 6.5: Transitional Police Reform 'From Below' in Indonesia**
> The security sectors in many developing countries in transition to democracy fail to provide the safe and secure environment required for sustainable economic and political development. Furthermore, in many countries, politicized or ineffective security bodies and justice systems are a source of instability and insecurity.
>
> The rocky transition from authoritarianism to democracy in Indonesia has been marked by the rise of communal violence [for example, Kalimantan, Maluku, West Timor and Riau] in many parts of the archipelago. This phenomenon can

be perceived as a symptom as well as a consequence of the poor performance of the security forces during the early stages of the Indonesian transition period. Security sector reform that began soon after the collapse of the New Order regime has brought about progress in some security sectors, including the police force. However, many of the steps taken by the government have approached the problems from a 'top–down' perspective. ... ineffective security bodies and justice systems are a source of stability and insecurity... .

At the same time, the process of transition in Indonesia has generated demands for more equality, justice, citizen participation and greater decentralization to local government. These are serious challenges for the new democratic government of Indonesia and need to be addressed consistently.

The issues of participation and decentralization are important as both are methods of expanding and improving public services. This would in turn help the government to gain legitimacy in the eyes of its citizens, and thus help to maintain a stable democracy. It is also part of the deepening of democracy that involves democratizing the state by allowing citizens more direct participation in deciding public policy, and by ensuring that public services reach those at all levels of society.

Key informing principles for action:

The first is a reorientation to the ethic of police professionalism. This reorientation includes a change away from a militaristic ethic towards a civilian ethic, back to a role as protector and servant of the community.

The second is reorganization of the police institution to make it more independent (from the military), accountable and decentralized.

The third is the development of institutional management so that the police can provide for staff and personnel specialization, staff development and adequate payment ... .

A further challenge for those attempting police reform 'from below' in Indonesia is to empower and encourage the community to engage with, trust and approach the police.

Source: Extracts from the study by Arifah Rahmawati and Najib Azca in Volume II.

The training described in this case included an introduction for police to considerations of conflict dynamics in their specific locations of work. This helped understandings which moved away from stereoptying and the notion of taking sides towards an orientation of balance in approach, and hence towards more professional policing and increased trust and respect from the community.

Local-level democracy networks are coming into their own in a revitalized way, for example via the creation of the new association of local governments around the world, United Cities and Local Governments (<http://www.cities-localgovernments.org>), the World Urban Forum, and the Global Network on Local Governance (<http://www.gnlg.org>) based at the the Institute of Social Sciences, New Delhi, India. The latter offers studies on the relationship between decentralization and poverty reduction; innovations such as the introduction in Bangalore of a 'municipal report card' whereby citizens can rate the services and delivery functions of local governance; information and resource sharing; advocacy tools, events and conferences; and capacity-building and training programmes. It promotes social justice and in particular women's participation.

> The process of transition can generate increased demands for more equality, justice, citizen participation and greater decentralization to local government. These are serious challenges for any democratic government and need to be addressed with a broad base of stakeholders.

One field in which the linking up of global networks with local NGOs is well developed is that of election monitoring. As Eric Bjornlund writes, 'The involvement of multilateral organizations in election monitoring has helped them to strengthen their commitment to promoting genuine democracy among member states. Meanwhile, non-partisan domestic election-monitoring groups in developing countries have not only deterred fraud and improved public confidence in important elections but have also encouraged citizen involvement in political life more generally' (Bjornlund 2004: 304–5). In other words, international engagement in monitoring of electoral processes has also had salutary effects on strengthening local capacities.

2.2. Building Viable, Democratic States

Democracy building at the level of national states has become more prominent as an area of concentrated efforts and programmatic activity by international and bilateral donors since the end of the cold war. Their focus has included national-level institutions and processes —such as elections—and the ways in which society can oversee and restrain power.

Many of these efforts have tended to focus on electoral processes, and in particular the strengthening of independent electoral management bodies, monitoring of electoral processes such as parliamentary or local election events, voter education campaigns, voter registration and the drafting and review of electoral laws. Increasingly, there have been fruitful efforts to develop international codes and guidelines for the functioning of EMBs. However, much electoral assistance has been directed towards individual high-profile electoral events on the immediate political horizon. This has often given visibility to donors, but not necessarily addressed either the desirability of building the capacity for locally sustainable electoral administration in the longer term or the relationship between electoral assistance and the wider process of development support. Indeed, support for an electoral event has sometimes been seen as an exit strategy by the international community. In addition, while international observation has played a crucial role in some elections, it needs to conducted effectively and professionally throughout the electoral process and demands substantial resources. There has also been a danger of it being used as a low-risk option by international actors.

Other areas in which democracy-building support has grown include:

- electoral processes, and in particular the strengthening of independent EMBs, monitoring of electoral processes such as parliamentary or local election events, voter education campaigns, voter registration and the drafting and review of electoral laws;
- strengthening of parliamentary capacities, to include capacity building for oversight of executive behaviour, committee processes, legislative drafting, budgeting, constituency relations, rules and procedures, and parliamentary ethics;
- rule-of-law programmes to improve judicial independence and oversight, access to justice, alternative dispute resolution processes, community-level justice processes, legal training, awareness of and participation in adjudication under international law, and citizen-level training on human rights;
- support for the media, to include protection of the free speech of reporters, opening access to international communications and especially the Internet, and protecting newspapers, broadcasters and other media outlets from undue control or interference by political authorities;
- building strong national civil society organizations and interest-group structures such as private sector associations; interest group representation on functional issues such as health, education, employment, or the interests of young people; and
- creating mechanisms for civilian control and oversight of the armed forces and police, to include professionalization programmes, oversight machanisms, military ethics, community and public order policing, and the strengthening of citizen capacities for oversight.

The expanding international engagement on this theme has led the Development Assistance Committee (DAC) of the Organisation for Economic Co-operation and Development (OECD) to define the basic principles of security system reform, calling for greater consistency in what has traditionally been an area of different branches of donor action, ranging from development and humanitarian aid to defence and trade departments. With particular reference to this as part of the broader human security agenda (OECD DAC 2005: 11), the study 'Security System Reform and Governance' emphasizes the importance of a shared vision on the part of internal and external stakeholders, and both a 'whole government' (rather than single sector) approach and the development of civilian control and oversight. This builds on the established DAC Guidelines for assistance which link conflict prevention, peace building and democracy (see box 6.6).

Box 6.6: The OECD DAC Guidelines Linking Conflict Prevention, Peace Building and Democracy

34. A central focus of assistance should be to improve the general economic, political and social climate in partner countries, by supporting measures to improve the legitimacy and effectiveness of the state as well as the emergence of a strong civil society. Such efforts should facilitate the building of consensus on central economic, social and political issues. Assistance for the promotion of democracy, participatory mechanisms in the political system, and the rule of law can all be elements of a peacebuilding strategy helping to integrate individuals and groups into society, building their stake in the system and preventing their marginalisation and potential recourse to violence.

35. At the community level, donors can specifically help facilitate negotiations and reconciliation processes, particularly in the case of weak states or where large areas or regions are outside the control of the central government. Such assistance, having a primary peacebuilding and reconciliation objective, should focus on nurturing the appropriate social or institutional networks and organisations that can act as stabilising points in society in tandem with efforts aimed at the national-level. This can include support for the development of intermediary social organisations such as local NGOs, business associations, multi-ethnic committees, women's organisations and helping marginalised groups obtain better access to justice systems, the civil administration and the media. Realism requires donors to recognise that some governments may perceive active social or institutional networks as a threat and respond accordingly.

Source: Articles 34 and 35 of the OECD Development Assistance Committee's *The DAC Guidelines: Helping Prevent Violent Conflict* (Paris: OECD DAC, 2001).

Many transition countries have seen the development—often supported by international donors, particularly at the outset—of national-level NGOs which work for democracy promotion and implement programmes in different aspects of democratic development. A good example is the Institute for Democracy in South Africa (IDASA), which played a pivotal role in advocating for a transition to democracy, facilitated the transition through programmes and activities to build confidence among various domestic actors, and subsequently has played an important role as a promoter of accountability, good governance and civic education. The projects IDASA has developed in the democratic consolidation phase include parliamentary watchdog functions, advanced political party training, and extensive public opinion polling.

2.3. Regional Approaches to Democracy Building

Recent experience suggests that regional approaches may be effective in global democracy building. Regional organizations such as the EU, the OAS, the OSCE or the African Union (AU) have their origins in the efforts of a group of neighbouring countries to manage economic and security cooperation, and their roles have expanded in recent years to include democracy promotion. Among regional organizations, the OAS Unit for the Promotion of Democracy has been extensively involved in monitoring and country-level assistance efforts in recent years. Building on Resolution 1080 of 1991 (AG/RES. 1080 (XXI-O/91)), the OAS Secretariat is called upon by member states to automatically respond to instances of democratic crisis (e.g. a *coup d'état*) by organizing a collective response. More recently the OAS adopted a Democracy Charter for the Americas.

> Regional approaches to democracy building have their weaknesses and strengths, and may continue to grow in relevance for leadership and broadly-based consensus.

Box 6.7: Incentives for Democracy: The EU's Economic 'Magnet'

In addition to, and sometimes augmenting, direct bilateral aid, for East European states of the former communist bloc, the role of EU conditionalities and the effects of these stipulations for the further consolidation of East European democracies can hardly be overstated. The EU's economic pull is like a large magnet attracting states in the East, and improvements in democracy seem to be the key to entry to the club (see Zielonka and Pravda 2001). Possible EU membership and the associated access to finance (e.g. credit) and a larger market represent powerful incentives for the continuation of the democratic experiments. These states see compliance with these conditions as an important bellwether of their possible future full membership in the EU. The conditionalities are laid out the the 1993 Copenhagen Criteria, as follows:

- stability of institutions guaranteeing democracy, the rule of law, human rights and respect for and protection of minorities;
- the existence of a functioning market economy as well as the capacity to cope with competitive pressure and market forces within the Union; and
- the ability to take on the obligations of membership, including adherence to the aims of political, economic and monetary union.

For further detail, see the European Union web site at <http://europa.eu.int/comm/enlargement/intro/criteria.htm>.

The AU's Peer Review Mechanism is designed to provide a comprehensive governance audit process to help African states build democracy through constructive evaluation by eminent men and women from neighbouring states. (For an authoritative description of the Peer Review Mechanism's purposes and processes, see New Partnership for Africa's Development 2003. For a critique, see Ukeje 2005.) The AU saw particular success in the recent transition crisis in the West African state of Togo, where a non-democratic attempt to usurp power by the son of the president, Faure Gnassingbe, upon his father's death was reversed by quick action by AU and Economic Community of West African States (ECOWAS) countries, which imposed sanctions and gave clear signals that a non-democratic transition in Togo would not be legitimized. Nigerian President Olusegun Obasanjo was particularly influential in asserting a regional role in preventing a non-democratic and unconstitutional transfer of power.

Similarly, the OSCE has developed a significant capacity for democracy promotion among its more than 50 member states. The principal OSCE mechanisms for this purpose are the Office for Democratic Institutions and Human Rights (ODIHR) and the High Commissioner for National Minorities (HCNM). P. Terrence Hopmann writes that 'The OSCE has devoted considerable effort to promoting democratization [by assisting] new democracies in establishing fair procedures for holding democratic elections, [supervising] the conduct of those elections to assure that the procedures are followed, and [evaluating] their outcome. Since 1991, the OSCE has embraced the argument that the construction of stable democratic systems contributes in the long run to peace and security by reducing the risks of both intrastate and interstate violence' (Hopmann 1999: 16, 19). Similarly, the Council of Europe, since its inception in 1949, has been a consistent advocate of democracy promotion, and the conditionalities for membership in this pan-European institution have also been a significant factor in promoting democracy, especially in the states of Eastern Europe which aspire to integrate their political, social and economic futures more fully into Europe.

New forms of regional cooperation are emerging. The 2005 EU and Association of Southeast Asian Nations (ASEAN) monitoring for the Aceh Peace Process is an example. More than 200 monitors from the European Union and ASEAN shared a joint monitoring mission for the first phase of disarmament by separatist rebels in Indonesia's Aceh province, under the 2005 Memorandum of Understanding, which ended 29 years of armed violence. This was the EU's first peace-monitoring venture in Asia. Along with its European participants, the Aceh Monitoring Mission included unarmed military representatives from the ASEAN nations of Brunei, Malaysia, the Philippines, Singapore and Thailand. In political terms each regional body is of particular acceptance value to the parties to the conflict. In post-settlement Aceh the Indonesian Government gained legitimacy and support thanks to ASEAN's visibility, and the Free Aceh Movement (Gerakan Aceh Merdeka, GAM), which had long appealed to actors outside the region in the course of its armed struggle, voiced confidence in a mission also including European monitors. Genuine democratization, the development of local government, and visible development progress in Aceh, a province of about 4 million people, will be key to the peace process.

ASEAN's 2005 Kuala Lumpur Declaration heralded the ASEAN Charter initiative which may mean a new regional constitutional framework for both aspirational and operating principles and values. This would be a new departure for ASEAN and a mark of maturity and potentially deepening regional influence.

Ágora Democrática in the Andean region has the purpose of helping to develop party systems that lead to consensus and more responsive governance, fostering more effective political parties, and encouraging political leaders from the regions within each country, and especially women and young people, to increase their knowledge of decentralization, the political party system, and public policy themes, including poverty reduction and social cohesion.

The SADC has committed itself to principles including human rights, democracy and the rule of law, 'Equity, balance and mutual benefit' and the 'Peaceful settlement of disputes' (see the study on Southern Africa by Khabele Matlosa in Volume II), and Electoral Guidelines including voter education and gender provisions that are intended to anchor African Union declarations firmly in sub-regional and local practice.

Regional NGO networks have emerged as major forces for democratization. Among these non-profit organizations are CODESRIA (Centre for Democracy and Security in Africa), based in Senegal, and the Electoral Institute of Southern Africa (EISA), which has its headquarters in South Africa. These organizations run regional programmes to promote democratic practice and transnational networks of local NGOs, election administrators, political parties and the mass media. The West Africa Network for Peacebuilding (WANEP) features organizations from seven states which work on early warning, development and democracy, featuring the publication of policy papers and monitoring. They work on conflict issues and the cultivation of a democratic culture, for example, analysing the coup in Togo and the response by the AU and ECOWAS, as well as the rest of the international community.

FORUM-ASIA represents over 33 member organizations in 13 countries of South, South-East and North-East Asia, working on human rights and democracy. Red Interamericana para la Democracia (RID) is a network of civil society organizations working to strengthen democracy in the Americas.

2.4. Global Approaches: Transnational NGOs

Charitable organizations that usually have their origins in the estate of wealthy and idealistic benefactors have been key players in the democracy promotion network. These foundations, such as the Ford Foundation, the Soros Foundation and the Aga Khan Foundation, have far-reaching global programmes for democratic development or for broader promotion of 'open societies'. A central strategy of the work of the Aga Khan Foundation is to create or strengthen an institutional structure at the village level through which people can determine priority needs and decide how best to manage common resources in the interests of the community as a whole. Private foundations directly support programmes that promote civic education, develop pluralistic civil society, enhance free media, train opposition parties, enhance legislative and parliamentary processes, and advance human rights causes such as gender equality and women's participation in political life.

Among the NGOs involved in the global democracy promotion network, several have come to the fore as important and dynamic actors in the network: the Washington-based IFES (formerly the International Foundation for Election Systems), the US-based party institutes (the National Democratic Institute and International Republican Institute), and the German party foundations (e.g. the Hans Seidel Foundation, the Friedrich Ebert Foundation or the Konrad Adenauer Foundation). Other significant NGOs with global programmes include the Carter Center, which has become the standard-bearer for organizing non-official election monitoring missions around the world which are perceived as being neutral.

2.5. Global Approaches: The International Financial Institutions and the United Nations

There is increasing awareness of the strain between structural economic reform and political reform in transition settings. In post-war settings this can be particularly acute, requiring a re-examination of prevailing conditions, appropriate measures and desired impact. James Boyce examines this in depth in box 6.8.

Box 6.8: International Financial Institutions, Post-war Peace Building and Democracy Assistance

There are important complementarities between peace building and the more conventional goals of efficiency, economic growth and poverty reduction. But these goals are not perfectly congruent, and it cannot be assumed that peace building can be secured simply as a by-product of 'business as usual'.

Two sorts of innovation are needed. The first involves modifications of existing policies and practices to take into account the special circumstances of post-conflict environments. This requires the willingness and capacity to do some things differently. The second involves efforts to address issues that may be absent or avoidable in 'normal' contexts but that must be faced squarely in post-conflict settings. This requires the willingness and capacity to do some different things.

Horizontal Equity Impact Assessment
The World Bank has acknowledged the need for 'integrating a sensitivity to conflict in Bank assistance', and its Conflict Prevention and Reconstruction Unit has developed a conflict analysis framework for this purpose. Perhaps the IMF and the regional development banks will follow this lead. *However, conflict analysis cannot simply be tacked onto standard operating procedures and added to the job descriptions of current staff members.* To carry out such analyses, and to reframe assistance strategies and redesign projects in the light of the results, will require a deliberate and sustained process of capacity building.

A critical area for such capacity building is in assessment of the 'horizontal equity' impacts of policies and projects. 'Horizontal equity' refers to disparities

---

across social groups, defined in terms of ethnicity, region, religion and race, whereas 'vertical equity' is defined in terms of differences between rich and poor regardless of group identities. Horizontal disparities are often viewed as playing a central role in inciting or perpetuating violent conflict (see Annan 1999; and Stewart 2000). In this connection it is important to distinguish between levels of inequality and changes or trends in inequality over time. The latter can spark greater antipathy than the former. In Rwanda, for example, widening economic inequalities in the late 1980s and early 1990s have been cited as one factor in the escalation of ethnic tensions that preceded the 1994 genocide (see Uvin 1998; and Colletta 2004).

In 'post-conflict' transitions, the risk of renewed outbreaks of violent conflict remains high: World Bank studies report that there is a 44 per cent chance of a resumption of conflict in the first five years after a civil war (Collier et al. 2003: 83). Although horizontal equity impact assessment is especially important in these settings, the international financial institutions (IFIs) and the donor community more generally lack adequate capacity for this task. 'Donors have not been very good at understanding the underlying political economy of many of the countries with whom we deal', the chair of the OECD Development Assistance Committee recently remarked. 'We underinvest badly in history' (Manning 2003: 11). In addition to history, capacity building will require investments in political science, anthropology and sociology, and the application of economic analysis to this important but unexamined dimension of income and wealth distribution.

Recommendation
The IFIs should invest in the development of capacity to assess the impacts of policies and projects on horizontal equity and social tensions, and should incorporate conflict impact assessment into policy formulation and project appraisal.

Rethinking Macroeconomic Stabilization
'Macroeconomic stabilization' refers to the goal of stabilizing prices and the exchange rate by means of fiscal and monetary policies. In the division of labour among the IFIs, this is mainly the province of the IMF. During post-conflict transitions, stabilization is not only a matter of macroeconomics: political stabilization is at least as crucial. While there is a broad complementarity between the goals of macroeconomic and political stabilization, there can be important trade-offs, too. The IFIs—particularly the IMF—need to develop greater capacity to evaluate these trade-offs so as to incorporate them into policy design.

More specifically, the relationship between budget deficits and social tensions requires careful analysis. The IMF generally assumes that the inflation associated with larger budget deficits would fuel social tensions, whereas critics of its programmes generally assume that budget deficit reduction measures exacerbate tensions. Both arguments are plausible: there may be a U-shaped relation between budget deficits and social tensions, wherein deficits that are too high or too low both lead to greater social tensions. If this is so, the IFIs need to explore (a) how to identify the turning point on this curve, which may vary from country to country and over time; and (b) how the curve can be shifted so as to relax tradeoffs between macroeconomic stability and social tensions (see Boyce and Pastor 1997).

This issue surfaces in recent World Bank research that finds that 'social policy is relatively more important and macroeconomic policy is relatively less important in postconflict situations than in normal situations' (Collier et al. 2003). Apart from the direct benefits of social expenditure, the World Bank suggests that 'by prioritizing social inclusion, the government may indirectly reassure investors' and thereby encourage private-sector investment. 'If opportunities exist for modest trade-offs that improve social policies at the expense of a small deterioration in macroeconomic balances', the Bank concludes, 'growth is, on average, significantly augmented' (Collier 2003). The same logic can be applied to public investments in new democratic institutions.

In addition to assessing such trade-offs, rethinking macroeconomic stabilization during post-conflict reconstruction and peace building could extend to reconsideration of the indicators by which macroeconomic performance is measured. Rather than targeting inflation, as is the standard practice today, policy makers could target the purchasing power of the population. The main argument for controlling inflation during post-conflict transitions is that it would erode the real incomes of the poor. If this is so, why not target purchasing power directly? This would require investments in capacity to monitor not only the prices of basic necessities but also wages and other incomes.

Recommendation
To reconcile macroeconomic stabilization and political stabilization—goals that should be mutually supportive—capacity should be built to monitor indicators of social tensions and alternative macroeconomic indicators (such as the purchasing power of the population) and to assess potential trade-offs between them.

James Boyce, University of Massachusetts, Amherst

The United Nations, with its mandate to promote global human rights, including government by the 'will of the people' (as outlined in the 1948 Universal Declaration of Human Rights, and other norms such as the 1966 International Covenant on Civil and Political Rights), has become a leading advocate of democracy. In particular, within the UN system, the Secretariat and the UNDP have become increasingly involved in democracy promotion in the pursuit of international peace and human security and as a pivotal element in human development. (For a comprehensive evaluation of the UN role in promoting democracy, see Newman and Rich 2004.)

The UN Electoral Assistance Division (EAD) assists in electoral design and the administration of elections; however, it is somewhat constrained in its activities as it requires a member state's invitation to become involved in any given electoral process, and states are sometimes reluctant to invite the UN in to what are deemed internal affairs. Nevertheless, the EAD has played an important role in bolstering information sharing and capacity building for electoral processes in the situations in which it has become involved.

In several peacekeeping operations—notably in the United Nations Transitional Authority in Cambodia (UNTAC), more recently in the UN-sponsored transitions in East Timor and Afghanistan, and presently in Liberia—UN authorities have been called in to actually structure and administer major electoral processes (see e.g. Chesterman 2004). This role borders on aspects of trusteeship, in which the UN performs tasks normally reserved for sovereign states, to include the organization and implementation of electoral processes. A more common role for the UN, however, is the extensive election monitoring missions that have been carried out in many different states beginning in the early 1990s, as in Namibia, Nicaragua, Angola and South Africa, to name only a few. In this capacity, the UN is also often called upon to organize and accredit monitoring by other intergovernmental organizations (such as the Commonwealth).

2.6. The Democracy-building Regime: A Functional Overview

Global efforts to promote democracy raise questions of agendas, of norms, of knowledge, and of responses when local implementation is found wanting.

- *Agenda setting.* While it is clear that democracy building has become a cornerstone of the second Bush administration in the USA, it is also clear that demand for democracy comes from within and below. Whether in Togo, Ukraine, Nepal or Lebanon, the agenda of democracy is also set by those citizens and advocacy groups within states who are willing to demand free and fair elections, to demand accountability by their political leaders, and to demand the freedom to participate in policy making.
- *Negotiating norms.* As noted in chapter 3, there is an international right to democratic participation, codified in various instruments of international law. (For a comprehensive review of international law pertaining to democracy, see Ibegbu 2003.) New norms of democratic participation continue to evolve, particularly within the context of regional organizations such as the OAS and the AU, and in sub-regional organizations such as the SADC (see Matlosa 2005). The regime has also seen the development of 'soft law' norms such as the authoritative statement of UN Secretary-General Boutros Boutros-Ghali in his 1996 *Agenda for Democratization* (United Nations 1996) and in virtually every major statement of Secretary-General Kofi Annan since then.
- *Monitoring compliance.* Capacities for monitoring the progress of democracy are

in widespread use and are found in local NGOs and the private sector, the media, transnational NGOs, and regional and international organizations. (For a country-by-country overview of recent monitoring of democracy, see <http://www.worldaudit.org>.) From the human rights NGOs which monitor and report on country situations, to organizations such as Reporters without Borders which monitor press freedoms, to Transparency International which seeks to track problems of corruption, information technology aids to monitoring capacities are improving rapidly. Global news brings instant attention to selected concerns. New instruments for assessing the quality of democracy have been created to take a more holistic view of the quality of progress towards democracy's goals in any given setting. (See International IDEA's State of Democracy Project, and especially Beetham et al. 2002.)

• *Gaining compliance.* The international community generally employs incentives to promote democracy norms, for example through direct assistance to electoral processes; or by directly funding international NGOs to support the creation and sustaining of monitoring and implementation capacities, and funding domestic NGOs for activities such as capacity building, training, the media, labour union activism and human rights advocacy; and in some instances by providing direct support to ruling and opposition political parties. Often there are ideological strings attached to such aid, for example, the combination of sanctions against the government of Slobodan Milosevic in 1998 and the subsequent assistance to anti-government political parties and movements in the (then) Federal Republic of Yugoslavia.

• *Reacting to non-compliance.* The most difficult choice the international community faces is in situations of non-compliance with international norms. Zimbabwe, for example, since 2000 has seen three consecutive electoral processes in which many observers saw serious irregularities, intimidation, fraud and repression. Many organizations in the democracy promotion network have criticized Zimbabwe and implemented sanctions.

There has been relatively greater consensus about imposing sanctions on Myanmar, which has held democracy activists such as Nobel Laureate Aung San Suu Kyi under house arrest: both the USA and the EU member states have imposed similar 'smart' sanctions against Myanmar's military junta. The trend towards the use of smart sanctions was reinforced in early 2006 when the EU and the USA accused leading members of the government of President Alexander Lukashenko in Belarus of violations of regional and international norms of fairness during the contentious 2006 elections.

• *Refining international aid and development policies.* Both World Bank and IMF conditions now contain a requirement for participation of wider stakeholders in the development of PRSPs. By February 2005 PRSPs were being implemented in 45 countries and there is ample evidence and research documenting and assessing the participatory processes utilized. The question 'Who speaks for the poor?' is problematic; the answer is often devised as a joint project of the IFIs, bilateral donors, and Northern NGOs who find local partners with pro-poor platforms. Thus a process that is meant to make external aid policy more 'democratic' has implications for internal democratization.

3. The Future of Democracy Building: Recommendations for More Effective Action

The recommendations presented here have emerged from research and reflection on the nexus between democracy, conflict and human security. They seek to link the pursuit of human security and human development more fully—strategically and operationally—within the international community's democracy-building strategies, options and instruments. While the essential right to democratic practice is clearly codified in core instruments of international law, the further development of international norms is needed, particularly on the level of regional norms and in non-binding but sensible operational guidelines or 'soft law'.

These recommendations reflect a concern for improvement in global policy and consensus on the utility of democracy assistance in attaining human development *and* human security. They highlight a need to re-evaluate problems evident in the current network, which hinder assistance to building effective, nationally owned democracies.

1. *Demonstrate the linkages between democracy and human security:*

- document successful initiatives which link local communities to meaningful participation in decision making, influence on elected representatives, access to justice, police reform and a voice on education and health measures;
- support innovation for decentralization of power, 'knowledge banks' on approaches to democratic land reform measures, resource revenue sharing, and civic education; and
- cultivate improved 'participation' in community projects concerning clean water and housing as active citizenship exercises in relation to rights and roles.

In short- to medium-term settings of international human security crises, expand the representation of women in peace support operations, in vulnerability and needs analysis, in specific national recovery and constitution-building processes, and in decision making on interim governance arrangements:

- seek to improve and refine the ways in which local communities can identify factors they see as intrinsic to their resilience and human security, avoiding the imposition of 'blueprints' from outside which may prove inappropriate;
- work towards enabling state responsiveness to human security needs—away from technical good governance criteria to longer-term lower-profile support, as in mentoring and skills training approaches; and
- capture the importance of context and process; assistance to local-level democracy and the meaning of citizenship in national settings, including the gendered factors which influence active or passive citizenship; and expectations for demobilization and training.

In the longer term, pursue the attainment of the Millennium Development Goals' focus on improved, participatory governance as essential to the realization of 21st-century efforts in order to:

- reduce and eradicate extreme poverty; and
- address problems of inequality (especially when such inequality mirrors ethnic, religious, or other identity cleavages such as gender).

Democratize global governance and other transnational regimes by opening up multilateral decision making to more genuine public consultation and dialogue. If the world is grappling with interdependences and issues that transcend national boundaries, democracy itself must go global.

Provide greater support to parliaments and other decision-making bodies to enable citizens and their representatives to participate effectively in global negotiations that directly affect their daily lives.

2. *Broaden the vision of democratic practice with sensitivity to context.*

- *Norms and operational guidelines for democratic practice at the regional level need to be supported and further developed.* The international community should seek to demonstrate the application of standards, and emphasize compliance with clearly defined existing international norms that reflect a right to democratic, accountable governance, respect for minorities, and tolerance of different religions and beliefs.
- *The international community needs to more fully agree on accountability measures for international intervention* and explore the issue of accountability for new security actors such as private security firms; reaffirm the universality of international human rights law and the Geneva Conventions; and recognize the 'modelling effect' of older democracies in behaviour, for instance, regarding the prohibition of torture, or in attitudes to the reception of asylum seekers or refugees.
- *Emphasize that there is no 'one size fits all' approach to democratization,* building on local structures that are conducive to representative and participatory forms of government, as in the (modified for gender equality) Shura in Afghanistan, or the Somali convening of elders. Improve understandings of democratization processes as an avenue towards strategic peacemaking in contemporary armed conflicts, as in Nepal, Sri Lanka or Colombia. Democracy assistance may be an effective lever in mediation to encourage parties to settle the conflict at the bargaining table rather than on the battlefield.
- *Translate and educate.* People can better make their own choices and design their own action and desired outcomes when they are well informed as to a range of debates, experience and possible avenues for national futures.
- *Design comprehensive country-level strategies: further the development of assessment and monitoring capacities for fragile or conflict-prone states.* The 2005 *Peace and Conflict Report* by US scholars (Marshall and Gurr 2005) argues that 50 per cent of the world's states reflect indicators predictive of inequality and scarcity-induced social conflicts. In countries where democracy promotion has been extensive, actors in the

democracy-building network have teamed up to provide country-level assessments of the challenges to democracy, options for transition, and recommendations. International IDEA, for example, has produced detailed assessments of the prospects for improving democracy in Burkina Faso, Romania, Guatemala and Nepal, and contributes to the same for Bolivia. The World Bank has completed a major country-level assessment of conflict in Nigeria in 2003 following the country's transition to democracy in 1998 and 1999; the report identifies a number of ways in which democracy and development are critical to future conflict mitigation in this complex and multicultural society (see World Bank, at <http://lnweb18.worldbank.org/ESSD/sdvext.nsf/67ByDocName/ConflictAnalysis>).

3. *Improve coordination among democracy builders from global to local levels.*

• *Empower regional organization structures* and approaches to monitoring conflict situations, understanding the sources of human insecurity, and promoting inclusive, participatory democracy in regions where they are strong or more fully developed, such as Europe and the Americas; extend the writ of the European mechanisms to enable them to engage more deeply in the Caucasus and Central Asia in much the same way as the EU has developed a systematic approach to democracy assistance in the Maghreb states and the Middle East in the Barcelona Process. ASEAN is well positioned to move in a credible manner on human rights and develop informed framework guidelines for democratization processes based on national experiences.

• *Encourage the institutionalization of democracy building in regional organizations* that are presently weak or stymied in efforts to achieve regional solutions to governance crises in South-East Asia, Central Asia, South Asia and the Middle East. For example, further enable the development of the African Peer Review Mechanism and link it more fully to the involvement of international democracy assistance networks through information sharing, capacity building, and financial resources. (Encourage democracy assessment by citizens themselves, for example, through the State of Democracy methodology.)

• *Build coherence and consistency among donors' approaches.* Review macroeconomic reform measures and the impact of privatization in order to reconcile macroeconomic interventions and political democratization, goals which should be mutually supportive. Build capacity for monitoring indicators of social tensions, and develop alternative macroeconomic indicators (such as the purchasing power of the population), to assess the impacts of policies and projects on horizontal and vertical equity and social tensions. Support the assessment of potential implications for well-informed choices. Cultivate coherence of approach on the different policy areas that impact on human security, including trade and natural resource management.

4. *Refine and further develop promising institutions and instruments.*

• *Improve existing instruments for democratization-related conflict prevention and reactive capacities in situations where democracy is the strategic or 'political' approach to realizing peace, and work to develop a set of guidelines to inform the work of the new UN*

Peacebuilding Commission created at the 2005 World Summit. The Peacebuilding Commission may benefit from a comprehensive assessment of lessons learned on how peace-to-democracy transitions address challenges such as electoral system choice, electoral violence, the sequencing of elections, constitution-building processes, and the ways in which UN-coordinated peacemaking, peacekeeping and (peace-building) strategies can be applied to improve the design of transitional processes.

• *Avoid the 'elections as exit strategy' trap*; build in measures as far as possible to ensure consistency and long-term developmental relevance, including support to elected parliamentarians for their roles, and the strengthening of domestic capacity for follow-up and accountability measures.

• *Enhance the capacities of legislatures and political parties and improve linkages between parties and their societies, through training that builds transparency and accountability, and offer options for conducting participatory policy making*, and through more effective management of aspects of governance such as judicial process and access to justice. The Inter-Parliamentary Union (IPU) produces useful and highly relevant tools (Inter-Parliamentary Union 2006). Parliamentarians for Global Action has provided opportunities for training newly elected legislators in law-drafting procedures—an often overlooked issue in the workings of parliamentary democracy.

• *Enhance information sharing* on best practices, comparative information, and specific consulting. Because of the highly technical nature of some aspects of democracy, such as constitutional design and electoral system choice and administration, a key function of the democracy-building network has been to provide information and specific consultative advice on these often complex issues. In 1995, for example, the UN's Electoral Assistance Division helped sponsor the work of the Fiji Constitutional Review Commission, which toured the globe meeting with scholars, NGOs and officials in states to examine best practices for constitutional design in multi-ethnic societies (Fiji Constitutional Review Commission 1996).

• *Further professionalize election administration.* The powers, responsibilities, capacities and professionalism of EMBs are critical to processes of democracy worldwide. In recent years, organizations such as IDEA, the UNDP and IFES have teamed up to provide 'one-stop shopping' on electoral costs, election administration, and all other election management issues. The ACE Electoral Knowledge Network (<http://www.aceproject.org>) provides online, up-to-date information on best practices, options and issues in the rapidly growing world of election management. This knowledge base is combined with careful work with EMBs to share information, develop professional standards, and train new cadres of professional election managers.

• *Promote civic education.* International NGOs have been extensively involved in mounting civic education campaigns in transitional societies, from 'get out the vote' campaigns to 'street law' (practical applications of human rights) to promoting awareness of constitutional concepts and the meanings and purposes of democracy. The aim of such activities is to work at the grass-roots level to generate the capacity to participate and enhance awareness among the public of the meaning of human rights and ways in which the public can directly pursue their promotion and protection.

• *Foster South–South support and South–North education.* South Africa offered electoral assistance to the Democratic Republic of the Congo for its planned 2006 elections, but highly skilled (and overstretched) South African representatives commented how useful it could have been to invite India to contribute expertise and experience, as well. Experience, challenges and insights from the global South could benefit and revitalize approaches for sustaining democracy in the global North.

4. Concluding Remarks

The democracy–conflict–human security nexus is clearer than ever before. In 2005 the Comprehensive Peace Agreement between the government of the Republic of Sudan and the Sudanese People's Liberation Movement and Sudanese People's Liberation Army spoke of addressing the root cause of the conflict and establishing a framework for governance through which power and wealth shall be equitably shared and human rights guaranteed. The people of Aceh wait to see whether self-rule in the form of decentralized local government will address their deep-seated needs and inequalities, and enable new political representation and ways to deal with past abuses. Liberia and Sierra Leone tackle questions of impunity and justice while facing a demographic 'youth bulge' and the desperate need for jobs and economic development. Bosnia and Herzegovina faces the challenge of newly negotiating a social contract; Kosovo awaits final status; and unrecognized Somaliland may well one day lead the (democratic) way for Somalia in a positive scenario for the future, depending in part on the force of wider regional politics.

India is one of the largest contributors to the UN Democracy Fund. New leadership is emerging in Latin America which claims redistribution as paramount in priorities. ASEAN will debate a new charter in 2006 which may address democracy and human rights in an unprecedented fashion. Meanwhile, popular street protests are capturing media attention and influencing election timing in cities as distant as La Paz, Bangkok and Manila, while headlines about political corruption appear in London and Nairobi. Globalization itself has impacted heavily on local human security needs and awareness, as evidenced in rural protests and mass migration in China.

Democratization does not move according to seamless or set pathways, but rather in incremental and messy fashion. The test of 21st century democracy will not be limited to the cultivation of widespread free and fair elections (a challenge in its own right), but will be determined equally by whether human rights standards are reclaimed as universal, inequalities reduced and social justice furthered. It will be determined and measured from the viewpoint of delivery—whether it seeks to meet human needs, and whether it recognizes that human insecurity is one of the main root causes of the many violent conflicts the world is facing and that insecurity is often linked to exclusion and lack of access to resources and power. New thinking and behaviours will be needed globally. The challenge is for democratic practice, in action, to move from formal to broadly-based, locally owned democracy and to create legitimacy and ownership in support of sustainable democratic development tailored for specific contexts.

Notes

[1] Both context and the quality of dialogue used will be huge variables. The Overseas Development Institute (ODI) in London has prepared a series of working papers on PRSP strategies, including a review of the process in Bolivia. See also Booth 2003.

References and Further Reading

ACE Electoral Knowledge Network, <http://www.aceproject.org>

Annan, Kofi, 'Peace and Development: One Struggle, Two Fronts', address to World Bank staff, 19 October 1999, <http://www.reliefweb.int/w/rwb.nsf/0/4eea64265493fc048525680f006deaf5?OpenDocument>

—, 'Why Democracy is an International Issue', Cyril Foster Lecture, Oxford University, 19 June 2001, available at <http://www.escwa.org.lb/information/press/un/2001/word-pdf/19june.pdf>

Arabi, Hooman (Tehran), letter to *Guardian Weekly*, 21–27 October 2005, p. 14

Beetham, David, Bracking, Sarah, Kearton, Iain and Weir, Stuart, *International IDEA Handbook on Democracy Assessment* (The Hague: Kluwer Law International, 2002)

Benner, Thorsten, Deng, Francis, Reinicke, Wolfgang and Witte, Jan Martin, *Critical Choices: The United Nations, Networks, and the Future of Global Governance* (Ottawa: IDRC Publishers, 2000)

Bjornlund, Eric, *Beyond Free and Fair: Monitoring Elections and Building Democracy* (Baltimore, Md. and London: Johns Hopkins University Press, 2004)

Booth, David (ed.), 'Fighting Poverty in Africa: Are PRSPs making a Difference?', London, Overseas Development Institute, 2003

Boyce, James K. and Pastor, Manuel, 'Macroeconomic Policy and Peace Building in El Salvador', in Krishna Kumar (ed.), *Rebuilding Societies After Civil War* (Boulder, Colo.: Lynne Rienner, 1997)

Brown, Mark Malloch, 'Democratic Governance: Toward a Framework for Sustainable Peace', *Global Governance*, 9 (2003)

Brown, Michael E., Lynn Jones, Sean and Miller, Steven E., *Debating the Democratic Peace* (Boston, Mass.: MIT Press, 2004)

Carothers, Thomas, 'The Backlash Against Democracy Promotion', *Foreign Affairs* (March/April 2006)

— *Critical Mission: Democracy Promotion* (Washington, DC: Carnegie Endowment for International Peace, 2004)

Chesterman, Simon, *You, the People: The United Nations, Transitional Administration, and State-Building* (Oxford: Oxford University Press, 2004)

Chopra, Jarat and Hohe, Tanja, 'Participatory Intervention', *Global Governance*, 10 (2004)

Colletta, Nat J., 'Human Security, Poverty and Conflict: Reform of the International Financial Institutions', in L. Chen, S. Fukada-Parr and E. Seidensticker (eds), *Human Insecurity in a Global World* (Cambridge, Mass.: Harvard University Press, 2004)

Collier, Paul et al., *Breaking the Conflict Trap: Civil War and Development Policy* (Washington, DC: World Bank, 2003)

Cousens, Elizabeth and Kumar, Chetan, *Peacebuilding as Politics: Cultivating Peace in Fragile Societies* (Boulder, Colo.: Lynne Rienner 2001, p. 7

Diamond, Larry, *Promoting Democracy in the 1990's: Actors and Instruments, Issues and Imperatives*, Final Report of the Carnegie Commission on Preventing Deadly Conflict (Washington, DC: Carnegie Commission on Preventing Deadly Conflict, 1998)

—, 'Universal Democracy?', *Policy Review* 19, January 2005, <http://www.policyreview.org>

Dobriansky, Paula J. (US Undersecretary of State for Global Affairs), 'Democracy Promotion: Explaining the Bush Administration's Position', in Thomas Carothers, *Critical Choices: Essays on Democracy Promotion* (Washington, DC: Carnegie Endowment for International Peace, 2004), pp. 75–82

Fiji Constitutional Review Commission, *Towards A United Future*, Parliamentary Paper 34 (1996)

Franck, Thomas M., 'The Emerging Right to Democratic Governance', *American Journal of International Law*, 86/1 (1992)

Fraser, Alistair, 'Four Ways of Thinking about PRSPs, NGOs and Democracy', *Ontrac,* no. 31, September 2005, <http://www.intrac.org>

'Hague Statement on Enhancing the European Profile in Democracy Assistance', European Conference on Enhancing the European Profile in Democracy Assistance, The Hague, 5–6 July 2004, <http://www.nimd.org/upload/publications/2004/the_hague_statement_july_2004.pdf>

Hopmann, P. Terrence, 'Building Security in Post-Cold War Eurasia: The OSCE and US Foreign Policy', United States Institute of Peace, Peaceworks, Occasional Paper, Washington, DC, October 1999

Ibegbu, Jude, *Right to Democracy in International Law* (London: Mellen Press, 2003)

Ignatieff, Michael, 'What are Americans to Think that Freedom is Theirs to Spread?', *New York Times*, 26 June 2005

International IDEA, *Democracy and UN Peace-building at Local Level* (2005), <http://www.idea.int/publications/democracy_un/index.cfm>

Inter-Parliamentary Union (IPU), *Parliament and Democracy in the Twenty-first Century: A Guide to Good Practice* (IPU Secretariat, Geneva, 2006), see <http://www.ipu.org/english/handbks.htm#democracy>

Manning, Richard, Remarks reported in World Bank, 'Structuring Aid to Sustain Governance Reform in Low-Income Countries Under Stress', 21 September 2003

Marshall, Monty G. and Gurr, Ted Robert (eds), *Peace and Conflict 2005* (College Park, Md.: University of Maryland Center for International Development and Conflict Management, 2005), available at <http://www.cidcm.umd.edu/inscr/PC05print.pdf>

Matlosa, Khabele, 'Democratization at the Crossroads: Challenges for the SADC Principles and Guidelines Governing Democratic Elections', Institute for Security Studies Occasional Paper no. 111, Pretoria, Institute for Security Studies, October 2005

Minxin Pei, *China's Trapped Transition* (Cambridge, Mass: Harvard University Press, 2006)

New Partnership for Africa's Development (NEPAD), 'The African Peer Review Mechanism (APRM)', September 2003, <http://www.dfa.gov.za/au.nepad/nepad49.pdf>

Newman, Edward and Rich, Roland, *The UN Role in Promoting Democracy* (Tokyo: United Nations University Press, 2004)

Organisation for Economic Co-operation and Development (OECD), Development Assistance Committee (DAC), 'Security System Reform and Governance', DAC Guidelines and Reference Series, OECD, 2005, <http://www.oecd.org/dataoecd/8/39/31785288.pdf>

Piron, Laure-Hélène and Evans, Alison, 'Politics and the PRSP Approach: Synthesis Paper', Overseas Development Institute Working Paper 237, London, March 2004

Schraeder, Peter J. (ed.), *Exporting Democracy: Rhetoric versus Reality* (Boulder, Colo.: Lynne Rienner, 2002)

Simmons, P. J. and de Jonge Oudraat, Chantal (eds), *Managing Global Issues: Lessons Learned* (Washington, DC: Carnegie Endowment for International Peace, 2001)

Stewart, Frances, 'Crisis Prevention: Tackling Horizontal Inequalities', *Oxford Development Studies*, 28/3 (2000)

Ukeje, Charles, 'Rethinking Africa's Security in the Age of Uncertain Globalisation: NEPAD and Human Security in the 21st Century', Paper submitted to the 11th CODESRIA General Assembly, Maputo, Mozambique, 6–10 December 2005 on the theme *Rethinking African Development: Beyond the Impasse, Towards Alternatives*

United Nations, *An Agenda for Democratization* (New York: United Nations, 1996)

United Nations, General Assembly, 'Support by the United Nations System of the Efforts of Governments to Promote and Consolidate New or Restored Democracies', UN document A/50/332, 7 August 1995

United Nations Development Programme (UNDP), *Human Development Report 2002: Deepening Democracy in a Fragmented World* (Oxford: Oxford University Press, 2002)

— *Human Development Report 2005: International Cooperation at a Crossroads. Aid, Trade and Security in an Unequal World* (Oxford and New York: Oxford University Press, 2005)

— 'Governance for the Future: Democracy and Development in Least Developed Countries (LDCs)', Joint report of the UN Development Programme (UNDP) and the UN Office of the High Representative for Least Developed Countries, Landlocked Developing Countries and Small Island Developing States (OHRLLS), 2006, <http://content.undp.org/go/newsroom/may-2006/good-governance-20060519.en>

Uvin, Peter, *Aiding Violence: The Development Enterprise in Rwanda* (West Hartford, Ct.: Kumarian Press, 1998)

Willett, Susan, 'Development and Security in Africa: A Challenge for the New Millenium', in Geoff Harris (ed.), *Achieving Security in Sub-Saharan Africa: Cost Effective Alternatives to the Military* (Pretoria: Institute for Security Studies, 2004), pp. 101–20

World Audit, <http://www.worldaudit.org>

World Bank, *World Development Report 2006: Equity and Development*, <http://web.worldbank.org>

Zielonka, Jan and Pravda, Alex (eds), *Democratic Consolidation in Eastern Europe Volume 2: International and Transnational Factors* (Oxford: Oxford Scholarship Online, 2001), <http://www.oxfordscholarship.com>

About the Authors

Judith Large is Senior Advisor for Democracy Building and Conflict Management at International IDEA. Before coming to IDEA in 2003 she combined lecturing in international relations, political economy and conflict theory/analysis with being an independent consultant/practitioner in conflict analysis and strategic planning for United Nations agencies, the UK Department for International Development (DFID) and international non-governmental organizations (NGOs). She has taught and assisted with programme development at the University of Kent's London Centre for International Relations, the Centre for Conflict Studies at the University of Utrecht (Netherlands), and the University of Lancaster, UK, also serving as a visiting lecturer for other faculties in the UK and Austria.

Her particular research interests, then and now, are the prevention and reduction of violent conflict. As a consultant she specialized in practical strategies for improved linkage between levels (from grass-roots to middle-range leadership, national and international) for transition from protracted conflict to just and non-violent outcomes. She has worked on post-war national- and community-level recovery programmes for the World Health Organization (WHO) (in Bosnia, Serbia, Kosovo), for the DFID (post-Dayton Bosnia, implementation, civil affairs), for the United Nations Development Programme (UNDP), for the British Council (in Indonesia—Ambon, Maluku, Kalimantan, Sulawesi, Sumatra including Aceh); also through the British Council with local partners on peace building in Mindanao, the Philippines; and for the UN High Commissioner for Refugees (Evaluation and Policy Unit) in East Timor. She has served on the advisory board for the UK Consortium on Complex Political Emergencies (COPE) research project with particular involvement in the work of the Agency for Co-operation and Research in Development (ACORD) and local actors in Northern Uganda (Gulu and Kitgum); on the Board of Trustees for the Centre for Security and Peace Studies at Gadjah Mada University, Indonesia; and as an advisor for the *Journal of Peacebuilding and Development*, and has published widely on related themes.

Timothy D. Sisk is Associate Professor in the Graduate School of International Studies, University of Denver, USA, where he is on the faculty in the Master of Arts Program in Conflict Resolution. He is an external Policy Advisor to International IDEA's programme on Democracy Building and Conflict Management, and was an early contributor to *Democracy and Deep-rooted Conflict: Options for Negotiators* (IDEA, 1998). His PhD (with distinction) in political science (comparative politics, research methods) was earned from the George Washington University, USA, in 1992.

Prof. Sisk specializes in the nexus between democracy and governance and the management of conflict in deeply divided societies, especially those emerging from a period of intense social violence, and his recent research culminated in a book entitled *Beyond Bloody Sundays: Violence and Negotiation in Ethnic Conflict*. A former Programme Officer and Research Scholar at the United States Institute of Peace (USIP) in Washington, DC, Sisk was a Washington-based scholar and analyst of international relations and US foreign policy for 15 years. As a programme officer at USIP in 1989–98 he organized international conferences, training in professional conflict resolution skills, and 'track two' peacemaking efforts, and conducted field research and unofficial diplomacy in Africa, Europe and the Middle East. He has also served as a consultant to the US Department of State, the UN and international NGOs on peacemaking in ethnically divided societies. He is the author of five books and many articles, including *Democracy at the Local Level* (IDEA, 2000), *Democratization in South Africa* (Princeton University Press, 1995) and *Power Sharing and International Mediation in Ethnic Conflicts* (Carnegie Commission on Preventing Deadly Conflict, 1995). Currently he is completing a study entitled *Negotiating Peace in Ethnic Conflict: Forging Settlements for Durable Peace* which will be published in 2007.

Reginald Austin is a Zimbabwean professor specializing in international and constitutional law who was directly involved in the constitutional and ceasefire negotiations leading to the transition from Southern Rhodesia to Zimbabwe. His work has included responsibility for elections for the UN in Cambodia (1992–3), South Africa (1994) and Afghanistan (2003–4). Prof. Austin has been a Director of the Legal and Constitutional Affairs Division of the Commonwealth Secretariat, and from 1998 to 2003 he directed IDEA's electoral and, later, Africa programmes.

M. Najib Azca is Deputy Director of the Centre for Security and Peace Studies and a lecturer at the Department of Sociology and Master's Programme of Peace and Conflict Resolution at Gadjah Mada University, Indonesia.

Feargal Cochrane is Director of the Richardson Institute for Peace and Conflict Research at the University of Lancaster, UK. Dr. Cochrane has published widely, researching and teaching in peace studies and conflict transformation, with a focus on the dynamics of ethnic conflict.

Olayinka Creighton-Randall is Component Manager for Informal Justice with the Justice Sector Development Programme (JSDP) in Freetown, Sierra Leone. JSDP contributes towards establishing safety, security and access to justice for the people of Sierra Leone especially the poor, the vulnerable and the marginalized.

Andrew Ellis is currently the head of the Electoral Processes Team at IDEA in Stockholm. He has led electoral and constitutional assistance activities in Indonesia, Cambodia, Bosnia and Herzegovina, Palestine and elsewhere, and has wide experience as a technical advisor on electoral and institutional matters in democratic transitions.

J 'Kayode Fayemi is the Director (International) of the Centre for Democracy and Development. for West and Central Africa. A civil–military relations scholar, Dr Fayemi is an advisor to various organizations on African affairs, including the British Parliamentary Human Rights Group, the International Crisis Group and the Norwegian Council for Africa.

Guido Galli is Principal Desk Officer in the Asia and Pacific Section of the Coordination Response Division, UN Office for the Coordination of Humanitarian Affairs (OCHA), Geneva. Between 2004 and 2005 he was based at International IDEA assisting with the development of the Constitution-Building Processes project.

Yash Ghai is a Kenyan who was the Sir Y K Pao Professor of Public Law at the University of Hong Kong until the end of 2006. Prof. Ghai has taught at various universities in Africa, North America, Europe and the South Pacific.

Enrique ter Horst, formerly a Venezuelan diplomat and Assistant Secretary-General of the United Nations, headed the UN peacekeeping operations in El Salvador and Haiti, and was UN Deputy High Commissioner for Human Rights. He now is a lawyer in Caracas.

Aziz Huq directs the Liberty and Security Project at the Brennan Center for Justice at the New York University School of Law. He was selected in 2006 to be a Carnegie Scholars Fellow. He has published widely and works internationally on the intersection of national security and human liberty.

Todd Landman is a Reader in the Department of Government and a member of the Human Rights Centre at the University of Essex, UK. He is the project leader for IDEA's State of Democracy project, which is run jointly with the University of Essex.

Gurpreet Mahajan is Professor and Chairperson of the Centre for Political Studies, Jawaharlal Nehru University, India. Prof. Mahajan has written extensively on multiculturalism and issues of diversity and discrimination in liberal democracy.

Khabele Matlosa is the Director of the Research, Publications and Information Department at the Electoral Institute of Southern Africa (EISA), in Johannesburg, South Africa. Dr. Matlosa is a widely recognized expert in political reform and electoral processes.

George Gray Molina served as a senior staff member on the Bolivian government's Economic and Social Policy Unit UDAPE, and now works with the United Nations. He is a leading scholar and analyst in the fields of development economics and the politics of popular participation.

Arifah Rahmawati is the Deputy Director for Planning and Development and a lecturer at the Master's Program in Peace and Conflict Resolution, Gadjah Mada University, Indonesia. She is also a researcher at the Center for Security and Peace Studies (CSPS) of Gadjah Mada University.

Paikiasothy Saravanamuttu is Executive Director of the Centre for Policy Alternatives (CPA) in Colombo, Sri Lanka, an independent and non-partisan public policy institute focusing on issues of democratic governance and peace through programmes of research and advocacy.

INTERNATIONAL IDEA
Supporting democracy worldwide

Created in 1995, the International Institute for Democracy and Electoral Assistance—IDEA—is an intergovernmental organization that supports sustainable democracy. Working globally, but with a current focus on Africa and the Middle East, Latin America and South Asia, IDEA seeks to improve the design and effectiveness of democratic institutions, and to strengthen democratic processes through:

- providing researchers, policy makers, activists and media representatives a forum in which to discuss democratic principles;
- blending research and field experience, developing methodologies and providing training to improve democratic processes; and
- promoting transparency, accountability and efficiency in managing elections.

Its main areas of activity include:

- **Democracy building and conflict management**. IDEA's work in this area focuses on constitution building, reconciliation, inclusive dialogue and human security. It targets societies in transition, particularly those emerging from periods of violence and weak governance.

- **Electoral processes**, including ensuring the professional management and independence of elections, adapting electoral systems, improving access and building public confidence. IDEA develops training modules and materials for election officials and provides comparative data and analyses on both the political and the technical aspects of designing, organizing and running elections.

- **Political parties, political equality and participation** (*including women in politics*). IDEA's work includes the review of political parties' external regulations, public funding, their management and relations with the public. It also includes identifying ways to build commitment to inclusive politics, especially those related to the inclusion of women in politics, through for example the provision of comparative experiences on the application of special measures like gender quotas.

Membership

Membership of IDEA is open to governments. Currently IDEA has 24 member states: Australia, Barbados, Belgium, Botswana, Canada, Cape Verde, Chile, Costa Rica, Denmark, Finland, Germany, India, Mauritius, Mexico, Namibia, the Netherlands, Norway, Peru, Portugal, South Africa, Spain, Sweden, Switzerland and Uruguay. Japan has observer status.

International Institute for Democracy and Electoral Assistance (International IDEA)
Strömsborg, SE-130 34 Stockholm, Sweden
Tel: +46-8-698-3700; Fax: +46-8-20-24-22
E-mail: info@idea.int
www.idea.int

Index

conflict:

  causes 13, 18, 27–35, 194

  democracy and 7, 97, 196

  economic dimension 30–31

  ethnic 101

  factors leading to 35

  gender and 18

  internal 13, 26, 27

    causes 27–35

    civilians 36

    consequences 36–39

    economic costs 36–37

    global consequences 38

    human rights violations and 38

    spillover effects 36, 38

  international 15

  local level processes 69

  lootable goods and 29

  new 1

  numbers of 26

  poverty and 34–35

  regionalized 36

  trends, global 26–27

  see also wars *and under names of countries*

Congo, Democratic Republic of (DRC):

  conflict in 29

  displaced people 183

  elections in 183–84

  electoral assistance to 219–220

  population transfers 182

  power sharing 182

  refugees 183

  Rwanda and 66

  voter registration 183

  war to democracy transition 154, 180

consociationalism 79, 100–1, 102, 188

constitutions 85 *see also under names of countries*

Convention Against Torture 143

Convention on the Rights of the Child 25, 166

Copenhagen Agreement 83

Costa Rica: electoral system 93

Cote d'Ivoire: conflict in 1

Council of Europe 134, 209

Creighton-Randall, Olayinka (Volume II) 51, 197, 198

crimes against humanity 38

Croatia 160

  Centre for Peace and Justice 103-104

Czech Republic: democratization 52

Czechoslovakia: velvet divorce 82

D

Dayton Accord, 1995:

  criticisms of 170, 173

  democracy and 42, 56, 170

  democratic deficit 175

  High Representative of the International Community 175

  inflexibility of 170

  international administration 173

  overview 173–75

  power sharing 175

de Klerk, President F.W. 56

debt relief 201

decolonization 78

democracratic institutions: building 5

democracy:

  with adjectives 132–33

  anti-terrorism and 144–46

  assessment 53, 113, 115

  assistance 193, 199, 217-218

  characteristics 78

  competition and 79

  complicated nature of 40, 49, 53, 120, 147, 220

  conflict caused by 3

  conflict and human insecurity linkages 2, 3, 6, 8, 34

  conflict management and 2, 3–4, 6, 9, 43, 50, 153, 169,

  consensual 132

  consensus-seeking in conflicted societies 100–9

oil: conflict and 29

Organisation of American States (OAS) 25, 83, 208

Organization for Security and Cooperation in
Europe (OSCE):
democracy promotion 209
election monitoring 134
High Commissioner for National Minorities 70,
83, 84, 209

Oslo Agreement 170

─────────────────────────────── P

Pakistan: coup 56

Paraguay: democracy in 134

Paris Minimum Standards of Human Rights Norms
in a State of Emergency 141

Paris, Roland 18

Parliamentarians for Global Action 219

participation:
broadening and deepening 103–4
conflict and 35
gender differences and 105–7

peace:
democracy and 3, 195
ecomonic growth and 66

Peace and Conflict Report 217

peace-building: democracy and 50, 184, 187, 193,
196–98

Peru: democratization 52

Philippines:
anti-terrorism 144
conflict in 29, 144
government overthrown 59
peace process 144
People Power 59

Pinochet, President Augusto122

Poland: Solidarity 59

police:
accountability 143
civil control of 69

political parties:
ethnic 95–96

women and 106

pollution 22

popular movements 33, 220 *see also* mass
movements

Portugal: 'Revolution of the Carnations' 52

post-Soviet states 60, 114

poverty:
democracy and 5, 114, 122, 123–28
dollar a day 1, 23, 195
HIV/AIDS and 129
reducing 195, 217
'Who speaks for the poor?' 215

Poverty Reduction Strategy Papers (PRSP) 201–2,
215

power sharing:
criticisms of rigid 100–3
flexibility and 101
lessons for 176
moving beyond 176
overview 187–90
varieties of 187–88
war-torn societies and 153, 169–77

privatization 8, 29, 66, 67

Przeworski, Adam 58

public opinion surveys 147

─────────────────────────────── Q

al Qaeda 143, 199

─────────────────────────────── R

Rahmawati and Azca (Volume II) 69, 203

Rawls, John 80

Red Interamericana para la Democracia (RID) 210

referendums 81–82

refugees 22, 129, 180–81 *see also under names of
countries*

repression, extreme 65

Reynal-Querol, Marta 36–37

Rodrik and Wacziarg 66

Ross, Michael 124

Russia:
democracy in 134–35

---- **Y**

---- **Z**